Ritchie on Carp
The Whole Story

by

Ritchie McDonald
and
Greg Meenehan

First published in March 2014

All rights reserved. No part of this publication may be reproduced, stored in a retrieval system, or transmitted, in any form by any means, electronic, mechanical, photocopying, recording or otherwise, without prior permission of the publisher.

© Text and pictures - Ritchie McDonald & Greg Meenehan

© Design - Mpress (media) Ltd

ISBN number: 978-0-9926062-2-0

Designed and published by m!press (Media) LTD.
Unit Four, Ashton Gate, Harold Hill, Romford, RM3 8UF

Dedication

This book is dedicated to John and Eileen Walker, who have been there for me for as long as I can remember, and who are still the only people who are allowed to tell me off and get away with it.

I would also like to dedicate it to my three kids, Danny, Steven and Lindsay, and to my brother, Michael, and me sis, Liz, who aren't allowed to tell me off, but somehow also manage to get away with it.

A special mention must also go to (in no particular order):
Essex John Watson, Les Bamford, Johnny Allen, Dougal Gray, Len Arbery, Bob Buteux, Scott and Eve Conroy, and the late, great Bill Quinlan and Ivan Marks.

Acknowledgements

I would like to thank all of the people whose help made this book possible, including Chris Ball for his pictures of the Richmond Park Forty, to *Angler's Mail* and *Angling Times* for the use of black and white photographs and newspaper cuttings, to all at Mpress for their hard work in putting this book and DVD package together, and to all those people who agreed to take photos of fish that I'd just caught when I held out my camera or rang them up at home, among them Chris Yates, who also designed the cover of the first book. I owe you one. Last but not least, a very special thank you to Greg Meenehan, for without him, this book would not be possible.

Accompanying this book are a free DVD video recording of me on the bank holding the Yateley North Lake fish at 45lb 12oz, from October 1984, and an audio recording made at one of my slide shows following the Cassien trip. The whistling and cheering at the start is because I came on stage dressed in stockings and suspenders!

Contents

Introduction 7
Foreword 9
Comments from the forums 10

PART ONE – Ritchie on Carp

Preface 21
1. Early Days and Late Nights 23
2. Ashlea Antics 33
3. Redmire - A Dream Come True 45
4. Redmire - A Dream Turned Sour 55
5. 1981 - A Year Without Equal 67
6. Four-legged Friends 85
7. Loony Lads and Savay Thirties 91
8. Forty-five Twelve 99
9. Cassien - the Beginning 107
10. Cassien - Success at the Second Attempt 123
11. Big is Beautiful 135
12. The Famous Four 151
13. One Last Cast 163
Glossary 165

PART TWO – The Whole Story

Foreword 1 by Chris Ball 170
Foreword 2 by Mark Starkey 173
1. Finding a Forty 177
2. Two in a Week 193
3. The Royal Forty 207
4. Plumbing the Depths 217
5. Trouble and Strife 225
6. The Good Old Days 233
7. Carping – Then and Now 247
8. The Last Word by Greg Meenehan 255

Introduction

My name is Ritchie McDonald. Way back in 1988 I wrote a book called *Ritchie on Carp* that sold thousands of copies and gave me writer's cramp signing my name in it for people at shows.

Twenty-five years have gone by and a lot has changed. Back then, Thatcher was Prime Minister, the internet as we know it hadn't been invented and you could count the number of 40lb carp in the UK on the fingers of one hand.

It's been twenty years since I've fished seriously for carp, and from what I hear now, if you haven't had a 'fifty' by lunchtime you can go to the geezer who owns the lake and ask for your money back!

And as for tackle… I went to a show to see what was occurring and when I walked in it was like I'd stepped into Dr Who's Tardis and travelled through time. Blokes were buying bivvies the size of small houses and walking round with radio controlled boats under their arms!

I'm not an internet geek, but friends have shown me a few of the things about me on-line, in particular on the chat forums. There's been lots of speculation as to what became of me. I discovered from reading a few comments that I'd moved to Thailand, which was news to me; that I was planning to make a comeback in carp fishing, which I'll be having a word with my agent about; and that I was sharing a house with Lord Lucan and riding Shergar at weekends.

I also discovered that people remember me fondly (I got a nice Christmas card off Essex John, from Belmarsh, where he's doing a seven-stretch). One bloke wrote on the internet that going to see one of my slide shows back in the day was "almost up there with Hendrix at Woodstock"!

And when I went to a carp show there were guys looking at me and nudging their mates and whispering: "D'you know who that is?"

I also found out that the price of second-hand copies of my book were changing hands for about £90 each!

It made me think that maybe the time was right to bring it out again, but this time updated with all the things that have happened to me since it was last published.

That way a few more people would be able to afford to read what I wrote all those years ago, and I could tell you the full story of what I've been up to since the last book came out, and how things went very right and then went very wrong.

So that's why the whole text of *Ritchie on Carp* is here between these covers, along with all the new stuff. If you've read the first book before, I'll forgive you if you want to skim through that, but if the last time that you looked at it was twenty-five years ago, I'd say it's worth another go.

One bloke put on a forum that it was "a fantastic read", and: "if you are lucky enough to see a copy for sale, then buy it. It's one of my favourite books." So here it is, and more besides. And the other reason for writing this is that I turned sixty last September, and maybe it's time to come back in from the cold and get involved in angling again after too many years away.

I may not be able to climb trees quite as quickly as I used to, and my breakdancing shoes don't get dusted off quite as often as they once did. But what age takes away in vitality it gives back in experience and, as you'll find out when you read this book, you don't spend half your life on the banks of our lakes and rivers without learning a thing or two.

Be lucky,

Ritchie

Foreword

It's funny how you form an impression of someone before you meet them. Like with Ritchie McDonald. I'd heard the name; I'd seen the reports; I'd heard the rumours: from a distance he was larger than life, full of confidence, a Jack the Lad who liked to smell the roses, could talk a bit, and could catch big fish. When I met him I found out it was all true. You couldn't invent Ritchie.

I've got to be honest, I think I was developing a bit of a mental block about big fish when I met Ritchie. My personal best of 32lb 8oz had been caught at Redmire in the early seventies and remained at that figure for a whole ten years – although I've since discovered that the Avon scales I was using only weighed up to 32lb 8oz! I'd hooked bigger fish in the in-between years, but fate seemed to be against me and they always came off.

I fished with Ritchie for a season or so, and although I don't think I did anything different with the bigger fish, somehow his confidence, or perhaps his knack, seemed to rub off. Whatever the reason my personal best went up by stages from 32lb 8oz to almost 40lb, and this was before I started fishing abroad; figures took on a whole new significance with the Cassien fish.

If our spell of fishing together helped my confidence, it didn't seem to do Ritchie any harm either: he capped all my efforts by landing the Yateley North Lake fish at 45lb 12oz in the autumn of 1984. His patience and confidence and self-belief had paid off again and rewarded him with the second biggest carp ever to be caught in this country.

Ritchie's success is based upon hard work and dedication. Dedication to a particular fish he has in his mind's eye. He says: "I'm going to catch that fish, no matter what it takes." If it takes a thousand hours, to Ritchie it does not matter, because he knows he will get his reward in the end, and he'll thoroughly enjoy every moment after that fish. He is, in every sense of the word, a true specimen hunter.

That's the Ritchie I know and have spent some terrific times with. Ritchie the grafter; Ritchie the pleasure seeker; Ritchie the carp angler; and now Ritchie the author. The book portrays the man as he is; a bit naughty, and a bit special. I hope you enjoy reading it as much as I have done and that Ritchie does for your self-belief what he did for mine.

Good on yer, Ritch; get 'em in.

Rod Hutchinson

Comments From The Forums

WHAT HAS HAPPENED TO THE GREAT RITCHIE MAC?

••••••••••

Last I heard he had grown his hair and beard really long and gone to live in the jungle. Oh no, sorry. That was Lord Lucan, wasn't it?

••••••••••

imho one of the top five ranking anglers ever.

••••••••••

Very clever man – even better carper.

••••••••••

Ritchie McDonald is a legend from the days when carp were hard to catch.

••••••••••

Ritchie is what Ritchie is, a loveable rogue and an extremely gifted angler. You might call him a bit of a 'Rock n Roll' carper, very much a man of his time...

••••••••••

Great angler, colourful character and one that people will revere forever.

••••••••••

Ritchie on Carp is a cracking read and an insight into the man's character. I got two copies as I wanted to make sure I never lost one (I'm like that). I'm going to have a word with him and tell him he needs to start writing, the lazy git.

••••••••••

Comments From The Forums

•••••••••••

I love his book, one of my real fav's, that one.

•••••••••••

Was a colourful character… still is… never in those days did I meet anyone as determined as Ritchie... inspired me no end.

•••••••••••

I had a set of Ritchie's rods back in the day, till they got nicked. Also have his book. Good read, but it would be nice to see him bring out another. More pages, a warts an' all book. I think the carp world owes the guy something at least, and a proper book should line his wallet with the amount it would sell.

•••••••••••

Watched his slide show at an old CAA meeting at Aquatels just after he had caught Bazil from the North Lake. Very funny. He was selling videos of Bazil's capture that night. I bought one. £12, but I've frigging lost it.

•••••••••••

Definitely my biggest influence in carping. Absolute legend.

•••••••••••

It would be great to see him back on the bank. Looked up to him 25 years ago. Got me into big carp fishing.

•••••••••••

Enjoyed a great week-end with Ritchie and Albert Romp in Loughborough one year, when they held the N.A.S.A shows at Loughborough Uni. We went into town Sat night for a few (yeah right) and a meal. I don't think I've ever laughed so much. We were all aching. Can't remember the year off hand, but it was the year he brought his book out, as I've a signed copy. Top blokes both of them.

•••••••••••

•••••••••••

Seeing Ritchie in *Angling Times* with the Yateley North Lake 40 as it was known then at 45 plus, was one of the reason I took up carp fishing. It looked immense on Ritchie, much bigger than 45. Used to pop down to the old Penge Angling where he was working at the time just to see him, and gawp at some of the old black & white photos of some of the Cassien fish he had on the wall down there… sad, I know.

•••••••••••

Ritchie and Tim did our first ever Carp Society show in Exeter round about 1981. As usual he needed a few voddies to get him going and to be honest at one point we wondered if he'd ever manage to stand upright, let alone talk. Yet we needn't have worried. He had the audience in stitches, specially with his tale about the Redmire eel! Top man.

•••••••••••

Ritchie on Carp, 1989. If anyone has a copy willing to sell please pm me. The cheapest I have seen on the web is £40.

•••••••••••

Good luck. The dearest was £105 for a 1st edition.

•••••••••••

Ah Ritchie McDonald, a legend in his own lifetime. Would love to read his book.

•••••••••••

His slide shows were awesome, the best I've ever seen - big fish after big fish and very entertaining... and who can forget the series of articles in *Angling Times* when they followed Ritchie to Lake Cassien in pursuit of a new world record carp, and ended up with the exclusive on Johnny Allen's monster catfish - terrific stuff!
At a time when many other folk's slide shows were little more than a boring parade of similar fish, Ritchie's used to be a breath of fresh air. Everyone's lovable rogue and chancer, had a real flair for giving the audience a good time.
I particularly loved the one about JA's Cassien catfish!

•••••••••••

Comments From The Forums

••••••••••••

How I would have loved to have attended one of Ritchie's Carp Society slide shows… guess that's almost up there with Hendrix at Woodstock. Geeeezzzzaaaaaa!!

••••••••••••

Only managed to see him once, at a Stoke carp do about '88 I think… when the book came out. Awesome Cassien slide show… Christ, could he tell a story… Well large geeza! Come back, Ritchie. Get on the slide show circuit again!!!

••••••••••••

He did one at Wye Road, Newcastle, Staffs, about '88-89. He had the audience eating out of his hand, the ultimate big carp man and showman combined.

I won a Nutrabaits t-shirt. I went up to get my prize from Ritchie and he was giving me the old shadow boxing routine because I was quite a bit bigger than him.

••••••••••••

I remember his slideshow at Wye Road, Newcastle-under-Lyme in the 80s… it was simply top drawer, from both a fishing and humour perspective.

••••••••••••

If you are lucky enough to see a copy of *Ritchie on Carp* then buy it, one of my favourite books by someone who was a real hero to a keen young carp angler.

••••••••••••

Read it cover to cover at least 20 times – best carp book ever written imo.

••••••••••••

The first carp fishing book I ever read and it is still one of the best. I got a copy out from the library in Partington and just paid the fine with my paper round money after I said I lost it!

••••••••••••

••••••••••••

Last time I saw Rich was at Peter Broxup's funeral, and like most carp anglers he's still as mad as a bag of snakes… God bless him.

••••••••••••

Ritchie was a real inspiration to carp anglers of my generation and I was fortunate to meet him a few times. He was one of the first anglers to specifically target a particular fish and to target big carp in general and was bloody good at it, too!

••••••••••••

I have just finished reading *Ritchie on Carp* – what a great book. Just wanted to know whatever became of him as he is no longer on the carp scene.

••••••••••••

A vastly under-appreciated book IMO, one of the funniest reads ever.
Never met the guy but he comes across really well from the book: sort of Chris Yates if he had been raised by wolves!!

One of carp fishing's true legends… a rubbish shot with a sawn off shotgun though. Which is good, otherwise me and Thicky wouldn't be here!

••••••••••••

Is he still wearing that camou jacket, tartan cheese-cutter, leather moccasins/bivvy slippers and listening to Capital Gold? Used to enjoy his nuggets of carpy wisdom when he was at `ounslow Angling.

••••••••••••

I'm fairly sure he netted a carp for me at Farlows in 1992 that I'd caught feeder fishing on double maggot on a size 18. He fell in twice getting round to my peg and smelt of hemp, can't imagine why!
I'd never have got it into my silly pan net and he was almost as chuffed to see me catch as I was. Nice bloke.

••••••••••••

•••••••••••

Worked at Penge Angling for a bit. Went and sat by the kid with a coma's bedside if I remember rightly, too. Great guy. Working class hero.

•••••••••••

Someone did say he was into playing darts, big time. Any truth in this? Internet rumours, eh! Apparently he was turning professional at darts.

•••••••••••

This bloke called Ritchie McDonald is almost like a folklore legend. It amazes me the whirlpool of interest that surrounds this geezer. I admit I am fascinated, too. He is like Robin Hood! The man could write another book about what he has done since his last book and it would sell tonnes. Even if it was about his adventures down the local and playing darts, as one poster mentioned earlier. Cult figure for sure.

•••••••••••

What a living legend, and huge inspiration.
I'm not surprised he's given up! Things where a lot different back then. Ritchie was one of the original pioneers and achieved what most mortal carp anglers only dream about. I suppose once you've tasted the Holy Grail what's left? It's time to bow out gracefully having been there, done that, and wrote the book!
It is a great, great book.

•••••••••••

I liked Ritchie Mac… faults and all… and no matter what anyone else thinks, his determination was second to none.

•••••••••••

The guy was an exceptional angler, very helpful towards anyone who asked advice regarding the fishing side of things, and was generous when it came to putting his hand in his pocket at the pub while helping to celebrate another's success on the Yateley complex – now that's the kind of angler whose company you don't mind!!

•••••••••••

•••••••••••

Ritchie's capture of Bazil is the reason I started carp fishing, and I know a few others who say the same thing. I had the privilege of learning a lot from him when I was just a kid on the Yateley complex. I witnessed him catch Jumbo and Heather. He was the original superstar of carping, before Terry took over that mantle.

•••••••••••

I hope he does take up carping again. He is more than welcome to come and have a dabble on my lake whenever he wants. He was an inspiration for a generation. I just wish I could get a copy of the picture of him with Bazil to stick on my wall.

•••••••••••

Will always remember meeting Ritchie at Stanstead Abbotts big lake at the time. It was clear that the guy was just in a different fishing league in terms of his methods and determination. One of only two moments I've been in awe of a very, very special angler.

•••••••••••

The guy basically showed me how to carp fish when I was a kid and he was on the Copse all those years ago. Was less about rigs and bait and more about a different way of thinking about things. I liked him a lot and will always be grateful for all the help. Wish him well wherever he is and whatever he is doing these days.

•••••••••••

I met him on the Kennet a few years back now. What a gent he is. I chatted with him for about 45 minutes and then started fishing. When he packed up he came over to shake my hand and say goodbye. The 45-minute chat was very eventful, to say the least… Attended a lot of shows he was at and he (when he was not largeing it up) was a true gent to me. It was a proud day when I had my picture with him, Rod, Tim and John W. Can never take away what he did and how many he inspired, but he will tell you that it is not all it seems to be and you do have to balance it or pay the ultimate price…

•••••••••••

It was a real buzz to meet him. I was only 13 at the time, had just had my first 20 and Ritchie and Rod Hutchinson were the main men!!! Whenever I saw him since that day at carp conferences and meetings he always said hello and was a really genuine top bloke.

•••••••••••

Comments From The Forums

••••••••••••

Have been fortunate enough to meet him on the bank. He's a true legend and character in my carping lifetime. He probably started a lot of carpers' careers that fella did single handed with his capture of Bazil. It did mine.

••••••••••••

Cor, it's like seeing your target fish in the bottom of your net having Ritchie back in a modest limelight. Welcome back, Ritch!!!!

••••••••••••

Ritchie McDonald is one of the most sensitive, funny, knowledgeable men I have ever met. A True Gent, and it is a privilege to be working with him.

••••••••••••

I had the privilege of watching him angle on Yateley for many years, and witnessed some of the bigger fish captures. The man was awesome. Would have given Terence a run for his money over the past few years. Let's hope he is back angling. He would be a welcome addition to the collective pool of carp angling wisdom, and he was a gentleman, to boot.

••••••••••••

I had a flick through his book last night... fantastic read. Looking forward to the 16th June even more now!

••••••••••••

One word 'LEGEND'.

PART ONE
RITCHIE ON CARP

Preface

It was a steaming-hot day in July – the sort we used to get all the time before someone half-inched the British summer. A cloud of dust rose behind my car as I drove up the track that runs alongside Horseshoe Lake, in Gloucestershire. There was no sign of my mate's Saab Turbo, so I took my time unloading the tackle from the car and selecting a suitable swim.

There had been a few carp caught during the previous week, all to a 16-year-old lad. He had been giving everyone else a pasting, adults and youngsters alike, and I was hoping he would still be there, so that I could check him out and watch him in action. So when the very same boy appeared while I was setting up, I was pleased to see him.

"Just arrived have you?" he began, and I nodded. "Have you fished here before?" I could see he was bursting to tell me about his catches, so I decided to pretend I knew nothing about the water. Here was my chance to find out just how good he was.

I asked him where he thought I should cast, how deep the water was and even whether there were any gravel bars, and he trotted out the answers without hesitation. He told me the bait he had been using and the type of rig, so I unhooked mine from the butt-ring and asked him what he thought of it. He pulled it and twisted it, moved things around a bit and then gave it back, saying it was better now. I couldn't resist going all the way and started asking him what he thought of my tackle. A few of his friends wandered along the bank and sat down on the grass at the back of the swim to watch him handing out advice.

My mate arrived soon afterwards and he gave me some very funny looks when he heard what I was asking, but I tipped him the wink without any of the boys noticing, and he joined in.

"Could you cast out for me?" I asked, adding that I wasn't much good at casting and that if he did it for me I could watch and try to copy his style. He picked up one of the rods, reeled the lead to just short of the tip, folded back the bail-arm and had taken the rod up to the casting position when he saw printed on the underside of the butt the words 'Ritchie McDonald'.

His face was a picture. "You're not, are you?" he asked, but he knew from my smile and the laughter behind him that it was true. He never did show me how to cast. He just closed the bail-arm, put the rod back in the rest and started to walk away, his face as red as a beetroot.

I called after him and reluctantly he came back. I said: "You've got nothing to be ashamed of. You were willing to help me when I said I didn't know much about fishing, even though you had nothing to gain by it. I wish there were more people about who were prepared to do that."

I thought of this boy as I started to write this book, and I realized that, for me, catching carp is only part of the pleasure of fishing. If someone is struggling and I can give them some help that puts a fish on the bank, I'm as pleased for them as I would be if I had caught the fish myself.

So if, with this book, I can help others by recalling the lessons I have learnt over the years, and a few of the laughs, then I will have achieved what I set out to do. For I believe natural skills such as watercraft, fish-spotting ability, instinctive decision-making and perseverance when others have packed up will give a good angler an edge over other good anglers, not secret baits or rigs. If you help others, they will help you, but if you are the secretive type, you will get left out in the cold.

Part One

Chapter One
Early Days and Late Nights

The first carp I ever saw made my eyes pop out like organ stops, It was lying in the bottom of another angler's keepnet, as golden and gorgeous a common as you could wish to see. And although it sounds corny, from that day onwards no other fish has held the same fascination for me as carp.

It is like falling in love with someone at first sight, and knowing you'll never feel the same way about anyone else. I've fished for other species, but carp always have been and always will be my first love.

I don't even know the name of the man who was holding the keepnet. But the content of that net captured my imagination. Moreover, the man promised to teach me all he knew, and from that day to this I have never set eyes on him.

But he provided me with a memory that has lasted a lifetime, and on that warm summer day he turned a non-angler into a would-be angler. It was my first day of fishing and, like most people, I will remember it until my last.

It wasn't even my idea to go, it was my mum's. I was dead against it, but I had been getting in a bit of bother and she thought it would keep me out of mischief. She'd had a win on the bingo and splashed out on a 'Junior Fishing Kit'.

It contained a very short rod, a tiny reel, a float, line, some split shot and some hooks. It might as well have been a car aerial, a cotton reel, bent pins and a bit of string for all I knew, or cared, about angling.

With my fishing kit and a packed lunch, I was handed over to my friend's dad, who was a keen angler and who had offered to take me to a local lake.

At nine years of age I would rather have been out messing about with my mates, and when we got there I soon got bored and started wandering around looking for trouble. There was a bloke fishing a little way from us and he had his rod propped up in the air and was fishing in the lily pads. I asked him what he was doing and he said he was legering for carp. I asked him if he had caught anything and he said he had one in the keepnet.

I remember him bending down to pull the net out and then suddenly before my eyes was this massive fish. He didn't seem even proud of it as it lay in the bottom of his net, but my eyes were popping out of my head. It looked enormous and I thought there and then: "I've got to catch one of these."

I asked him if he would help me catch one, and even before he agreed I had gone to fetch my tackle. He cast out for me and although I didn't catch, he said he would be there again the weekend after.

He wasn't, and I have never seen him since, but although I felt let down at the time, I have him to thank for getting me started on a lifetime of carp fishing.

From that day on I was only interested in catching carp, and apart from three years off, when I met and married my missus, I have spent most of every season trying to catch them. Once I'd got her down the aisle, it was back on the bank, and carp, and still more carp.

My mum was right in thinking fishing would keep me out of trouble, and she was just in time. Moving from Acton was not a good idea. In Acton you could get into trouble if you went looking for it, but where we moved to trouble came looking for you, and found you.

Until I moved I didn't know what a swear word was, but within a week of arriving I was nicking money from the washing machines in the block of flats where we lived.

I got my first taste of villainy and my first smack in the mouth, and I hadn't even turned eleven. No wonder my mum was worried.

In a lot of ways I've got fishing to thank for keeping me out of trouble. When I hear about some of the people I used to spend time with and the things they have got up to since, I realize how close I came.

Don't get me wrong, I'm not trying to make out I've led a blameless life. I've tried wearing a halo, but it just doesn't go with my designer sweatshirt and break-dancing boots, but I do try to keep my nose clean.

Even when fishing took me away from bad company, I still had to find the one shilling day ticket money for Gunnersbury Park Lake, near Chiswick, and the easiest way to get it was certainly not the most honest.

But what really held me back was not being able to read or write properly until I left school, so books were a bit of a problem, and with no one to teach me how to fish, I struggled to catch anything for a couple of years. In truth, not having had a father to teach me, I didn't even know there were books written on fishing.

Bait had to be one thing: cheap. That meant bread or worms, but I made out that worms were the best, so that my mum let me out after dark to get them. I spent half an hour getting them and two hours messing about with my mates. She must have thought we had the leanest worm picking patch in West London.

Everything had to be learnt as I went along, and it was like being shipwrecked and trying to catch fish from a desert island. When I tied a knot I used a shoelace bow, because it was the only knot I knew, so the fish I managed to hook stayed on for about ten seconds.

My tackle was up-market, though, or at least more up-market than the Junior Fishing Kit. Now I would turn heads at the lake with a six-foot sea rod, and instead of the tiny, green fly-reel I had begun with, I was now the proud owner of an Intrepid Black Prince reel, price 15 shillings (75p if you weren't around then), with a ratchet that stayed on all the time.

But despite my fumbling attempts at fishing, my lack of knowledge and my laughable tackle, one capture gave me the confidence to carry on, and made me think, even in those early days, that I might have the luck to come up with the goods when it mattered most.

I was fishing for carp with bread, and was reeling in when the line went tight and I felt a tug at the other end. I played the fish out, or rather cranked it towards me until it refused to come in, and then cranked it a bit further, and was surprised to see it was a perch.

I landed it and I can remember the weighing as if it were yesterday. On someone else's scales it went 4lb 15oz, a fish well over the British record, although I didn't know it then.

Part One

Since that day I have never been far away from big fish for long, sometimes by design and sometimes, as in the case of the 3lb roach I landed on a boilie, by accident.

But that one capture made me think I might be able to get good at this sport and I started to struggle through angling papers, reading with difficulty, but learning quickly.

Another problem presented itself. If I was going to fish regularly I needed some sort of transport. I couldn't afford the bus, and I had got fed up with walking. Now in those days you had things called butcher's bikes, and everybody had one except butchers, because people kept nicking them. All you had to do was wait until a delivery boy came by and parked one in front of a house, and as soon as he had turned his back and started up the garden path, you jumped on and pedaled away like mad.

For most people one bike was enough, until they bumped into the owner, and were 'persuaded' to give it back. I managed to get through quite a few, though, mainly because I was night fishing the park lake, which was not allowed, and so I had to lift the bike over the locked gates and drop it, to land with a crash six feet below on the other side. This did wonders for my shoulder muscles, but the bikes didn't stand up to this treatment for long, and I was soon on the lookout for another.

I can tell you're wondering how I managed to get permission to go night fishing at the age of twelve. Well, I asked my mum if I could go and she wouldn't let me, so as we lived on the first floor of a block of flats I waited till she had gone to bed, which was usually when the dot came up on the TV, and then opened the balcony door and lowered my gear down to the ground.

I did this every Friday, and told my mum I was going fishing early in the morning, so she didn't get suspicious when she saw me packing my tackle, and didn't wonder where I was in the morning. She liked her kip too much to be up early enough to find me out.

So there I was, out without permission, on a stolen bike, breaking into a park and night fishing, when it wasn't allowed. I should have realized a halo would never suit me.

I may as well make a full confession and tell you about my first car, which I had to get when butchers started buying padlocks and the supply of bikes dried up.

I was fourteen at the time, and I bought it, a blue Anglia, from a Jehovah's Witness for £10. He told me I could have it if I went to one of their meetings, so I took him at his word, went to exactly one of the meetings, and then drove off into the night unconcerned that I was three years under age.

It had wonderful wide wheels, and I drove it around the flats car park at 4am when no one was around, just for practice. Driving took a bit of getting used to, but I didn't hit any other cars, just walls once or twice.

I took it on fishing trips, and escaped from the noise and dirt of the city streets. Maybe it was because I was always surrounded by people shouting, cars stuck in traffic jams and aeroplanes roaring overhead that I found night fishing so wonderfully peaceful.

Every sound seemed louder and every silence quieter than during the day. Everything in nature was happening around me. Birds were rustling in the trees, animals moving through the grass, the whole waterside was alive with the kind of sounds I had never heard before on the busy streets where I lived.

Night fishing frightened me as well as exciting me, and I felt drawn to, and yet threatened by, that secret world, sitting alone, wide-eyed and alert, listening to the squeak of voles and

At seventeen I caught my first double.

the rustle of hedgehogs as they went about their nightly business.

I thought even then that it was a shame most of my friends couldn't experience this. It seemed, as children, all we heard were adults shouting at us, and there was no quiet time for us to be alone with our thoughts, unless they, like me, went fishing and escaped.

It wasn't long before I liked that world better than the one I lived in during the day, and I began to spend more time fishing and less time with my mates. The town just seemed so noisy, and when we went up to the East End, there were doors being thrown open and people arguing and shouting or running, and you were always on your guard. But by the waterside, although you heard animals moving through the grass and foxes fighting, these were things that were not going to hurt you.

One evening my mate said he was going to a disco and asked me if I wanted to come, but I said I was going fishing. At 2am he and the rest of them turned up at the lake, girlfriends and all, and started messing about. I saw a different side of them, and didn't have anything to do with them after that.

So I branched out on my own and I suppose the fact that I enjoyed my own company and didn't feel the need to drag others, who were less interested in fishing, along with me meant I was something of a loner. Certainly, judging by the people I have met in fishing over the years, I would say the sport attracts more than its share of loners. And the people interested in fishing for big fish seem to be able to spend the longest time in their own company.

I can spend any amount of time on my own on the bank because when I wake up to hear the birds singing, or coming to the front of my bivvy to take food, I never feel alone. I'll probably get locked up for saying it, but I talk to the fish and try to persuade them to move over my baits. So if you hear me on the bank, chatting away, all alone, you'll know what I'm doing.

Some of the people I respect most in fishing are like that, none of us minds being on our own for days. We will be there, season after season, all on our own except for the ducks and geese, until we have done what we set out to do.

Perhaps that's why you get more good guys in angling than bad guys. It's something I've noticed over the years, for every bad person involved in fishing, there are 20 or 30 good ones, and the majority of the people in the sport are genuine.

Part One

The most successful people often have the right woman behind them. They say behind every good man there is a good woman, well that applies to anglers as well. My early success came at the same time as I was courting my missus.

At seventeen I met her and caught my first double. At nineteen I got married and had my first 'twenty'. I didn't need telling that I had found the right person, and ever since then she has been there, helping me in whatever I wanted to do.

Women I can understand, but I've never been able to understand bosses. When I first left school I would do a week's work, go fishing at the weekend and on Monday there would be the boss waiting at the gate with my cards. The only thing I can think that might have upset them is not telling them that my weekend started on a Thursday evening, but then surely they knew you had to get down to the lake before everyone else if you wanted a choice of swims.

It took me a while to cotton on. My first go at window cleaning lasted three weeks, then I was a cutter for about the same time, a label printer for a shorter time, a sheet metal worker for even less, a coffee machine cleaner for a couple of days and even a dressmaker's assistant.

But the record for the shortest lasting job was on night work. I thought I had it sussed. I would work all night, and fish and sleep all day. Great. I'd cracked it. First night on the new job, I got there late in the evening and worked for about an hour. Then suddenly I felt really tired, the sort of tiredness that makes you feel like propping open your eyelids with matchsticks.

I was working a machine and soon it got to the point when I was almost asleep. In the past when I had left I had asked for my money, but I thought it was pushing it a bit after one hour's labour, so I got up and walked out and never went back.

The trouble with work was it interfered with fishing, but there was one job I couldn't have done even part-time, it was so boring.

At nineteen I got married and had my first 'twenty'.

I had to take four corners off thousands of square plates using a ball press. After three or four rounds of this I thought there must be a faster way, so I started doing two at a time. This worked a treat so I had a go at three, and then four, and then five.

I think I was on six at a time and had piles of finished plates next to me when the foreman came over, and without even raising his voice said: "Go and get your cards." Apparently they had to be finished one at a time to get them right, and I had ruined about £2,000 worth of stock in a couple of hours.

But I always went back to window cleaning. The beauty of it was it started early, finished early, and if you didn't turn up for a couple of days, some sweet talking would get you your job back afterwards. And if you were good, you didn't clean many windows either.

Office blocks were the best. The object was to do nothing and then present your bill for one of the big-wigs to sign. You've heard of stitch-one-purl-one, well this was do-a-floor, miss-a-floor. Some people got wise and checked up, but there are always a few people like that in life, and most times if I got away with it, I was fishing by 11am.

Then there were women getting undressed… and more. The worst experience I ever had with regard to nudity was when I was up this double-twenty ladder (forty feet high). The curtains were closed and I was just starting to clean when they were whipped open, which in itself is a frightening thing at that height, and there was this geezer, standing there totally naked. I didn't know where to look, with my nose almost pressed against the glass, and all I could think to do was mumble: "Sorry mate" (which was a bit daft because he couldn't hear me through the glass), get slowly down the ladder and wait for him to go.

Another time I was dangling from a cradle at sixty feet when a pigeon came from nowhere and flew straight at my face. I fell forty feet straight onto some rose bushes. A few seconds after I landed, a woman poked her head out of one of the windows and said: "Mind my roses!"

Have you ever been cleaning a window and come across a bit you just can't reach. At forty feet up it's even harder, yet there's always someone in the room who comes to the window and points out the bit you've missed. This woman made me reach a bit too far one day. I knew I couldn't get to the spot, and the woman that did it knew I wouldn't be able to reach it either, but she insisted.

So I stretched across, and over I went. I can remember thinking: "I knew that would happen" as I toppled off the ladder and crashed into this bush. I had thorns in my back and thorns in my side. I now know what it must be like for those geezers who sleep on beds of nails.

The next thing I knew she had rushed out of her flat, down the stairs and out into the garden. "At least she's good enough to come and help me," I thought, but she only told me off for damaging her bushes. I must admit I lost my rag. I gave her a right earful and, as anyone who has got on my wick and been on the receiving end of one of my ear bashings will tell you, I don't mince words. Well, she ran indoors and I went after her and I must admit I did a bit of damage to her front door, but then she shouldn't have slammed it in my face. I thought we were quits, but when I got back to the office, there was the boss with my cards. She'd only rung them up and told them.

Judging that the best form of defence is attack, I enrolled with another lot and got a round where I could learn to use a sixty footer. It was a while before the others would let me go up all of it, and even longer before I was left alone with the ladder. But the time came when they were at lunch, and I had reached the end of a building. Here was my chance to show off my skill.

I decided to have a go at moving it. After all, the principle was the same as a forty footer, surely.

I still say I would have been all right if the wind hadn't caught it just as I got it to the corner, but once it started falling there was no stopping it. I felt like shouting: "Timber!" as sixty feet of aluminium ladder crashed through the roof of this car on the corner. I looked all around me, saw no one, and did the only thing I could think of in that situation… I ran away.

I remember a short time as a mini-cab driver. This bloke got in the cab at 5.30pm and said I could have a tip if I could get him to where he wanted to go by 5.40pm. I've always liked a challenge, so I roared off into the traffic. I got him there, looking a bit pale, and he gave me the tip, but I also got the sack for "putting lives at risk," thanks to someone who reported me.

Fork-lift truck driving was the best. We used to have high-speed races around the yard, but they gave me my cards after three weeks. They said I wasn't safe behind the wheel of a pedal car.

I filled in the gap after that with some scaffolding, and a spot of demolition, but working at the brewery was an experience; I got the sack for working too hard.

My philosophy has always been: Get your work done and go home. It even applies to my carp fishing, in that I do everything in my power to put the fish I want on the bank, and when I've succeeded I pack up and go home.

They told us to move some barrels from one place to another. We got going and we weren't working particularly hard or fast, but a couple of hours later this bunch of blokes came round and said we had to slow down because we wouldn't get any overtime. I told 'em where to go, but then things got rather heavy and I decided my future with the company looked a bit bleak, so I left.

The British Rail parcels job lasted three weeks, which was quite a long time for me, so I took them to the industrial tribunal over my sacking, and won. I didn't like the job much though, so I left anyway. Then I became a driver, but I kept getting lost so they gave me the sack, too.

But by now I was getting good at getting the sack, and I'd timed it to happen on a Wednesday or Thursday, so I could go fishing. No wonder my fishing improved, the number of free weekends I had.

With the money I earned from the bit of work I did manage to do, I bought a Mitchell 300 reel, and I saved up Embassy coupons to buy my first carp rod.

The postman just left it standing on the doorstep, so I wrote to the firm and said it hadn't arrived and they sent me another one. I know it was dishonest, but in those days I was even more strapped for cash than I am now. Anyone who saves Embassy tokens has to be desperate.

In those days we used a Heron bite alarm, a dough bobbin and a penny on the reel spool with a plate underneath. You get what we called a "buzz-bong" run from the sound of the Heron, and then the penny on the plate. This could be heard all night long from various parts of the lake.

I remember agreeing to go fishing with a bloke I had met. He seemed to know what he was doing, and I thought it could be a good chance to learn a thing or two. The first hint I got that I had misjudged him was when he struck a run and fell backwards off his seat. He knew even less than me, but at least he boosted my confidence.

Mind you, I can talk. The first time I fished the Grand Union Canal I struck at a roach and sent it sailing into someone's back garden, after being told to: "Hit it as hard as you can when the float goes under". The worst bit was having to ask the bloke pruning his hedge if I could have my roach back.

Early Days and Late Nights

Tackle was basic, with a coin and a dish as a bite 'alarm'.

But I got keener, the sessions got longer, and the tackle got better. I once fished Thursday, Friday, Saturday and Sunday without any sleep. On another occasion I fell asleep while driving back. I don't know how long I had been asleep, because it was a straight piece of dual carriageway, but I woke up when I hit the roundabout and missed some houses by a few inches.

Experimenting with tactics brought success.

One of my Embassy rods was replaced with my new pride and joy, a Richard Walker Mark IV cane carp rod, which set me back 14 guineas. But if my tackle was getting better, baits were still very basic: catfood, polony and a mixture of sausage meat and white rusk were all used at some time, but the best bait was cheese paste. When I went fishing with my missus I made up a 4lb lump and we put it between us, working our way through it during the 'long weekend'.

But I was beginning to experiment with my tactics and learn a few lessons. I thought I would catch a bigger fish by using a bigger bait, so I put on a lump of paste the size of a small football (I've never been one for doing things by halves). Within ten minutes I had a run and it was a carp of about 8oz, hooked in the mouth.

Years later I was fishing with a friend and he was catching so many small carp that his arm began to ache, and he decided to do something to give himself a breather.

Opening a tin of luncheon meat he put half the tin on a hook and threw it out, but he'd hardly had time to put the silver paper on the line when off it went and he landed a carp of 4lb, again hooked in the mouth.

The more I fished, the more I learnt, and the more people I met to learn from. At Stan Talbot's Lake I met John Allen, who went on to catch the 200lb-plus catfish at Lake St. Cassien, in France, and at Cut Mill I caught my first 20lb carp, on luncheon meat, although spuds were the best bait at the time.

At Longfield I blanked for a long time, until I met John and Eileen Walker, who taught me all they knew about carp fishing, which was a lot. I was fascinated, and they became more than friends, they were like an adopted father and mother to me. John, whom I call the Old Man, and Eileen have influenced my fishing and helped me get my priorities right. They taught me to appreciate the rights of other anglers, and to be happy in my fishing and never to take it so seriously that I couldn't have a laugh and a joke.

We three fished together for several years, until it was time for me to move on. I was hungry to learn more, and to catch bigger and better fish, but I still keep in touch and they are both still dear to me.

Of all the hundreds of people I have known in angling, I have never met anyone, perhaps with the exception of Rod, who could take their place.

So with three 'twenties' under my belt I was keen to catch a 'thirty', but when an invite came to join the Ashlea Pool syndicate in Gloucestershire, Mike Starkey and I, who were fishing Cut Mill together, turned it down, because we had heard there was a lot of arguing going on among the members. But when the invite came again the next year, we knew we couldn't afford to turn it down again. It was 1976, the year before Kevin Maddocks joined.

Luncheon meat worked at Cut Mill, though spuds were the best bait at the time.

At Longfield I blanked for a long time until I met John.

Although I had been a British Carp Study Group member for three years by then, my personal best stood at just 22lb 3oz. I knew the water held a 'thirty' though, and that was the one I wanted to catch.

From the start of my carp fishing I wanted to catch a bigger 'single', then a bigger 'double' and then go one better still. Numbers of fish have never been an attraction, just the biggest in the lake. It would have been better to have joined Ashlea with a list of 'twenties' under my belt, but there was no telling when, if ever, the offer would come again.

Maybe I should not have spent so much time on a hard water like Longfield. On an easier water I might have learnt more quickly, but then just maybe I would not have learnt how to be patient while fishing, an investment that has paid regular dividends over the years.

Chapter Two
Ashlea Antics

The instructions on how to get to Ashlea Pool said: "Don't blink or you'll miss it." It's the smallest carp water I have ever fished, but that wasn't what struck me first about the place, it was the amount of weed.

The water is full of the biggest underwater cabbages I have seen, before or since. If you could have entered them for gardening competitions you would have walked away with the prizes.

Now this would worry some people. If they haven't got gravel bars to cast towards, they don't know what to do, but these surroundings don't bother me. I prefer these sort of waters to gravel pits.

The gin-clear water and enormous carpet of really thick weed looked like problems, but view the lake from the top of a tall tree on a sunny day and you will see four or five tiny clear patches dotted around.

The fish swim between the cabbages, feeding under their leaves, where they are hidden from view, and appearing in the clear patches like grey ghosts, disappearing just as suddenly. It is an uncanny experience watching this from twenty feet up in a tree.

The first time I set eyes on the lake, which I estimate is about three-quarters of an acre, although others put it as large as two acres, was on a working party in May 1976.

I had paid my £43 syndicate fee and been told we could only visit the water on this one day in the Close Season, and only on our rota weeks from June 16, because the lake was in the grounds of the owner's house.

The water wasn't very deep, and with good climbing trees all the way round you could see almost all of the water when the sun was in the right place. This made the task of catching fish from there seem easy, like fishing in your garden pond. But the lake was then, and I believe still is today, one of the hardest waters in the country.

I had a good look around that first day, and spent a lot of time thinking over my tactics for the start of the season. Some people said you had to fish the clear spots, but I knew the fish avoided these as much as possible because they could spell danger.

Others reckoned the thing to do was fish in the weed, using a heavy lead cast high in the air to get it through the cabbages to the bottom. They tied the bait to the bomb with PVA string, which John Roberts had just brought out, and it was carried through to the lake bed with the lead.

I decided not to choose one or the other, but fished both, one rod in the weed and the other out of it. What I lacked in experience I made up for in confidence, and I was sure that if I didn't catch at the start, I would get something eventually.

The first session was in the last week of June. Armed with tic beans from the health food store, I also had a good supply of soft catfood pieces bought from the supermarket, which often brought some strange looks from the shop assistants, and made into a paste.

I headed down the M4 in Vic Gillings' car. I remember that trip as the first and last time Vic let me drive his car. Now I don't know about you, but when I get behind the wheel I'm only interested in wasting as little of my life as possible. Sitting in traffic jams is not the game plan. If I can save myself a few seconds by taking a short cut, or even by pulling the odd stroke, I'll do it. I once beat an E-Type Jag back to London by driving down the central reservation of a dual carriageway to get past a tailback of traffic.

But I must have got a bit carried away in Vic's Rover, because I snapped the gear stick clean off. Somehow while changing from first gear into second I managed to slam it into reverse, which I can really recommend if you want to get the full attention of your passengers. Anyway, getting it out of reverse the gear stick came off in my hand and we had to finish the journey with a screwdriver stuck in the hole where it had been, which meant we had to drive all the way back in second gear!

The car was in a pretty bad way before, but this knocked the final nail into its coffin, and it sat outside my house for months, long after Vic had got another car.

He bought this Morris 1000 van and we shared the petrol, but not the driving. I remember one day we were on our way down and right out of the blue he said: "This car's going to fall apart any minute now." Seconds later there was a clanking noise and the prop shaft buckled.

We stood there by the side of the road, both penniless and stranded, and at the same time we both saw a breakers yard in the distance on the other side of the motorway. We dodged the cars and got across to it, searched the deserted yard until we found the right car, an old Morris that they had been taking to pieces. When we got back, the part fitted perfectly, and the car went like a dream.

I remember being so pleased with the way it was going that when some Hell's Angels on bikes came into view, I reached across and started blowing the horn as we overtook them. Vic wasn't at all impressed and said he thought they would chase us, but the motor didn't let us down.

I've had cars that have never let me down, cars that never did anything but let me down, and cars that were brilliant one minute and terrible the next.

One time I offered to take my missus, Yvonne, down to Selsey Bill in the car, which meant going along a road that was just one hill after another. The car was in a bit of a state, and every time we went up one of the hills it got slower and slower, until first the posh cars were overtaking, then the old cars were overtaking, and then the people walking on the pavement were going faster than us.

We must have been doing about five miles an hour, but when we got to the top, I put my foot to the floor and we went down the other side at 80 miles an hour, passing everything that had passed us on the way up.

The wings on the front were loose, and as we belted down each hill, the wind got under them and made them flap up and down just like the ears of Dumbo the Elephant.

At this point I would like to give you a bit of advice. If you're one of those blokes with a car, who gets put upon by his mates asking for a lift, I've got the perfect solution. I agreed to give these lads a lift to Longfield on a fishing trip one time. "Yeah, pile in," I said. "The more the merrier." They must have thought they'd found a free bus pass, because they packed into the back all smiles.

There weren't too many smiles when I got there, though. I'm a bit of a daredevil when I get behind the wheel, and some people call me Procol Harem, because all my passengers go a Whiter Shade of Pale. I think most of those lads were that colour when we got there, but just in case there was one with a cast-iron stomach among them, I did a handbrake turn in the car park, as a sort of finale. You should have heard the language as they staggered out. Every last one of them vowed never to get in a car with me again, which is funny, because those were the exact same words my brother said to me after my stunt-man impression on an aircraft runway.

I'd been watching *Fall Guy,* that programme where the blokes drive their cars on two wheels, and when we were taking him back to this air base, it seemed a good chance to have a go. I don't really know now what made us drop back the right way up, because at one point we were perfectly balanced on two wheels and it was only by luck that we came down the right way up.

I gave Roger Smith a lift to Savay once and for months afterwards he was going around in a daze and saying to people: "We went sideways." It became his catchphrase, but I still think he was a bit harsh on me, after all, it was he who suggested I see how fast we could go.

I thought it sounded like a good idea at the time, but perhaps the handbrake turn as we roared into the Savay car park was a mistake. We must have gone about 30 yards sideways in a cloud of dust and grit, though I don't know how he knew about it, he had his hands over his eyes at the time.

But I almost learnt my lesson in a big way at Yateley. They say that fate catches up eventually with everyone who lives dangerously. I had got permission to go down a private road at the back of the Copse Lake, and it was snowing as I drove along.

The road was a series of steep slopes, and in the slippery conditions the only way I could get up was to drive fast. I was enjoying myself because, as you've probably gathered, I like a bit of rally driving, but then the steering went soft and I had no control of the car as it flew all over the place. The inevitable happened and it went off the road, coming to a halt just a couple of feet from the edge of the lake. If I had tried to drive out, I'm sure it would have slipped into the water.

I wandered around until I found a couple of blokes who would push me out, but I thought at one stage I might have to call my brother-in-law, who has pulled me out of so many soft spots, he has a tow rope permanently attached to his car. He used to pull me out of the mud down this Lovers' Lane I visited regularly late at night. Why was I there? Why do you think? But it was a bit embarrassing ringing the police to get me out. I did that once and they wanted to know what I had been doing! I said I had gone down to look at the river, but they found that hard to believe in the dark.

Anyway, I was telling you about Ashlea. There were four of us on that rota: Vic Gillings, Geoff Booth, Dave Powell and myself, and ten anglers in the syndicate. When Vic and I arrived for the first three-day session we got a shock. The water was low, far lower than when I had been there in May, and in the swim I chose, known as Jack's Hide, the wooden rod-rest frame built by Jack Hilton was so far away from the water's edge that I used the front rest to hold the rod butts. But worse was to come that year. I'm sure anyone who was fishing in 1976 remembers it as the year of one of the worst droughts for over a decade. Water levels dropped, shallows became deoxygenated and the last thing the fish were interested in was food.

I didn't realize how important that first trip was, coming before the drought got a stranglehold. If I had, I would have been paying attention when the bottle-top-and-isotope indicator rose up to the butt ring at 1am on the first night.

I fell out of bed, picked up the rod, and I couldn't believe what happened next. I was literally dragged along by an incredible force on the other end. I was fishing with a closed bail arm, and the hook pulled out before I could give any line. I shook for hours afterwards. What I didn't know was that I had missed my one and only chance of the season at Ashlea.

I fished three sessions, each lasting three days, and one single-day session, but conditions got worse and worse, as they did on a lot of other waters, and before long we were spending our time in the pub. It was so hot in the day that we knew we stood no chance of a run, so we drank beer and talked fishing, often as much fun as fishing itself, and then went back to the lake to sleep in the sun.

It gave us a chance to get to know each other well and find out each other's strengths and weaknesses. The lads soon decided I should be cook, and this suited me fine. They always had lots more grub than me, so in return for handling the pots and pans I got some of their nosh.

Maybe that's why I got on so well with Vic. He loved his food. No matter how bad something turned out, he would always eat it. If the egg sarnies ended up on the floor, Vic would be the one to pick them up, dust them off, and get them down his neck. No wonder we called him the Human Dustbin.

I don't know if the lack of action brought us all together, but I can't remember anyone having an argument. There were only two fish caught on our rota: Dave had a 28lb 12oz fish, and Geoff one of 17lb, but there was no jealousy or back biting.

I wasn't too disappointed at my results in the first year of Ashlea. These two fish were the only ones caught by the entire ten-man syndicate, all very good anglers. I'd had the chance of a fish, despite the freak weather, and was keen to get back the following year. It just had to come good for me.

In the first year I hadn't put much bait in, mainly because I like to feel my way into a syndicate and find out other people's likes and dislikes on things like baiting up and using a torch.

But on Ashlea they were easy to get on with because no one interfered with anyone else's fishing, so I decided to attack the water and put a lot of bait in. In 1976 I had been using particles and catfood paste, and thought that in such a small area of water the fish would have to visit your swim at least once a day, so there was no need to bait heavily.

By the following year I had some protein boilies to try, given to me by John Perkins, and this Strawberry flavoured stuff had produced good results for him at Darenth the year before.

I made them up, golf-ball sized, lightly skinned and coloured red, and took three hundred along with me to the May working party visit. Once again this was my only chance to see the water before the start of the season.

A new area had been dug out of the lake, forming an extra bay, and knowing how curious carp are of anything new, I put most of the bait in there. I noticed two or three of the other members also baiting up, although no one put in as much as me.

Part One

    I will always remember that day because of one incident. I had been keeping my eyes peeled for signs of fish, but had seen just one when I was called over to help pull down an old hide which was beginning to look as if it might fall down on its own and do some damage. We had been banging away with sledgehammers for four or five minutes when someone said: "Look at that!" We turned round and saw every fish in the lake right in front of us in the margins. Every visit after that I banged my rod rests in with a mallet in the hope the fish would do the same again. I think they must have been curious as to where the noise was coming from, because it was normally such a quiet place.

    Fish are definitely curious. There have been times when I've cast out over and over again, trying to get into just the right spot, and then had a run straight away. Other times I have cast to the right spot first time and got no action. I've put out twenty or thirty baits and seen fish roll over the same area before I've finished. I'm pretty sure it's not just the smell of the bait, but the noise of it going in as well that attracts the fish. It's certainly worked for me on occasions, although I wouldn't make a habit of casting fifteen times on purpose.

    But that sighting of fish at Ashlea was like someone carrying a tray of food in front of a hungry man. Now I had seen the fish, most of them over 20lb, and all I had to do was get them in the mood to feed.

    I felt more confident on that working party than ever before. The lake level was back up to normal, the fish were showing themselves more freely, and the new bay looked full of promise.

    When June 16 arrived and no one headed for the bay, I was surprised but glad, and even more sure that success would soon follow. Vic picked one of the hides, while Geoff fished further off to my left along the same bank.

    I was the only one with protein baits, because in those days you couldn't walk into a tackle shop and buy the good gear you can today. You had to have friends in the food industry. But the atmosphere in our rota was such that we agreed to share bait if one of us was catching and the others were not.

    I couldn't see my swim because there was a mound of earth in front of me, and I had to kip on one side of it and set the rods up on the other. All I could see were the handles. I cast out for the first time and had started clearing up some bits and pieces, the way you do when you have just set up, when the buzzer sounded.

    I couldn't believe it was a fish, so I pulled the bobbin back down to the ground, muttering about tench being a nuisance. I don't know what made me decide just to have a quick look over the mound, but when I did, I saw this carp swimming off and I realized I had just pulled the bait out of its mouth. After last season I wondered if I might have just blown my only chance of the year.

    I joined the others for a pint when everything was tidy, and in drowning my sorrows I overdid it a bit. When I got back I cast out, I don't know where, flopped into bed and was just drifting off into dreamland when one of the buzzers went off.

    The bobbin went up to the top, but then stopped, and stayed there. I pulled it down again, got back into the sack and had just shut my eyes when the same thing happened again. At any other time, a run would have been a dream come true after just one chance in a year, but with a few pints inside of you, as I'm sure you know, your interests don't extend much further than a good, long kip.

I pulled the bobbin back down, climbed back into the soft, warm depths of my bed, and up it went again. I lost my rag. I fought my way out of the sleeping bag, stumbled across to where the rods were, and pulled it back down hard. All of a sudden the line was whipped out of my hand, and the whole lake erupted. Still well drunk, I can remember thinking I had hooked into Jaws, as the fish steamed across the lake and leapt out of the water with the pressure I was piling on. It jumped again in Vic's swim, knocking both his rods off the rests, at which point he woke up, also the worse for wear, and thought he was in.

Geoff came along the bank to help me and I haven't got a clue how long I played the fish for, but the next thing he was sliding the net under a beautiful leather carp of 32lb 12oz, known as Lucky.

I didn't care what else I caught that season, I had achieved an ambition, and this one capture made up for everything that had gone before. The blank sessions of the previous year didn't seem all that unpleasant. I was well chuffed.

It's amazing how a big fish like that can sober you up, and I couldn't wait for first light, to get some photos. When the sun got up and the lads gathered round, I got the camera gear ready and had just picked the fish up when one of the rods went off. I told Vic to hit the run, but he said he wouldn't because it wasn't his rod. I put the fish down, covered it up, and ran across to the rod, but by the time I got to it, the fish had dropped the bait.

I went back, got the photos, and was just putting the fish back when the other rod went off, and this time Vic agreed to hit it. He was just picking the rod up when he saw the fish,

I can remember thinking I had hooked Jaws, as the fish steamed across the lake and leapt out of the water.

Part One

Lucky at 32lb 12oz.

a common of about 18lb, belting off down the lake away from the bait. I couldn't believe it. Last season I had one run all year. This season I had one fish on the bank, two other runs, and I had been on the water only twenty-four hours. I was shaking, partly from the excitement and partly from the hangover.

I almost didn't notice when the third rod went off. I reached for it and hit this one fair and square. After a good fight I slid him over the net, and looking down into the folds I recognized the fish as the one I had spooked the day before. Little Fatty, as he is affectionately known, weighed 20lb 8oz.

With a personal best and a 'twenty' under my belt, it wouldn't have bothered me if I hadn't caught anything else all season.

The big 'un was also a record for Ashlea Pool. It was caught by Vic a few weeks later at 8 oz lighter, but it went on to reach 38lb, which was when Kevin Maddocks caught it to set up the present lake record.

I think I was the only one to get action on the first trip, because I pre-baited heavily and chose to fish in the newly-dug bay. The fish were certainly keen to make up for the lost feeding time of the previous season, and in July Alan Downie had a 30lb 8oz fish on his first visit, the same day that Vic had his 'thirty'. Of the nine fish caught by the syndicate that year, three were thirties, five were twenties and one was a double.

I had one other chance, on a floater. It was when the weather again made fishing hard in July and August. I had tried floater before at the start of the season, but hadn't got any response, so I didn't bother taking any with me.

Little Fatty, as he is affectionately known, weighed 20lb 8oz.

Part One

The owner's wife, Mrs Perry, came out to the bottom of her garden one afternoon and threw a load of bread on to the pool. Straight away fish appeared and started slurping it down. I went around for a look, and they were all whackers, so I got a bit of bread from the food in the car and threw a slice out. As the crumbs started dropping through the water a fish followed the trail up and all of a sudden this whole slice folded in three and disappeared.

I was dumbfounded. I'd never seen this happen before, and once again my hands began to shake like a plate of jelly on a high-speed train. I got my rod from the swim, picked up a slice of bread, folded it in half three times, and put my hook through the middle.

I cast out, throwing a couple of other pieces around, and as soon as the line hit the water, the fish stopped feeding. I sat there for a bit, but nothing happened and I remember looking at this bird tweeting in the tree next to me. When I looked back the line was peeling off the spool, and I was so surprised I fumbled the strike. I just saw this fish belt away, and I knew it was one of the bigger ones.

I cast out again, and as soon as the bait hit the water, a fish took it. I struck straight away, far too soon, and missed it, pulling the hook out of the bait and leaving the fish with a free offering.

That was my last session, and I couldn't help thinking it could have been a very memorable one. I wasn't going to make those mistakes again in a hurry.

Money was short and I was fishing Longfield at every opportunity, keen to get a big one out of there. I was more than happy with my achievements at Ashlea, but I had caught the biggest fish in there, and when I have taken the best fish, not necessarily the biggest, from a water, I move on to a new place and a new challenge.

Gloucestershire is an expensive place to go fishing when you live in Surrey, so I said goodbye to the Pool and took advantage of an offer to fish a water in the Colne Valley as a guest.

It led to one of the best set of sessions I have ever had. I had been to Yeoveney with Geoff Spooner, and on the way back he popped in to one of his other waters, which was the Con Club, and we saw a guy catch three 'upper twenties' in as many minutes on luncheon meat, sausage meat and catfood.

That really got me excited, and I asked if there was any chance of being able to fish as a guest. I couldn't help wondering what a protein bait and Robin Red would do if this bloke could clean up on ordinary baits. Geoff agreed, and I gave him some bait to put in before we fished it. The first session was a disaster. I expected the fish to go absolutely crackers on the bait, but we had one run each, Geoff landing a 23lb mirror, and me breaking off on a mussel bed.

We could only fish nights because he had a full-time job, and on my way home that morning I was beginning to think the bait might not be as good as I thought, so I changed to the Strawberry I had used at Ashlea.

The effect was incredible. In eight one-night trips we landed twenty-one fish over 20lb, Geoff catching the most by a long way. I felt I was unlucky. Almost every fish I hooked was lost when the line parted on a bed of freshwater mussels. Sometimes I wouldn't even get to the rod before the line dropped slack. It was driving me crazy, but meanwhile Geoff couldn't go wrong.

In eight one-night trips we landed twenty-one fish over 20lb.

A switch from Red Devil baits, made with Robin Red, to Strawberry, worked a treat.

At one stage I saw him strike, so I went along to his swim to watch. By the time I got there his other rod had also gone off and he had struck that as well, and I was about to help when I heard my rod go off. I ran back and hooked a fish, but the line hit a mussel bed again and back it came. I looked down and the other rod, which I had dipped into the water, was going, and this time I landed the fish, a mirror of 23lb 2oz. All the fish, the biggest 27lb, which fell to Geoff, took the Strawberry boilies.

Not surprisingly I was keen to get on the water myself. I got to know the bailiff during these visits as a guest, and by keeping my nose clean and making him cups of tea (I can be an artful devil when I want to be) I got him to put me forward, and I was accepted for the following year.

Unfortunately I didn't get the chance to thank him, because he died before the start of the season, but I will always be grateful for the chance he gave me. Thanks to him I now had another top water to fish after pulling out of Ashlea, but even better was still to come.

That winter I was at a British Carp Study Group meeting when John Carver approached me and asked if I would like to fish the famous Redmire Pool. I said: "Who doesn't?" and he set up a meeting between myself and Tom Mintram, the syndicate boss.

All sorts of questions were asked, to see if I was prepared to help the syndicate or just wanted to fish for my own gain. I felt pleased with the way it had gone, and a few days later the phone rang and it was Tom to say I had been accepted.

It was like catching a big fish. Like many other anglers, I had always held an ambition to fish the water, but never thought I would ever achieve that aim. I really couldn't afford to go, but I took out a bank loan to pay the syndicate fee of £177.

Suddenly, two top waters were open to me, but there was no contest when it came to deciding which one would be given the most attention. Redmire was easily the tops.

Part One

Chapter Three
Redmire – A Dream Come True

I've only ever had three ambitions in fishing: to catch a 30lb carp, then to catch a 40lb carp, and to fish Redmire Pool.

Just to see the place, to drive down the lane, like Richard Walker had twenty-five years before in his battered Ford 10, and to sit in the swims fished and written about by Jack Hilton and BB was a dream come true. It sounds corny but I wouldn't have cared if I'd not had a single run all the time I fished there, but I felt so proud to see the lake and so happy just to sit quietly on the banks that setting foot in the place was pleasure enough.

But Redmire wasn't going to be all nostalgia and no action. When the time came to say goodbye, she had provided me with a few stories, a few fish and a chance to catch a record carp.

I felt so happy and proud just to sit quietly on the banks of Redmire.

Redmire - A Dream Come True

My first sighting of the carp fisherman's Mecca came on a warm, late-April day in 1978 when the syndicate gathered for a working party. John Carver and I let the car roll down the lane in the famous fashion, and the first thing we saw was the start of the Dam and the corner of the pool.

It was a fantastic feeling, simply incredible, and I just didn't have enough time to soak it all up on that first visit. The other members had all fished before, and I didn't have time to sit down and drink in the atmosphere while there was work to be done, but all the same I loved every minute of that first day.

The Dam rail had to be repaired and swims cleared, and while most of us were working hard, we didn't miss an opportunity to get up a tree and look for signs of fish when we thought no one was looking.

We slaved away from 9am till 6pm, tidying swims and getting the famous Redmire punt back in good condition. I saw a few fish that were probably 'twenties', but because they were so close to the bank they looked like monsters.

My next visit was three weeks later, when there were some willows to be planted. I didn't have to go, but I took every opportunity to pay the lake a visit.

The carp fisherman's Mecca, in 1978.

Part One

By the time June arrived I was full of the place, having soaked up the atmosphere and history, and re-read Jack Hilton's *Quest for Carp*. I didn't have any great plans on how I was going to fish Redmire. I just wanted to cast out and sit quietly, imagining what it must have been like in the olden days. When I fished in a famous swim, I would pretend I was there at the time that Walker or Hilton were playing one of the fish that made them famous, remembering the words from their books.

Our rota had the first week of the season, which was perfect, and I left very early in the morning in my old Cortina, zooming along the empty roads on one of those sunny summer mornings that make you vow to get up early every day from that day onwards. I was nervous, and I went to look for Tom, but as it was 6am, he and my two other rota members, Dave Short and Chris Seager, were still asleep. I walked past them up to the shallows, but didn't see anything, and when I came back, Tom was just getting up.

We shared a cup of tea, and I can honestly say I've never had tea made that way before or since. He would put a cup on the stove, put a tea-bag and some milk and water in it, and wait for the whole lot to boil.

Maybe I was still half asleep, or nervous, but I didn't expect it to be hot when he handed the cup to me straight from the stove, and I burnt my fingers. Tom had set up in the Willow swim and I decided to fish opposite him in the Evening Swim. I had seen three commons on a tiny patch of gravel while watching the lake from the top of a tree. I waited for them to move off, and then climbed down, baited the area and set up my gear.

The pitch was overgrown and I couldn't cast where I wanted to because of overhanging branches, so I got into the water to make sure my baits were on that patch of gravel. I put three rods out: one in the middle of the channel, one this side of it and one to my left, then just sat back to take in the atmosphere of the famous lake.

No one had seen any action, but at 10.30pm the line started peeling off the right-hand rod. The first run of the Redmire season and it was happening to me. I picked up the rod, struck into the fish, and soon had a 22lb 4oz common lying beside me on the bank.

I was over the moon. My first night at the water and the first fish of the season, a 'twenty', falls to me. The Strawberry protein baits that had worked so well at Ashlea had brought me success again. I made a mental note to buy John Perkins a pint the next time I saw him.

I sacked the fish for photographs the next morning, re-cast, and straight away started to get twitch bites. Instead of seeing line stream confidently from the spool, the bobbin would lift and drop back. There was no way I was going to hit them from inside a sleeping bag under canvas, so I went to the car and got out a huge folding chair, a bit like an armchair, and sat down next to the rods.

All the time I knew there was something funny going on, but I was determined to hook the fish responsible. With my hand hovering over the rod butts, I almost willed the line to move, and when it did, I struck with the speed of a gunfighter going for his holster. Clint Eastwood would have been proud of me.

There was no doubt that I had hooked something, but what a funny fight. I couldn't see what it was even when I got it into the margins because the night was so black, but when I lifted it up against the sky, I found to my horror I had caught an eel.

Redmire - A Dream Come True

Now some people don't mind eels, the same as some people eat frogs' legs and sheep's eyes, but I'm not in that club. No matter what size they are, the horrible things make my skin crawl, and how blokes can actually go out with the sole intention of catching them I'll never know. Anyway, this thing was writhing around on the end of my line and I decided the only way out was to cut the line. My scissors and torch were in the bivvy, so with the eel dangling there, I edged slowly back to reach for them.

I must have forgotten what I was doing with the rod, for all of a sudden this slimy snake hit me in the face. I dropped the rod in fright, dived into the bivvy, grabbed a torch and knife, and went for the eel before it could get me.

I chopped it in half, and after digging a hole and burying one half, I went back for the other bit but it had gone. It must have wriggled away. I recall I put an ice box on the 'grave' of the first half, to stop it burrowing back to the surface, and stayed awake all night watching it. It's silly really, but there's something about eels that does me up.

The morning couldn't come quickly enough. I would forget the eel saga and enjoy the photo session of my first Redmire fish. As far as I was concerned, I didn't care if I blanked for the rest of the season. I had caught a 20lb carp from the legendary pool and I could now die happy.

My first fish from the water, on my first night, was the first of the Redmire season.

Part One

The corner of the dam beside the outfall.

I moved to a swim nearer the car, but it took two days for me to get keen again, and I began to think how I could catch another. I don't feel happy in a swim that I haven't seen fish in at one time or another, and I decided a creep around the lake wouldn't go amiss. I picked up a rod and headed for the shallows, where I started peering into the water from different angles. Lying down on a platform, I could see under a patch of weed, and moving among the weed were two enormous fish.

One was the old 38lb carp, which was carrying a lot of extra weight, and looked about 44lb, the other was a big mirror, heavily in spawn, which looked as if it could top 40lb.

I went to see Tom and he came back and confirmed that the fish was the thirty-eight. Dave joined us, and trying not to tremble too much, I took the half ounce Arlesey bomb off my line and broke open one of my boilies, which were as soft as paste in the middle, and smeared some on the shank of the hook, making a barrel shape.

The fish kept appearing under a hole in the weed, which was about eight inches round and about ten yards out. I cast carefully and the bait went straight through the hole and rested on the bottom. The thirty-eight appeared a moment later, stopped, picked up the bait, and line started peeling off my spool. With a feeling of: "This is it!" I cupped my hand over the front of the reel and hit the fish with a firm, controlled strike, It made one mad dash and had only gone a few yards when the hook pulled out. I know this sounds ridiculous, but it didn't really bother me. I remember saying: "Look at that!" as the hook came flying back, and I could swear Tom and Dave's lower jaws fell open in amazement at my reaction.

I just rebaited, cast to exactly the same spot, and the other fish appeared straight away, stopped and picked up the bait. Wallop! I hit the run in text-book style and was giving the fish line across the shallows when the hook fell out again. My exact words were: "I don't believe that. I have never lost two fish in two casts like that ever before," and I haven't done so since.

Redmire - A Dream Come True

I spent a long time thinking about that incident. The hooks were razor sharp, the tackle was sound, and the strike perfect. At that close range you don't expect to lose one fish, and certainly not two.

The only explanation I could come up with is that both were foulhooked. When I struck, the bait must not have been in the mouth of the fish, and in the shallow water they could have touched the mud and picked up the hooks with their bodies. I'm now satisfied that must have been what happened.

I spent the next three days thinking about those few moments when I had two fish of about 40lb each on the end of my line. They were the last takes I had in opening week, but to have come so close to an incredible catch made me feel that the lake's biggest fish were within my capabilities as an angler, and with patience and perseverance I could hook a fish that would rock the carp world.

The next time I visited the water was in a steady drizzle, the sort that lasts all day, and I was delighted. Two anglers had shared an incredible catch in just the same conditions and I felt I had a chance as long as the weather stayed the same.

I always take lots of clobber with me because I'm always getting into scrapes. I was glad I did on this trip because after one creep round the lake spotting fish and a bit of mooching

Set up in the in-willow swim. Note the old-style cooking burner.

about in one swim, a new one called the Stumps, I was well wet. It's surprising how wet you can get sitting in a tree in the rain.

I got set up, changed clothes and sat next to the rods for a couple of hours, thinking it was going to happen at any moment. By the next morning the indicators still hadn't moved, so I decided to do a bit more tree climbing. I could see fish moving about, but after three hours up in the branches I was wet through again. Back to the car and another change of clothes, and without any sun to dry the first lot out I was down to my last set.

I was beginning to wish the rain had never started when I heard a fish crash out over to my right, under Bowskill's Tree. Grabbing a handful of bait I climbed up the tree and could just make out these two fish, one a mid-twenty and the other about 8lb. Every now and then they would move into a patch of surface reflection and I had to lean right over to keep them in sight. The branch I had hold of was rotten and... well, you can guess the rest. When I hit the water, on top of the fish, I don't know who was more shaken, the carp or me. But my main worry was my clothes. All I had left were the ones I was standing up in, doing an impression of a drowned rat.

There was no choice. I had to drive down to Ross-on-Wye to get some dry gear, wearing the same clothes I had been wearing when I fell in. I'll never forget the look on the shop assistant's face in the clothes store. I was second in the queue at the counter and the bloke in front was rabbiting away while I was dripping. There must have been a dip in the lino where I was standing because a pool of water started to form at my feet.

The shop assistant was trying to concentrate on what his customer was saying, but he kept giving me funny looks. Finally the bloke in front of me left.

"I want some waterproof clothes," I said.

"It's a bit late for that," he said, looking me up and down. I went into the changing room, pulled off my wet things and then realized I had nothing to dry myself with. I thought about using the curtain, but if people were watching, they might have got an eyeful and I might have got arrested. Anyway, I took off all my gear, put these nylon waterproofs on and they fitted okay, so I asked if I could wear them straight away, as I didn't fancy climbing into my wet gear again.

The bloke took my money and put my wet stuff in a bag, but he was still giving me strange looks. He must just have a dodgy eye or something, I thought. But as I walked back along the busy street, people were also staring at me. I didn't realize until I got back to the car and looked down to see just what they were looking at. Being wet underneath the nylon, the clothes had gone see-through, and I might as well have been walking along the street naked. By the time I got back the rain had stopped and the sun had come out, so I was able to put up a washing line to get everything dry and end my afternoon as a streaker.

Redmire was a place where you needed to use your noddle to catch fish. You couldn't choose a method at random and expect to catch fish on it, you had to give them what they wanted at a particular time, because they were always too stubborn to meet you half way.

I made the mistake of trying to get fish feeding on floater. Now, when I do a thing, I do it properly. No half measures for me, and when I say I covered most of the lake in floater, I mean it. The fish must have thought it was snowing floater, but apart from the odd nose appearing above the surface, they just weren't interested. So I decided you couldn't force them to do what you wanted them to do, and went back to bottom baits.

For half-an-hour after night had fallen there was a sound like a thousand drains being unblocked, as the whole lake got stuck into my free offerings and I sat there unable to see what was going on.

So I decided to find the fish, and think out a way of catching them. I went on the prowl for something to test my theory on, and eventually came across a few fish by the corner of the Dam.

They were patrolling just beyond a bed of weed and I thought if I waited for them to go past and anchored a piece of protein-cake floater off the bottom I would be in with a chance. The cast was accurate, a fish appeared, it seemed to like what it saw, and soon a 23lb common was on the bank. The fish was so long I thought it was a 'thirty' when it picked up the bait, and it fought like a demon.

The fourth session was a milestone, for me and, I'm proud to say, for the lake. It was November, when most of the members had put away their carping gear and retired to the fireside. People still didn't believe you could catch carp in the coldest months, and they didn't fancy fishing in frosts and snow. But I wanted to see Redmire in its winter clothing, so I put some corn in with my tackle and headed for Herefordshire. I hadn't expected to catch, so I didn't bother to make up any boilies, but to my surprise I found feeding fish as soon as I arrived, in front of Bramble Island.

I decided to fish from Greenbanks opposite, which meant setting the rods up on one side of a barbed wire fence, and putting the bivvy on the other. I draped a sack over the wire so that I could make a grab for the rods in the dark without spearing myself.

I set up at 3pm, and I hadn't been fishing more than half-an-hour before I got a nice slow run. I struck, played the fish, and landed what I believe to be the first 20lb carp ever landed in winter from Redmire Pool. It weighed 20lb exactly, and Barry Mills arrived just as I was netting it.

The only other winter fish I know of before that was one of 17lb. To make history at the place, even in a small way, was something very special to me. I couldn't believe it when at 6.30pm line started peeling off the other rod, and after a short battle I landed a 25lb 4oz common.

It was the same fish I had caught on that first evening in June, when I burned my hands on Tom Mintram's tea mug.

The last session of the season was in March, just a couple of days before the close of the season. I was in the Willow Swim when I noticed some activity under the oak. I reeled in and cast across to the oak tree opposite, before walking round to put a handful of bait into the spot. One hour later, away it went and I landed a 24lb common, my last fish of the season.

I did have a couple more encounters, but they were lessons learnt rather than fish caught. I had been told that if you get the fish feeding at Redmire, you were guaranteed a capture, so I spent quite a bit of time at the shallow end, throwing in bait and waiting for fish to appear. There's a spot in the In-Willow swim where the weed doesn't grow because the bottom is a bit deeper than on either side, and one day when I threw some corn into the hole, eight or nine fish, all over 20lb, appeared from nowhere and got their heads down on the bait.

When they had eaten the corn they drifted away, but when I threw in another handful, back they all came, only this time there were more of them. I thought I must be dreaming. It soon got to the stage where I had twenty fish all pushing and shoving to get at the golden grains, right in front of me. It was like feeding fish in a goldfish bowl.

Part One

I was there on my own so I decided to try a few experiments. I had been told that you had to be really quiet at Redmire, so I started talking to myself and watched the reaction of the fish. It didn't seem to bother them, so I tried shouting, and even that didn't put them off their food, although it made me feel a bit silly, shouting my head off all on my own.

Next I looked down at the log I was standing on and it was touching the surface of the water, so I started jumping up and down on it, and even that didn't stop them feeding. I soon realized that if I could get them feeding hard, I could afford to make a few mistakes and still be in with a chance of catching one. It certainly made me feel more relaxed.

But it was time to have a cast for one. I ran round the lake to get my gear and cast out, expecting a fish straight away. I couldn't believe it when the fish rushed in for the free samples and then drifted away, leaving just one bait, the hookbait, alone on the bottom.

The first 20lb carp ever landed in winter from Redmire Pool.

I repeated the process and the same thing happened time and time again. "It must be the line that's putting them off," I decided, and putting 1oz leads on all three rods, I positioned them so that the line never left the lake bed. But somehow I got the handles crossed as I set up all my gear and settled in for the night.

Nothing happened after dark, but the next morning I looked into the water and saw two fish, one of about 28lb to 30lb and the other about 8lb, feeding on the corn. Nothing happened at first, and because it was my last day I had the fishing log book that is kept at the fishery with me to fill in. I wrote: "Knowing my luck, I will get a run and catch the smaller one," and I had just managed to get it down on paper when one of the bobbins started rising. I picked up the rod, but it didn't feel right, and I thought I had picked up the wrong one. I struck, but there was nothing on the end. Then I saw that the line had gone tight on the other rod, but before I could do anything the big fish rolled on the surface and my line parted.

I was shattered. That evening was the worst drive home I have ever had, because I knew I had lost a good fish purely because of my own stupidity in not positioning my rods carefully. I'm not bothered if I lose a fish by chance, but if I'm to blame for the missed opportunity, I get annoyed with myself.

In all, that season I had landed five 'twenties' in five trips, well above average for the syndicate, and a great result in my first year. I had come to see the lake, and ended up finding the fish, and I couldn't wait for the next season to begin.

It was a fish called No Pecs, the same one that I had caught on that first evening in June.

Chapter Four
Redmire – A Dream Turned Sour

Where would we be without the Close Season, that annual opportunity to learn from the past, plan for the future and look forward to the glorious 16th. Time spent away from the water is useful for putting things in perspective, and looking back at my results I decided bait held the key to success at Redmire. All that Close Season I met up with the other members to drink and talk about fishing, and plan our tactics for next year. We all agreed it was down to bait, and as I was the one with the contacts, I agreed to order extra from Johnny Perkins to supply the other lads.

We didn't realize then how important rigs were in successful carp fishing, and I can remember Kevin Maddocks being desperate to get into Redmire. He kept saying that if he could get in, he would show us something that would double our catches. He was talking of course about the hair rig, the single most remarkable improvement in carp-fishing tackle in recent years, but we didn't listen. The secret had to be good bait.

I had noticed, though, from my tree-top expeditions, that fish could move into a baited swim, take all the free offerings, before picking up the hookbait and spitting it out again. Only rarely did they make the mistake of running off with the bait. If they did run, you didn't ever get a twitch bite.

Up until then I had used walnut-sized boilies, but for the new season I decided not to roll my baits, but to make them odd shapes, like the 'scatters' I threw in. Then I hooked them in the side, instead of burying the hook as I had been doing, and although the fish could sometimes still blow the bait out, quite often the hook caught in their mouth and they could not get it out.

Another thing I decided to do was carry a spare rod, already made up. The first thing everyone did when they arrived at the lake was to take a walk round, and quite often you saw fish and went back for your gear, only to find them gone on your return.

So I set up a rod with a float, before I left, broke it down into two with the line threaded through, and made sure it was the last thing to go into the car, and the first thing to come out as soon as I arrived, along with bait and landing net.

I was preparing for my fishing with a keenness I had never known before, I tried to be like Jack Hilton, who thought about his fishing, came up with new ideas and those ideas put fish on the bank.

I shall always remember 1979 for friendships made and friendships lost. It started badly, then became one of the happiest fishing times of my life, and then towards the end of the season the storm clouds that were to ruin my chances of fishing Redmire for another full season began to gather on the horizon. I even missed the chance of landing a record-sized fish.

Redmire - A Dream Turned Sour

When I arrived for the first session of the new season, I went for the customary wander, this time with rod in hand. I spotted a fish in the first swim, it took the bait straight away and was on the bank within five minutes of my arrival at the lake, a common of 8lb.

That was one of only two fish I caught with the ready-to-go stalking rod, and the only fish I landed until September. My big plans for Redmire had to be shelved when my son was taken ill and had to have an operation.

But when things settled down on the domestic front, I asked Tom Mintram if I could go on another rota for a week, to make up for the time I had lost, and he agreed. It was a decision that made me a friend for life, for Chris Yates was one of the other rota members.

Chris was so tall he had to kneel down when watching fish from the corner of the dam.

Part One

By the end of the week I had fish of 27lb 6oz, 24lb 4oz and 24lb to my credit.

A 24lb mirror carp photographed by Chris.

I fished with him and Barry Mills, and enjoyed every minute of it. I didn't need to cast out. Just to sit there and chat was fascinating, drinking tea and swapping stories.

Chris is a naturalist, a romantic and a damn good angler, but his idea of a high protein bait is a grain of sweetcorn. I could never convince him that protein bait was better, despite long debates into the early hours. During that first session I started with nothing to my name for that season, but by the end of the week I had fish of 27lb 6oz, 24lb 4oz and 24lb to my credit. "Maybe that protein bait is worth a try," said Chris. "You couldn't give me a couple, could you?"

Chris is an unusual angler. We were chatting one night and he just looked up at the sky and said: "I'll be back in a minute," and left. He headed for the shallows and came back a little later with a fish.

The Strawberry protein was working even better than before.

"I just looked up at the clouds and they looked right, so I thought there would be a fish down there," he said, and sure enough he was right. It was the first example I had come across of someone sensing when they were going to catch. I have seen it lots of times since, and felt it myself, although not as strongly as Chris did, but it still amazes me.

For me it is a smell. I have walked onto a lake on occasions and in one swim I have known I'm going to catch one or more, or if the smell is faint, I know I'm going to hook and lose a fish.

Chris gets a feeling that something is right with a swim and he has a sixth sense, which tells him if a fish is there. Talking to him about things like these made my week, and I know he enjoyed it, because at the end he said he hoped we could get onto the same rota together.

The Strawberry protein was working even better than before and I gave some ingredients to Chris to make up. I was surprised to hear he hadn't caught on it when I got to the lake a couple of days after him. Not to worry, though. I was confidant it would work eventually.

The first swim I looked into had little red baits dotted around everywhere, and the same was true of several other spots. I'd never known the fish leave bait uneaten for so long. I dropped into the Stumps and settled in for the night, not quite as confident as I had been.

By next morning nothing had happened. I had to have a look, and when some fish came into the swim they didn't even bother investigating the baits. Something was occurring.

I went round to see Chris and have a cup of tea. He was about to bait up and when he took the lid off the box that held his bait, the smell of Strawberry almost knocked me out from yards away. He'd used 20ml of flavouring instead of 5ml and spooked the fish off the bait. My confidence hit rock bottom. The only thing to do was to go to the shops for some corn. By Saturday nothing had happened and I had decided to pack up.

I had everything into the car except for the float rod when I saw a patch of bubbles. I had seen eels feeding in shallow water, pushing up the same sort of pin-head bubbles, so I wasn't over excited, but I decided to have one cast.

I got the float rod and a handful of my unused protein bait and decided to fish Yates style, casting in and putting three or four baits around the float. I remember thinking that this was the spot where he had caught his 38lb fish. Whilst I was doing so the float went under.

I struck, but there was nothing. On with another bait, out with the float again and a few free offerings to follow. Under it went again, and again I missed. "Must be eels," I muttered.

Now, I'm not too good at this float fishing lark, lack of practise I suppose, and I was just thinking that it was taking a long time to come up after my third cast when I saw the line snaking across the surface. I didn't need telling twice. I struck and the fish took twenty yards of line and leapt clear of the water. This was no eel.

I'd never seen a carp tail-walk across the surface before. I couldn't believe it. I told Rod Hutchinson about it a few years later, and when I showed him a photo of the fish, he said the same one had done the same thing to him.

When I slid it over the net I was glad I had gone back for that last cast. All my gear was packed away, so I walked around to Chris's swim with the fish in a sack, something I would never do now. It weighed 21lb 12oz. Chris and Dave were keen to know how I caught it. I told them to follow me, went back, cast out, and they had hardly got to the corner of the Dam when I was in again. This time the fish weighed 23lb 6oz, and as I was leaving, they asked if they could join me on the Dam. I drove away later, having seen fortune turn around for me in the dying minutes of the session, and vowing to always have that one last cast in future.

Chris and Dave were keen to know how I caught the fish...

Part One

So I went back and had another, this time 23lb 6oz.

But there was one last moment of excitement. On one of my last days at the lake, in Pitchford's, at the top of one of the two poplar trees that anglers use to scan the water, I caught sight of a big fish. At first I thought there must be a trick of the light, but when it came closer I realized it was enormous. It had to weigh over 45lb. I climbed down to get my tackle and Dave Short took my place in the tree, to tell me where it was.

Nervously I flicked a bait out and a few seconds later I saw the line twitch. Dave said: "He's got your bait." I looked down at the reel and the line had got round the back of the spool. I had to pull it clear or the fish would have broken me, and all the time I was fiddling, Dave was shouting: "He's got your bait in his mouth. Strike! Strike!" But I couldn't, and the same second that I freed the spool, the line dropped back across the water. The fish had let go. Chris Yates caught the same fish on opening day the following year, 1980, and it weighed 51lb 6oz. The rest is history.

Winter came and many of the members packed away their gear, but I went to the lake three times in November and twice in December without even a run. The fish must have known what was on the way, for soon after that the lake froze over and it was time to call an end to another season. I'd had five 'twenties' in nine trips, so I couldn't grumble.

Things were cold at the lake, but there were some hot tempers among the members, and rumours began to circulate. There was a lot of friction between myself and some of the other lads at the water, but I'm not going to go into that because I want people to enjoy this book.

Redmire - A Dream Turned Sour

It was only a minor problem at that time and everything else looked rosy for the following year.

I did have a rather heated argument with one of the other members in the Close Season, which left a nasty taste in both our mouths. The result was that I only had one week at Redmire in 1980, but I made the most of it, landing a 29lb common.

I almost lost it after I had landed it as well. The fish were moving along a patch of weed, and Chris Seager and Dave were fishing on one bank, so I set up on the West Bank on Bramble Island. I was fishing in the weed, and when I hooked the fish I had to manoeuvre it round this thick blanket of green weed. It took a bit of doing, but finally the fish was mine, and I must have got a bit over excited with a near 30lb fish in the net.

Chris Yates' record fish – the rest, as they say, is history.

Part One

To get to Bramble Island you have to walk across some planks laid across scaffolding, and I lost my footing and went for an early bath, tackle, net, fish and all. For a moment I thought it was going to get out, but the fish was wrapped in the folds of the net, and a Redmire personal best was carried ashore.

That was my last official visit to Redmire. It got to a stage with this other chap and I that we couldn't go on, and I was asked to stand down for a year, which I accepted, thinking it would all die away.

During the Close Season I had been to the lake on working parties and everything seemed okay. Then I went for a meeting with Tom, Dave Short and John Carver, and they told me my membership was not being renewed. I asked why and they did not seem happy that I had become friendly with Clive Diedrich and Malcolm Winkworth, although they never put that in print.

I left Tom Mintram's house that night with tears in my eyes. I have never forgiven that man for throwing me out of Redmire, and I never will, because I did nothing wrong. In fact it made me determined to do something wrong, just to get even.

Although I had made my last official visit to Redmire, I decided I would go up one last time, just to get my own back. I rang up a very good friend of mine, Dennis Davis, who had always wanted to go to the lake. "Do you fancy fishing Redmire?" I asked. He thought I was joking, but I had never been more serious in my life.

I only had one week at Redmire in 1980, but I made the most of it, landing a 29lb common.

Redmire - A Dream Turned Sour

"I've just been to Redmire and had a 31lb 8oz fish!"

We arrived at about 3am one night in the Close Season. There was no one around. We couldn't park by the lake without being seen, so we left the car up on the main road, with a note saying we had broken down.

At 8am the farm workers started in the fields around us. I told Dennis to keep his head down and let me do the talking. I could tell from the voices and rushing around that they knew someone was there, so I decided to bluff my way out, and went looking for them, hoping they didn't know it was the Close Season. Luckily the bloke I bumped into was one of the estate workers that I knew, and although he looked surprised to see me, he only asked if I was still in the syndicate. I said I was and that was that.

We fished, and although we didn't feel very comfortable, Dennis had two 'twenties', at 24lb and 21lb, which he was delighted with. I hadn't had an offer, so I crept round to where I had heard some fish moving and I hadn't cast out more than ten minutes when I hooked and landed a powerful fish that weighed 31lb 8oz, my first and only Redmire 'thirty'. Straight away I felt justified in what I had done. It had all been worthwhile, and after the long drive home, the first thing I did was ring Chris Yates and said: "I've just been to Redmire and had a 31lb 8oz fish!"

Dennis had two 'twenties', at 24lb and 21lb, which he was delighted with.

I will remember his words forever. He said: "Well done. That's justice for you." I had got even the only way I knew how, and although I don't agree with poaching, and know how wrong it is to fish in the Close Season, it was the only thing I could do to annoy the syndicate leaders. For that reason I told everyone about it and I heard in return that it had the desired effect.

Tom once said to me that a lot of people who leave Redmire don't go carp fishing ever again, but there was never any chance of that in my case. Although I was bitterly disappointed at what had happened, I spoke to Rod Hutchinson at a meeting and he told me about his troubles there. He had left before he had wanted to, but bounced back by refusing to let the b****** grind him down, and this was his advice to me. It worked, but although I have since gone on to other things, there is still a certain amount of pain when I think of the lake. Redmire was too beautiful and peaceful a place to be run by poisonous people who turned a person's dreams into nightmares.

Part One

Chapter Five
1981 – A Year Without Equal

Troubles never come in ones. When you're on the ground and struggling to get up, it's odds on fate will give you a couple of kicks, just for good measure.

When I was told I couldn't fish Redmire in 1981, I tried to bounce back by visiting my old favourite, Longfield, a notoriously hard water but home of some real monsters.

But it was an anglers' graveyard. My indicators seemed to be glued to the ground and my line gathered dust in the rod rings, while all around me others were catching left, right and centre. It was not as if I didn't know the lake. I had fished it since 1977, when I had a 'twenty', and added another three 'twenties' and a 35lb mirror in 1979.

But fish aren't fussy whose bait they pick up as long as it looks safe and tastes good, which got me thinking. Maybe the bait was at the centre of my problems, just as it had been when Chris Yates had overdone the flavouring at Redmire.

My first Longfield 'twenty', in July 1977. *Others followed, such as this 23-pounder.*

1981 - A Year Without Equal

The floating crust fish – 22lb 8oz. I threaded a piece of crust the size of a Swan Vesta matchbox on a hook and lobbed it out. Everyone laughed until a pair of lips sucked the whole lot down in one go.

It was another angler there who put the idea into my head. He told me he thought there was something wrong with the bait, saying: "You can't be on fish as much as you have been and not be catching." They were hauling them out all around me.

I decided it must be the type of casein I was using, so I switched to another sort, and having made up some baits to make sure it looked and tasted okay, I embarked on one of the longest pre-baiting sessions I have ever done, starting in January and leading up, week by week, to the start of the season in June.

Try to imagine what it feels like on June 16th when you have been visiting a water several times a week for almost six months. I was putting in six pounds of bait every week and the fish were loving it. I chose areas where there was no sign of fish, but before I had put out fifty baits they had come to see what the noise was about, and got their heads down on the free offerings.

On opening night that lake was full of people. I had put out two pounds of bait during the day and gone to the pub for a start-of-season drink. Everyone was in a great mood, as they always are before the season starts. It takes about three days for the faces to fall and for people to start to complain.

This bloke appeared in a suit and said he had wanted to fish, but there were too many people at the lake for his liking. I told him he was mad to miss June 16th and, of course, in a generous mood I said if he couldn't get in anywhere he could fish next to me. That was my first mistake.

When I got back to my bivvy I laid on the bed and lit a fag, to enjoy the last moments before the off. I could just imagine the fish feeding a few yards away. I couldn't see my swim from where I was, but all of a sudden I heard these baits going in and when I looked out, they were landing just where I was going to fish.

Part One

I tried to bounce back by visiting my old favourite, Longfield.

My indicators seemed to be glued to the ground.

35lb – suddenly all the hours spent mixing and rolling pounds of bait were worth it:.

Part One

I nipped round to the bloke in the suit a bit smartish and said: "You're putting your baits on top of mine." He said he was sorry and I couldn't really blame him for not knowing where I would be fishing, but the result was no runs at all for the first two days. I tried not to think how much time, money and energy had gone into preparing for that season, and instead convinced myself that the fish would come back before long

My first run came on the third day and it felt like a 'twenty'. There are more 'twenties' than 'singles' in Longfield so, you have to be a bit unlucky to get a small one. This fish went 11lb. It's about the only time I have been disappointed with a capture.

"Never mind. Forget about the bad start. Forget about last season's complete failure and stop thinking you're jinxed," I told myself. It worked. The next fish was a 26lb common, and before I had time to carve the first notch on my bivvy pole, I was into a really big fish, a mirror of 35lb.

Suddenly it was all worth it: the hours spent mixing and rolling pounds of bait, trips to the lake in freezing February, the lonely days of the Close Season, and the agony of the first few days, when I wondered whether I had just wasted six months of my angling life.

Later the same afternoon I landed a common of 19lb 8oz, and from then onwards I can honestly say I can't remember a time in 1981 when I didn't have a bend in my rod, as fish after fish came to the net, the best weighing 38lb 4oz, a fish I shall never forget.

It gave an incredible fight, and in the mesh of the landing net, lying there almost as tired as I was, it looked immense. But perhaps the best part was the moment it chose to pick up my bait, just as an old mate, Keith, who had given up fishing after one heartbreaking incident, turned up.

He had packed up after fishing hard for one huge carp on another water. When I say fishing hard, I mean he had lived on the lake for two years, fishing it round the clock, day in, day out, no matter what the weather. Now that's what I call dedication.

Eventually he hooked the fish that he had dedicated his life to catching, and it was the only fish I have seen in this country that comes close to Chris Yates' 51lb 8oz fish, and he lost it. I could understand why he threw in the towel after that. It's a wonder he didn't do himself in by falling on one of his bank sticks.

I was disappointed when he packed up, because he was a very good angler and a very nice bloke, and when he came strolling round the lake I got him interested in the developments since he had left the sport. He couldn't believe the hair rig and liked the boilies straight away. I could see the old twinkle of enthusiasm in his eye.

Just then the indicator shot up and line started pouring out. His mouth dropped open. In his day a two-inch twitch was the sign of a confident take.

As it tore off across the lake I set the hook and I thought I must have foulhooked a 'twenty'. I couldn't believe it when I saw the size of it. Keith was as pleased as I was, and watched the scales go round to 38lb 4oz. I suspect he was a little green with envy.

We sat down after the photos and were half way through the cup of tea I always have to celebrate a capture when off went the other rod, this time taken by a 10lb common.

Keith started coming out every other weekend after that, just for a chat and a walk round, and the more he came, the more interested he got. One day I arrived at the lake at midday and the fish were all up on the top. I put some free samples out and some bottom baits in an area to the right. I sat back and waited for them to take a few floaters.

1981 - A Year Without Equal

I couldn't believe it when I saw the size of it and the scales went round to 38lb 4oz.

It took a while for them to respond, so I started reading the copy of *Angling Times* I had brought with me, and just looked up now and again to see if anything was happening. Along came Keith and we sat there, discussing the paper, when suddenly he said: "There's a patch of bubbles coming up over there." It was right over my bait, but I didn't get up. I just picked the rod up to see if anything was happening and away went the indicator.

The fish weighed 26lb and it seemed that every time Keith turned up, the fish came along as well. He went away shaking his head, obviously thinking he must have been mad to have given it up, considering how easy it had become to catch carp.

But it was all down to the pre-baiting and my determination to catch fish after being asked to leave Redmire in such an unfair way. When you are determined to succeed, when you are hungry to prove yourself as an angler, you fish in such a keyed-up mood that everything seems more intense, and you don't miss a trick.

It doesn't often happen, but when you get in that frame of mind, you notice a tiny rise right out in the middle of the lake and your cast to it is inch perfect. The bubbler away to the right is also met with a perfect cast and soon both fish are on the bank.

They say that success breeds success, and when you are fishing like that and catching everything that comes near you, anything if possible. I think that year, if I had cast in the car park I would have had a run.

I've got lots of memories of Longfield, most happy, some sad, and lots of them funny, but one of the strangest is a few hours in the 1979 season. It was my second session of the season on the Goose Pool. I was fishing two rods baited with Apricot floaters and I had put some free samples around the bait.

It seemed that every time Keith turned up, the fish came along as well.

1981 - A Year Without Equal

The camera-shy 35. Kevin Maddocks caught it much later at 31lb and I had my picture taken with it for the album.

Part One

There were about eight or nine fish there and I decided to climb a tree to see if they were showing any interest in the bait. When I got to the top, the fish were circling my baits and it was a good job I came straight down again. As soon as my feet touched the floor, off went one of the rods and I landed a fish of 18lb 8oz.

This spooked the others, so I put this rod on the bank and left the other out, fishing a floater. Just before it got dark I decided to call it a day and had almost picked up the rod when I saw a back break the surface of the water. It looked huge and I was trying to guess just how big when I realized it had 'topped' right next to my floater. The line started sliding across the surface and I struck and hooked something very powerful. It didn't do anything spectacular, but it had no intention of coming to the net.

Eventually it gave in and I slid a 35lb mirror over the mesh. Magic! This was one for the photo album, so I sacked it up and nipped down to the phone box to get a few mates with cameras along. Chris Yates, Chris Seager and my brother-in-law all agreed to come in the morning. As you can imagine, I couldn't sleep after this excitement and I drank cup after cup of tea to keep me occupied.

Looking out across the lake I could see backs cruising up and down in the bay, I couldn't resist having another go. I took some tackle to another swim and put out some floaters. After about an hour I heard this sucking noise and I was sure that my bait would go at any minute. I sat there all night waiting for the run that just had to happen, but when dawn broke and the sun came up, I could see I had been fishing all night for floating rafts of weed, and the sucking noises were coming from rudd in the margins.

With the excitement of the chance of a fish gone, I began to feel tired, really tired, like only someone who has had no sleep for thirty-six hours can feel. By the time the first of the David Bailey brigade arrived I was feeling even worse and just sat and watched while about £1,000 worth of camera gear was prepared by seven or eight blokes.

The time came to get the fish out, and I was feeling even worse, so I decided to pose for the photos on the edge of the water and then I wouldn't have to carry the fish far. My brother-in-law offered to give me a hand getting the fish out of the sack, and I had just lifted it clear of the clinging black cloth when the carp did a neat flip out of my hands, and straight back into the lake.

No one said a word. They just started packing their gear away in silence, having not taken a single frame of film. I was gutted at having a fish of that size swim away without having its photo taken, and the lads must have thought I wanted to be left alone, for they went their separate ways.

After about ten minutes of sulking I got myself together, had a cup of tea and dozed off. The next thing I knew, Chris Yates was peering into my bivvy and taking a picture of me asleep. "Where is it?" he said. He hadn't been around for the 'photo call' and I told him the sad story and said I was going to design a zip-sack (later called the Mac Sack) so that something like this would never happen again.

I told the same tale to Brian McEwan when he came round later that day. We both noticed that the fish were still moving in the bay and he said he would go round the other side and have a go for one. Less than ten minutes later I heard him shouting for a landing net.

I picked mine up and ran round, and had just dipped it in the water to net his fish when I heard my buzzer go. "You'll have to do it yourself," I told him, and ran back round, but before I could get to the rod, the line dropped slack.

I was annoyed and disappointed. If he hadn't left his net behind I would almost certainly have had another fish on the bank. I went back to give him a piece of my mind and I found him unhooking a fish of 34lb 12oz.

Having caught my big 'thirty' the night before, now this one, and I had seen several big fish in the bay during the day, I have every reason to believe he cost me a very big fish. They seemed to have shoaled up in that area for some reason, and thanks to his forgetfulness I think I missed out on an incredible double.

He went home grinning all over his face and saying he would be back with all his tackle to fish properly. I shouted after him: "Don't forget your bloody net." Later in the evening I saw him walking round the lake with his tackle, stalking fish, and would you believe it, he still didn't have a landing net with him. Some anglers have no respect for other people's feelings. There's no way I would have lent him my net again, even if he had hooked the record.

Strawberry baits produced the best reaction so I scrapped Maple in favour of Salmon.

Part One

Talking of records, I was at Longfield when I heard that Chris Yates had landed his record fish from Redmire. Chris Seager came up to me and told me how much it weighed, and that it was the old '38' that had been caught down the years by Jack Hilton, Bill Quinlan, Tom Mintram and Bob Jones.

I felt pleased that Chris had been the one to catch it. He's the perfect ambassador for the sport of carp fishing, a gentleman through and through and I can't think of anyone better to hold the title 'Captor of Britain's Biggest Carp'.

Like most carp anglers I recognize this fish as the record, and it has always been a mystery to me why the British Record Fish Committee would not accept it. If it had been close to the weight of Walker's fish I would have understood them being worried about it, but at 7lb 8oz heavier — a weight difference that certainly showed in the photographs — there should have been no hesitation in accepting it.

Having said that, I'd like to think that if someone did catch a carp that beat Chris's Redmire fish, he (or she) would try to claim the British record, because I feel the BRFC are still important. Until that day, though, Chris's fish is the British best.

When things are going well I believe in riding your luck and making the most of the Midas touch while it lasts. After early success at Longfield I decided to visit a water in the Colne Valley for a few days. I took Pete Springate, whose usual fishing partner had gone on holiday to Ireland, chasing those flat, slimy things.

I had been to the lake several times already that season and had had fish in front of me, but I wasn't happy with the bait I was using. My Maple-flavoured bait didn't go down well on the first short visit. So on the second trip I took some of the Strawberry baits that had done me proud over the years, and used these on one rod and Maple on the other. I landed one 'twenty' and two 'doubles', and as the Strawberry produced the best reaction, I scrapped the Maple and replaced it with a Salmon-flavour that I had not tried before.

On the first outing with it I landed a fish of 28lb 4oz, on the next, one of 18lb 4oz, and then fish of 18lb, 32lb, 17lb and 9lb. The bait and the swim were starting to come alive and the fish I had seen in front of me were starting to get their heads down regularly.

By the time I took Pete there on August Bank Holiday weekend the fish had just got a taste for the new flavour, but I didn't tell him that. I just gave him some of the bait. We got there at dawn, because guests cannot fish at night during the week, and crept round the lake to the swim I had been fishing, known as the Silver Birches.

We put some bait out and half an hour later Pete was into a fish of 24lb 8oz. From that moment on it was one fish after another in the most incredible action I have ever experienced. At one stage we were both playing 20lb fish at the same time.

It was also one of the hottest days I can remember – the sort that makes even a sun-lover like me wish it was a little cooler. We could see fish coming across the surface into the swim and going straight down on the baits on a bar just fifty yards out. We didn't need indicators – we were often poised over the rods ready to strike, even before the line moved.

Pete couldn't believe it and neither could I. No one else on the lake was getting so much as a run. We kept the bait going in and while one person was playing a fish, the other was catapulting more bait in. I put about three times as much in as Pete and I think that was why I ended up with more fish. When they are having a bait it's hard to overfeed them.

1981 - A Year Without Equal

By the time I took Pete there on August Bank Holiday weekend the fish had just got a taste for the new flavour.

Part One

The total was eighteen fish up to 31lb, including ten 'twenties', caught between dawn on Friday and mid-afternoon on Monday. By the end, most of the anglers on the lake were in our swim trying to find out what we were doing that was different.

I gave Bob Davis some of the essence we had been using, which was the Salmon mixed with a Hermesetas liquid sweetener from Boots. He went home, made up some bait, came back and fished alongside us, but he still couldn't get a run, though we'd given them a pasting by then.

I'm sure the reason for our success was that we were using something different, but which had been introduced on a couple of visits prior to the Bank Holiday. Add to that the fact that Salmon is a damn good flavour and bingo! I must admit I didn't like it at first. I picked it out of a batch I was given, mainly because it was the most expensive, but it smelt horrible so I put it at the back of the cupboard. That was in 1977, and there it stayed until 1981.

After that memorable weekend the flavour was never quite as good at that lake again, though it worked on lots of other waters. I gave some to Rod Hutchinson and he got hold of a supply and called it Pukka Salmon. It has always been a favourite of mine for tackling a new water, and three years later it was responsible for the fish of my dreams.

The total was eighteen fish up to 31lb, including ten 'twenties'.

I couldn't have been more wrong about Salmon.

Another upper 'twenty' to Salmon Oil.

That weekend taught me a lesson. Until then I had decided whether I liked a flavour by one sniff of the bottle, but I couldn't have been more wrong about Salmon. Now I make up a batch of baits and give them a try before passing judgement. A new flavour can make all the difference on a hard-fished water, though it won't make a bad angler into a good one. Changing from Maple to Salmon gave me the edge at a difficult time. Don't get me wrong, I like Maple as a flavour, but so does everyone else!

When I went back to Longfield, Pete came with me, and while we were experimenting with a Cheese flavour, an unusual thing happened. Pete had just caught a 27lb fish from Yateley, Heather the Leather, and was full of confidence, but this time I was the first in action.

I had a fish of 25lb on our first night, but it turned out to be in a very poor condition, tatty fins and torn mouth, so I took a quick photo and slipped it back. Kevin Maddocks was fishing the far bank and he saw all this going on. He came round to my swim in the morning saying Pete had had a fish early in the morning but he had not weighed it, but had put it straight back. This didn't sound like Pete, so we went round to see him. He was sitting by his rods sipping a cup of tea and when Maddocks asked him why he hadn't weighed or photographed the fish, Pete said it only looked to be about 25lb! He explained to me when Maddocks had gone that he had caught the very same fish just a few hours earlier, so he had no need to weigh it, but it was worth winding our angling friend up just to see his face.

Things were going so well that summer that we decided to try the ultimate 'hard' water, Wraysbury, to see if we could catch carp where so many had failed, or whether our luck

1981 - A Year Without Equal

would desert us. We never felt confident enough to put up with all the blank sessions before, but now was our chance while spirits were high.

On the first weekend Pete lost a fish, but to get a run after only a couple of days at Wraysbury was a very good start. When I say that the following weekend we had eleven chances between us, you'll realize how special it was to get that much action.

Pete was the first to get a chance. I heard his buzzer sound in the night and went round to see him, but one of his rods was lying in the bushes by the time I got there, and he was back in the sack. By the look of the line flapping loosely from the tip ring and the way the rod had been thrown there rather than placed, I decided to go back to my bivvy.

In the morning it was my turn. It was still dark and the fish fought like a tiger, charging all over the place. Again and again I tried to bring it in close, but it wouldn't have it. When I finally got the net under it I was glad of a rest. Then I looked into the net and saw the fish was massive. I put the rod down, got hold of the mesh with both hands and tried to lift it out of the water. I couldn't. The fish was really long and suddenly I thought: "I've landed a 'forty'".

On the scales it went 28lb, but it wasn't disappointing. At last I had caught a carp from Wraysbury – something I had wanted to do for a long time.

When I went round to see Pete there was a second rod next to the first in the bushes. He was not in a good mood. I managed to get out of him that the fish had been one hundred and fifty yards away and still going strong when the hook had straightened. After a couple of mugs of tea and some breakfast he re-cast, and proceeded to land a 24lb common almost straight away!

The final fish of a memorable 1981 season at Longfield.

At last I had caught a carp from Wraysbury – something I had wanted to do for a long time.

The gravel bars were proving to be a problem. Previously we hadn't had runs and didn't realize how difficult it would be to play fish. Now we were getting chances, but the fish would dive into deep water beyond the bar after being hooked, and the 8lb line would part like cotton on the sharp pieces of gravel. The runs were all screamers and the fish were where we didn't want them to be almost before we could get to the rods. We put a lot of thought into overcoming the problem – using shock leaders and abrasion-resistant line – but when we went back the following weekend the fish had moved on and the lake was back to its usual quiet self.

That fish of mine remains my only one from Wraysbury, and that's after a fair amount of time trying. It's not a place for the faint-hearted, and though I haven't been back for a while, I keep saying I'll make it my 'retirement' water, when I've done all I want to do in carp fishing and am looking for somewhere where I can put plenty of time in without looking for a short-term result.

The water will be getting a lot of pressure in the next few years, after the capture of the record tench and stories in the angling press of massive pike. But that's not the sort of place to please the instant-success men. It is the ones who can stick at the task who will find the fish – people such as Pete Springate and Ken Hodder. They put a lot of time and effort into their fishing and are not put off by long, blank stretches. They will be the ones to reap the rewards.

Chapter Six
Four-legged Friends

"All things bright and beautiful, all creatures great and small, all things wise and wonderful, we anglers meet them all." You name 'em, I've had 'em in my bivvy – invited, uninvited and definitely unwanted. We must seem a funny lot to them, sleeping under big, green mushrooms for most of the night and part of the day, sitting around talking, drinking and climbing trees. No wonder they come for a closer look.

Take the creature I bumped into at Redmire Pool, for instance. There I was minding my own business, well away in the land of nod, without a care in the world, when I heard this incredibly loud "SLURP!" right next to my ear. It took me a few moments to get myself together. You know what it's like when you wake up, first you wonder where you are, then you wonder how you got there and then you try to find out what woke you up. "SLURP!" I could make out the outline of a huge tongue scraping up the side of the nylon, just a few inches away from my face.

Now, at Redmire there are a fair few cows and they wander past at certain times of the day. Being cows they are not too much of a problem. They're not the most intelligent of God's creatures and although they seem to like licking the paint off cars and scratching their backsides on wing-mirrors, they are pretty cowardly beasts and can be chased away. But, apparently there's something in the proofing of a bivvy that takes their fancy, some sort of wax, and if you let a herd of them have their way with your shelter, it'll be about as waterproof as a tea-bag by the time they've finished.

"SLURP!" A short, sharp tap with a bank-stick should do it. I wouldn't even have to get out of bed. I waited for the tongue to come out again and gave it a smack. "SLURP!" I couldn't have done it hard enough. Whack! "SLURP!" There was only one thing for it. Out came the mallet I use for knocking the bivvy pegs in and I gave the beast a right good bang on the nose, which I've heard is the most sensitive place on a cow. "SLURP!"

Now I was annoyed. I jumped out of bed, strode out through the front door and got half way round the back when I realized what I was dealing with – the biggest bull I have seen to this day. It had horns like elephants' tusks and enough meat and muscle to feed an army, or flatten one, depending on whether or not it could be caught. I was back in the bivvy before you could say "sirloin steak", shaking like a leaf.

I'd heard him bellowing from the next field on previous trips, but the farmer didn't usually let him out when there were anglers about. I could see the headlines now: "Farmer's error kills carp angler". I sat on my bed until it had licked all the proofing out of the fabric, wondering what I would do if it decided to taste the front panels and trying to decide whether it would be best to do the breast-stroke or the crawl across to the other side of the lake. I'm just glad I didn't get a run.

Mind you, cows can be a nuisance, too. I'd gone for a stroll round this lake one day, and when I came back my swim was occupied – by a couple of dozen of Farmer Brown's finest. They wouldn't have posed any problem normally; a short session of clapping and a few shouts like the blokes on *Rawhide* and the coast would have been clear, but they were between me and my rods.

Cows being cows, they will always head in exactly the opposite direction to a bloke waving his arms and shouting, and I could see a couple of hundred quid's worth of carefully made carbon-fibre (or was it fibreglass then) going for a burton. There was nothing for it, I would have to take to the water to make them move in the right direction. They watched me ease myself into the lake – which was cold enough to take my breath away – and make my way round in front of them. I didn't frighten them enough to make them smash through my tackle, but you could see (and hear) they were a bit worried because they did what a lot of worried animals do. I'm just glad I didn't have my fake-grass carpet down in the swim, I would never have got the stains out!

If anyone thinks I got off lightly because my gear was left untouched, they should try spending a few days and nights in a swim full of fresh cow-pats. It may be good for the roses, but wait until you slip in one when running for your rods in the dark, to say nothing of what it is like at meal times.

Don't run away with the idea that something has to be big to be a nuisance, though. Just wait until you've felt something land on your face while you're asleep and switched on the torch to find the inside of your umbrella covered in earwigs. I've often wondered what use earwigs are. Your bees make honey, your caterpillar turns into a butterfly and your spider spins a web, but earwigs are no use to anyone. In fact, if anyone thinks they know what useful purpose these 'orrible things serve, then I'd be pleased to hear from them. I've lain awake thinking about it and I can't come up with an answer.

Anyway, where was I? Oh, yes. Rats. Cows are bad news because of the damage they cause, but rats are just downright unpleasant. I was at Longfield once and it had been dark for a few hours. I'd had a few cans with some mates and, timing it just right, I said goodnight before I fell asleep and got back to my bivvy without falling over – that's years of practise for you.

There's always that wonderful moment when you pull off your shoes, slip into the soft depths of the sack, and pull the covers up over your head. Bliss! No need for counting sheep tonight – I counted cans of Fosters instead and was soon in the land of nod. Then it started… the patter of tiny feet across the groundsheet under my bed.

I turned over and it stopped. Great! Where was I, ski-ing down Everest with a carnation between my teeth, I believe. I'd just fastened my left ski when it woke me again. I shone the torch under my bed and again it stopped. Solved it! Then it started once more. This had to be sorted properly.

I dragged myself out of the bag, put my slippers on and started to search for the culprit. Every now and then I caught sight of a pair of eyes twinkling at me in the dark, but the little perisher wouldn't stay in one spot for more than a moment and I had as much chance of catching him as I would have had diving in the lake to catch a carp with my bare hands.

Part One

It was him or me, as anyone who has been desperate for a bit of shut-eye will tell you. I had to outwit him with my superior human intelligence, so I put the kettle on. I figured that if I kept very quiet he would appear and, with a kettle of hot water in my hand, I could splash some at him and put him off the idea of exploring my bivvy.

I laid out a trail of bait, leading to the front of the bivvy, and sat there as quiet as... a mouse, watching by the light of the burner. It wasn't long before I heard the scurry of tiny rodent feet and he appeared near the end of the trail. Making a grab for the kettle, I poured it over one of two dark furry shapes at my feet. It was about half a second later that I realized it was my slipper – with my foot still in it.

I don't know which way the rat went, but I sprang out of the bivvy and hopped up and down the bank holding my foot and cursing under my breath. I didn't have any trouble with rats after that, so, if you have the same problem, try pouring boiling water on your foot – it worked for me.

Of all the creatures we anglers meet beside the water, it is the bird life that causes us the most problems. If I had a pound for every time I've heard a carp angler complain about tufted ducks diving on his baits, I'd be able to afford solid-gold rod-rests and a silk bivvy. Yet I'd rather tangle with a tuftie than get anywhere near a coot. If you've accidentally hooked a tuftie you'll know they come in very quietly and look up at you with a wide-eyed innocence that even Bambi couldn't match. As you let them go and watch them swim away you feel like Superman when he saved the universe. Hook a coot and it's a different matter.

I remember one day I had run out of feed and after reeling in and asking a bloke nearby to keep his eye on my gear, I nipped into the village to stock up for a few days. When I got back nothing had changed, or so it seemed until I unzipped the door of my bivvy and looked in. I couldn't believe it. It was absolutely plastered in coots droppings.

I hadn't been away for more than half an hour and I couldn't understand what had been going on. At the back of the bivvy I found the culprit – tangled in fishing line and adding to the mess as I watched. I tried to get hold of him but the coot had other ideas and almost ripped my hands to pieces. The beak and claws of those things are unbelievably powerful, and I will never try to handle one again. In the end I had to corner it and throw a towel over it until I could get the line off and let it go. I couldn't believe one coot could make such a mess.

Mind you, the goose I saw at Yeoveney came close. At that time one or two swims there were fishing better than all the others, and one bloke was taking liberties. He had set up his bivvy in the best spot and, being a local, left it there when he went home so that he could still have the swim the next day. Sometimes he was away for a couple of days or more.

Not surprisingly, this swim-hogging gave a few of the other carp anglers the right hump, and so one day when he was away they cornered a goose, grabbed it and zipped it inside his bivvy. It was in there for about half a day, and when he got back and unzipped it the goose went crazy and flew at him, but that was nothing to what it had done inside. Everything had been turned upside down, from his pots and pans to his sleeping bag, and it looked as if someone had kept a herd of cows in there for a week!

But no chapter on Longfield would be complete without a mention of the fox. He, or maybe it was a she, was a legend in his/her own lifetime and the water even became known as Fox Pool. He was a thief and a scrounger, but everyone who fished the lake loved him.

On more than one occasion I woke up to find my slippers gone from in front of my bed. But I always knew when he had been, because I am quite a light sleeper and he smelt so 'high' it woke me up as soon as he came into the bivvy. He even came and slept under my bed one night; he certainly had no fear of human beings.

The first time he pinched my slippers it was a bit of fun, but I had to go into town to buy another pair, so when I woke to see him with one of the brand new ones in his mouth, I wasn't best pleased. As he ran off, I threw the other one at him and made him drop it. But by the time I had got my boots on he had hidden the first one and come back for the second, and I never saw either again. I couldn't get to my rods quickly without my slippers by the door, but I wasn't going to lose a third pair, so I decided to teach him a lesson.

I borrowed a pair from the Old Man, who lived nearby, and the next night I was ready for him. I smelt him coming, lying there awake, and when he grabbed one I gave him a good hard whack on the back. He dropped it, and although it didn't make him mend his ways completely, he never pinched slippers again.

Bruce Ashby was walking back to his bivvy one afternoon after a few pints at the pub and he just fancied opening a packet of biscuits he had bought the day before, and getting stuck in before felling asleep in the afternoon sun. It's funny how little pleasures mean so much when you are out fishing, at one with nature.

Anyway, enough of the David Attenborough stuff. Bruce was a few yards away from his bivvy when he saw this familiar furry tail poking out of the front door. The old fox must have heard Bruce coming because he turned just then, and in his mouth was the packet of McVitie's finest chocolate digestives. They hadn't even been opened. Anyone who comes between Bruce and his grub is in trouble, but he just wasn't smart enough for the fox, and the full packet of digestives went the same way as my slippers. "It's your own fault for leaving them near the door," I said to Bruce afterwards.

"I didn't," he told me. "They were at the back of the bivvy on my tackle box. He must have got on the bed and reached over for them."

Other things went missing. Every now and then you would hear a shout of: "Anyone seen my catapult?" or: "Anyone borrowed a bag of bait from my bivvy?" and it wasn't even worth replying. You knew who had 'borrowed' it and he wasn't ever going to give it back.

It made people who were new to the lake suspect the other anglers. People would accuse the bloke in the next bivvy and wouldn't believe him when he said a fox came round in broad daylight and helped himself to whatever he fancied. And we never found out where he stashed it all. There was probably some tramp walking round with a new pair of slippers, eating boilies and digestives and firing a catapult.

But it was only right that the old lad should share in the big nosh-up we had one evening. It was the most amazing meal I have ever taken part in, and probably as incredible a sight as anything a passer-by has seen at a carp lake.

Terry Dinsdale was going out with this girl who was a Princess back in her home country of Iran. She used to enjoy fishing, and made sure he didn't miss out on his meals while she was there. She would prepare these elaborate dishes, made up with delicate herbs and spices, and there was always enough to feed a small army. The fox was no fool. He was there faster than you could say "meat Madras," and often he would get half a chicken thrown his way, if he dived on it before we did. He must have thought it was his birthday every time she came.

Anyway, we were all gathered round one evening after the pub, drinking what we had bought from the off-licence and watching her cook his supper. She said: "Why don't we prepare a big meal for all of us on Saturday night?" and we agreed straight away.

So Saturday it was. Our mouths were watering already. We all chipped in and she came back with bags of stuff that took several journeys from the car to get round to Terry's bivvy. Everything went into one pot, and I've never seen a pot like it. It looked like a witch's cauldron, but she knew what she was doing.

There was an old barn nearby and we knew it had lots of old tables and chairs in it, so we borrowed these and put them out in front of the lake like a big banquet. When we came back from the pub there was this delicious aroma all round the lake, and the five of us, and the fox, all sat down to be served. There were bottles of wine, glasses, candles, even a candelabra, serviettes in rings, and expensive cutlery and plates. Finally out came the food and all six of us sat there under the moonlight on a beautiful summer night, eating this heavenly meal and watching the candle lights dance in the mirrored reflection of the flat-calm lake.

It was one of the best meals I have ever had, and certainly the most memorable. Only one mouthful was disappointing. There were some red chilli peppers left over and I had a bet with one of the lads that I could eat anything. He gave me one of these, and it looked harmless enough, but I knew the moment I closed my mouth that I had made a big mistake. I also knew there was no way I could back down after boasting about my iron-lined stomach and I had to chew it and swallow. I have never, ever, put a chilli pepper to my mouth since that evening.

The fox had a great time. He was kept busy with pieces of food thrown to him from the table and he had a bit of everything. We didn't want to spoil the evening by tackling the washing up, so we just left everything, candles and all, and staggered off to our-beds.

In the morning we all strolled round to Terry's bivvy to thank them for the wonderful meal, and we were just about to start clearing things up when the matchmen arrived for their Sunday morning stint. You should have seen the looks on their faces when they saw everything laid out for a banquet. "What's fishing coming to?" one of them said, but you could see he was envious. He'd probably left home without his sandwiches and flask of tea.

That was the summer of 1981, an unforgettable year in every way, and my last one at Longfield. After all, how could you follow a season like that. The fox disappeared about the same time, and someone even accused me of taking him home for a pet, but he smelt a bit too much for that.

We always used to moan about him, but he was great company because he was so tame and he was always up to his tricks. I often wonder what happened to him. I will always remember him for his love of bacon, and how he could take a piece off your finger so delicately, if you closed your eyes you wouldn't know it had gone. But like all the great times we share in angling, he came and went, and left us with a lot of happy memories that made that year very special to all who knew him.

Part One

Chapter Seven
Loony Lads and Savay Thirties

It's funny how fate sometimes takes a hand in fishing, and as one door closes, another opens without any need for work behind the scenes. After success at Longfield I wanted a new challenge, but hadn't made any plans. One month before the start of the season I was asked if I would like to join Savay, a syndicate famous among carp anglers from John O'Groats to Land's End for their antics on a Colne Valley lake of the same name. Savay holds more 'thirties' than anywhere else in the country; I couldn't wait. Little did I know I was to do less fishing there than on any other water, before or since.

The late notice didn't give me much time to prepare, but I knew Clive Diedrich and Malcolm Winkworth were both in the syndicate and using the same bait as I was. That would give me a head start. On the first trip down there I had a walk round and put some bait in near some reeds in a swim off the end of Alcatraz, the famous Savay island.

On the way back to the car I bumped into Andy Barker, who was plumbing the depths to decide where to fish. As it was lunchtime and still the Close Season, I decided a pint or two would be in order and left to find out what the local pub was like. When I got back you can probably guess which swim I found Andy in... the one I had baited up.

It may sound daft, but when I've decided where I want to fish, I find it hard to concentrate in any other swim. I feel as though I'm in the wrong place and spend more time wondering what the bloke in the other swim is doing than thinking about my own fishing.

At this point I would like to say it's a sixth sense I've got for sussing out the best spots, and that I've never caught anything from a swim that wasn't my first choice. But at 5.45 the next morning off went the buzzer and in came a 15lb carp. The next day the same, and in came a fish of 30lb 4oz. All I was expecting was a suntan and several nights of uninterrupted sleep, but then I've always liked surprises.

It was a good job I started well, though, because as soon as I got to know the other lads, we felt bound to keep up the ancient Savay tradition of enjoying a few drinks. It can be a fantastic place to fish, the best social life of anywhere in the country and fantastic fishing, but the pace of the late nights and heavy drinking sorts the men out from the boys, and only the best can be out every night and still concentrate on their fishing.

I thought the rota I was on enjoyed a drink and a laugh, but when I changed to the "Loony" rota and met Rod Hutchinson, Roger Smith and others, I realized I had been leading a sheltered life. I got to know Rod really well in those two years, which were the best two years of my fishing life, and easily the least productive in terms of fish.

All I was expecting was a suntan and several nights of uninterrupted sleep, but then I've always liked surprises.

Part One

When Rod and Roger got back from the Indian restaurant in the early hours they could cast out and be ready to hit a run at any time in the night. When I got back, all I wanted to do was sleep, and when my head hit that pillow I cared about as much for fishing as I do for tiddlywinks when I'm sober. It sometimes took so long to find my bivvy, on hands and knees in the pitch dark, that I had to sleep till midday before I had the strength to stand upright.

As a result, most of the fish I did catch were between the time I got up, usually about midday, and the time the pubs opened, about 6pm. And as this was the least productive few hours of the day, you can see why I didn't do as well as I should have done. I felt like a matchman, casting out when the sun was high in the sky and reeling in when it began to cool down.

I did have a few memorable moments, though. Keith 'the Tooth' O'Connor, so named because of his chipped front gnasher, was there when I got my best fish, and so were two young kids. It was a red-hot day, the sort you see on television in those spaghetti westerns when Clint Eastwood gets left in the desert without a horse or a water canister. The lake was as flat as a sheet of glass and even someone with specs like beer bottle bottoms would have been able to see the fish that were cruising in front of us.

I was in the swim that had produced the 'thirty' for me on that first trip. Suddenly I had a screaming run and found myself attached to a fish that fought like a lunatic. Only the smaller fish go quite that crazy, and I decided it must be a 'double'. I started playing up to the kids, digging my feet into the ground and letting it pull me along the bank. I should have gone on the stage instead of taking up fishing, for I really got them going with my Ernest Hemingway bit. They thought I had hooked Jaws.

I brought it round in front of me, bullying it with the rod almost bent double, and as I looked down the line for a glimpse of the fish, this massive common came into view. That wiped the smile off my face and I played it as carefully as I have played any fish in my life. But the best moment was when I got it on to the bank and those kids saw the size of it. They were over the moon, and just to see their mouths drop open made my day. On the scales she went 31lb 8oz and was, and still is, my best Savay fish and its most famous resident – Sally. I gave the boys some bait and they ran back to their rods, determined to sit there for hours if it meant they might catch a carp like that one.

I sacked the fish up and nipped round to see Roger about photographs. I almost ran into him hurrying round to see me. He had had a 19lb fish, which I photographed for him and he did the same for me. He went on to land several more fish to 28lb, although I had no more action on that trip, but I wasn't complaining.

Savay attracted the very best anglers, mainly because it was a hard water, which sorted out the 'stayers' from those who wanted success straight away.

And yet it managed to keep its fish from some of the best. Maybe that was why the social life was so good. There was always someone who had something to celebrate and a lot of others who wanted to forget another blank day or a lost fish.

When the word got round that we were meeting in such and such a pub it was too much of a temptation to resist. One day in November we heard that we were invited to go round to the Colne bank of the lake for tea. Now, that's not the sort you have at the Queen's garden parties, with buttered scones and crumpet (or is it muffins). The usual 'spread' was a steaming mug of PG Tips' best and a couple of fags before heading for the pub.

On the scales she went 31lb 8oz and was, and still is, my best Savay fish and its most famous resident – Sally.

Part One

For some reason we'd all gathered on the island, which meant getting across the water on the ferry. This was no big deal for a couple of blokes, even of Rod's size, but this day we must have had more to celebrate, or more to try to forget, than usual because when we got to the ferry there were rather a lot of us. A few of the blokes seemed a bit worried about the little raft, but their objections were waved aside with the sort of enthusiastic confidence that only comes from ring-pull cans.

I remember thinking I had better get in the front (I think it's called the bows) and they all got in the back (which must be called the arrows). I climbed on while everyone was chatting on the shore, six eggs in one hand and my slippers in the other. Then we started being pulled across and we were all laughing and singing the sort of sailors' song you wouldn't want your granny to hear, when the rail started to rise before my eyes. I grabbed hold of it with my slipper hand, dropping the eggs and my footwear not knowing whether I was imagining it or not.

When I looked round, though, the others were knee deep in water and going further in by the second. I looked at them, from my perch now high above the water, and looked at the land, and I knew we weren't going to make it across. They all tumbled out of the back of the boat one by one as it went underwater, but the man on the rope kept pulling and when we got to the shore, with me still sitting in the bows, I was the only one who hadn't had a ducking. In fact I hadn't even got my feet wet.

Pride of the Valley.

The rest staggered ashore with their clothes sticking to them, shivering from the icy November water and wringing large quantities out of their jumpers. It didn't half look funny when you were dry and warm. "I didn't even get wet," I laughed, and then realized they were all looking at me.

Someone said: "Let's throw him in," and that's when I decided to make a run for it. There are times when you are grateful you haven't let yourself go completely and developed weak legs and a beer gut, and this was one of them. I had no trouble leaving them behind, and slowed down when I couldn't hear the squelching of wet sneakers on the road behind me. I found the eggs and slippers the next day, beached where the wind had carried them, and not a single shell was so much as cracked.

That wasn't the first time members of the Loony Rota had got a couple of mouthfuls of natural water. With the pubs on one bank and the bivvies on the other it was inevitable that between swilling beer and sipping tea, someone would get an unexpected ducking, but next time it happened it was in my swim.

It happened in the same month, when Rod, Roger and I came back from the boozer (there must be something about November that makes anglers fall in). Now, Roger has this coat that is not really a coat but bits of a sleeping bag sewn together, with holes for his arms and legs, and he calls it his '5lb chub', because it is so big and bulky. He was wearing this and telling me a story and, being Roger, he had to laugh at his own funny lines. He had been sitting next to my rods, but the next moment he wasn't there at all.

He overdid the joke a bit and laughed and laughed and rocked and rocked and then he was gone, into my swim. We knew he liked to laugh at his own jokes, and that he had had too much to drink, but we didn't know he couldn't swim. It was only when we saw bubbles coming up that we realized it wasn't part of the story he had been telling.

I was aware that he was in trouble and grabbed him by the 'chub', which weighed a ton, being full of water, and we pulled him back up the bank. I sobered up in an instant because I realized he had come within seconds of copping it, and if we didn't get him warmed up from the icy water, he could still be in danger.

We got the colour back into his cheeks and when he came round there was a great grin on his face and his first words were: "I saw Sally the carp, eating boilies down there!" How can a man come that close to death and come out with a line like that? He's never normal. We warmed him up with tea and hot food and in a short time he was acting as if nothing had happened. He went off to change and as I climbed into my sleeping bag I remembered hearing the song Sally getting fainter and fainter as he walked away. Savay certainly sorts the men out from the boys.

I think I enjoyed my time at Savay more than any other because of the laughs we had. As we had no secrets from each other, we were all relaxed, and if something funny wasn't happening at the time, we were swapping stories of laughs we had had in the past, over homemade curries or pints in the local pub. It was like spending a week at a holiday camp with your mates, but with big fish thrown in. We were all willing to share our experiences, and no one minded making a fool of himself. If only carp fishing were always like that.

I remember looking a bit stupid in front of several members of the Loony Rota when I was still getting to know them. I had been on the lake for a couple of days without so much as a bleep from the Optonics. Rod turned up and within 24 hours he had three fish on the bank. This had to be investigated.

Part One

I wandered round for a chat and a cup of tea and part way through the conversation he stopped talking, looked at me, and then said straight faced: "You'll get one of those big 'uns soon". The words had hardly left his lips when I heard the scream of a buzzer. It was mine.

Line was still peeling off when I got to the rod and brought it back with a whack. Now, if you know a thing or two about carp fishing you'll realize that you can tell how big a fish is by the sort of fight it gives. The small ones go off like express trains, sometimes breaking the surface but tiring quite quickly; the medium sized ones are harder to stop and more difficult to gain line from; and the real lunkers move slowly and purposefully anywhere they want to if you let them.

The first thing I felt when I hit this run was a slow, steady, powerful thump, thump, thump as something moved away strongly. Rod and Bob Jones had run round close behind me, and even they were holding their breath, waiting for a glimpse of the fish. I swear that if the head of the Loch Ness monster had come up in my swim with my hook in the corner of its mouth they wouldn't have been surprised.

We all strained for a glimpse of my fish of a lifetime and then, suddenly, this branch appeared. We thought the fish must be snagged, so Rod volunteered to get in and free the piece of tree from the line. We managed it after a few attempts and the fish came into view. In perfect harmony we all said at the same time: "It's the Lizard", for it was he.

Now you won't see a picture of the Lizard in this book, partly because people are afraid they will damage their cameras trying to take one. It's got only half an eye in its head, one fin on its entire body, and just about anything else is missing damaged or deformed. Quasimodo himself would not be seen dead holding it.

I don't know who was more disappointed after all that, me or the lads who had been watching. It was like going to Wembley expecting to see the Cup Final and finding the Boy's Brigade playing the Venture Scouts. Rod scratched his head, Bob walked away looking puzzled, and although I tried to work out what had happened, I still don't know to this day.

That first year was great, but the second year was even better. Something about the place and the company made you want to let your hair down and do daft things. In the evening this was easy with a few drinks inside you and a warm pub fire to sit around, but I also felt like experimenting with my fishing.

I remember thinking that heavy baiting might be the answer to holding large numbers of fish in a swim, so I went prepared. I've said before that I never do things by halves, and if my actions seem a bit silly, at least they taught me how not to go about baiting up.

It was the opening week of the season and the Bramble swim looked just perfect, so I dropped in there and unpacked my gear. Out came the catapult, out came the bait, and I started firing, and firing… and kept it up for the next four-and-a-half hours! Rod turned up, chose a swim, set up and went back to the car for something and I was still putting bait in. He thought I had a screw loose.

What was the result? You've guessed it, I didn't have a touch all week, and in fact the first fish to be caught from that area that season came four months later in October. As Rod said: "That was a good swim until the day you fished it!" I have never baited that heavily since, and although it cost me a blank week, I learnt first hand what effect overdoing the baiting up can have. The only way to learn is to try things for yourself, in carp fishing just as in life.

There were times, of course, when Savay was in the doldrums and no one was catching, or likely to catch, but on those occasions we either paid a visit to another Colne Valley water while there was no action, or spent the time reliving past sessions.

On one such week at the lake in 1983, Rod and I decided to tour all the local waters we were in, on a sort of fishing version of a pub crawl; a daft idea that shouldn't have produced anything but somehow did.

I had started on Saturday at Bruce Ashby's syndicate water and caught mirrors of 16lb 8oz and 15lb 8oz soon after setting up. Then I moved on to Savay on Sunday and met Rod there on Monday. The lake was as dead as a doornail, so we set off for another local water on Tuesday, where Rod pulled out a fish of 26lb.

Wednesday saw us on yet another lake, which provided me with a 27lb 12oz fish, back to the previous lake and another fish for Rod, this time 23lb 8oz. Friday was spent on the same lake as Wednesday, and then we went back to Savay until Sunday.

Each day we had to pack up the full gear, carry it all, lock, stock, tackle, bed and water butts, back to the car, and set up at the next water. By the end of the week we knew as much about moving as the men from Pickfords and had shoulders like weightlifters from all the fetching and carrying.

When we got back to the lake it was exactly as we had left it. Not a single fish had been seen, let alone caught, and that's the way it stayed for the last day of our stay, when we caught up on some well-earned kip.

Sometimes you can get out in results what you put in in effort. It doesn't always work out like that because life isn't always fair, but I would rather be the man on the move with his baggage under his arm and hope in his heart than the stick-in-the-mud who stays put for the sake of convenience.

So 1983 was a fun year for all of us at Savay. I didn't realize it at the time, but it was also to be my last. I couldn't come up with the £100 when the time came to pay for 1984, but that's never been a problem, as I have very understanding friends who have lent me money in the past and helped me out of scrapes. Rod said he would pay for me, but somehow the cheque went astray, and when I rang up Graham Rowles to ask which rota I was on he said: "Neither." Once again I had to leave a syndicate before I wanted to, this time thanks to our good friends at the GPO.

Part One

Chapter Eight
Forty-five Twelve

Carp anglers want to catch big fish for the same reason that mountaineers want to climb high mountains – because they are there. When they've caught a 'twenty' they want to catch a 'thirty', and when they've done that, they want to catch a 'forty'.

That was what happened in my case. I remember the day I decided to try for the big one; I can even smell the fried mushrooms on Roger Smith's plate. We were in the café near Savay, getting stuck into full breakfasts of bacon, eggs, tomatoes, sausages, fried-bread, beans, toast and marmalade and two pots of tea, and in Roger's case, fried mushrooms whenever he had had a fish the day before.

In between mouthfuls, Rod was flicking through *Angler's Mail* and he stopped to admire the famous Yateley North Lake fish, caught at 43lb by a tench angler. Rod asked me if I had seen the picture, but I told him I wasn't interested because it was such a "big ugly bugger."

He said: "You must be joking!" and when he showed me the paper I had to agree I was wrong. It was a handsome looking carp. I'd only seen one picture of it before that and it must have been distorted – it had certainly given me the wrong impression. Rod and I just looked at each other and he said: "Shall we go for it?" I didn't need any persuading.

We decided to start in August. Richard Everson was going to join us and he had a couple of mates who were happy to make the bait for us. We gave them the Protein Mix and Pukka Salmon and told them which areas to start putting it in, two weeks before we were to arrive. They used 12lb of bait over those two weeks – 2lb at each visit.

When I went down to have a look at the lake I concentrated on one area, near the Christmas Tree swim, where the fish had been caught before. I fancied two swims, the Christmas Tree one and another bar between two islands at the other end of the lake. This one would be best if the lake got crowded for, being a long walk from the car park, it didn't get the same sort of attention.

I thought the fish was a "big ugly bugger" but when Rod showed me the paper I had to agree I was wrong.

Then the problems began. The first setback came one week before we were due to go. Rod rang up to say his wife was ill and that he wouldn't be able to make it. Richard was going to join me later, so I was on my own. I arrived on August 22nd – a good time to begin serious carp fishing, as I have found in the past – just before the fish begin their heavy autumn feeding.

I arrived for the first session expecting little to happen for a while. It usually takes the first three or four short sessions for me to understand the movements of the fish and find out how they feed. The first-choice swim was taken, so I carried my gear round to the distant swim and had just lifted the rucksack from my back when I heard a buzzer sound.

I was lying there, half asleep, when a golden-coloured carp leapt out of the water thirty yards out.

Part One

The next thing I heard was someone shouting: "Give us a hand!" I thought at first that the tench bloke fishing at the far end had hooked a carp, but when I got down to his swim I could see it was Sam Fox, one of the Yateley regulars, and he was standing on the island playing a fish.

By the look of him he'd swam across from his swim with his rod, to prevent the fish going behind the island. His mate swam across with the net (that's what friends are for) and when he landed it my heart sank. I could see from the size of it that it was a very big fish and that could only mean one thing – he'd just landed the fish I had come to catch.

I helped Sam with the photos of the fish, which went just over 43lb, and then I couldn't see much point in staying because there was no way it was going to come out again the same day. But Sam said a couple of the fish feeding with this one had been spooked towards the corner of the lake, and when I went back to my swim, sure enough there were fish feeding on the bar. I set up and later had a fish of 18lb 4oz, which was very pleasing because Yateley carp of any size are hard to catch.

That first session lasted five days, but the second visit was over in twenty-four hours. It just didn't feel right or look right. There didn't seem to be a movement anywhere in the water or on the land; even the birds seemed quiet and the lake was flat calm. There's only one thing to do when it's like that and that's to pack up and go home.

On my third visit I got there late and only had time to set up and cast out before darkness fell. The Christmas Tree area had been free, so I dropped in there, knocked back a couple of cans of Paul Hogan's "amber nectar" and was soon asleep.

I'll say one thing for carp fishing – you get plenty of time for a good kip. With early nights, late mornings and siestas, you can get more shut-eye in a couple of days by the waterside than in a week at home.

I was lying there, half asleep, when a golden-coloured carp leapt out of the water thirty yards out and along to my right and then fell back with a crash. My glimpse of the fish and the ripples it sent across the lake told me it was a good 'un.

I leapt out of bed, reeled in and cast to where the ripples had come from. An hour later I had a run and landed a beautiful, golden mirror of 23lb 12oz – I believe, the same fish that I had seen.

I was delighted with the fish, but not so happy with the conditions, and decided to call it a day. There's little point sitting around feeling miserable when you don't think you're going to catch anything. Far better to save your patience for the times when you're in with a chance.

I was back the following weekend, and this time I chose the swim on the point of a peninsula that forms part of the Christmas Tree area. I could get a bait to the Christmas Tree from there and put another bait on the area in front of me that had produced the 18lb mirror on the first session.

I felt a lot more confident, and during the four-day session I had a 28lb 4oz mirror from the back of the Christmas Tree. On the next visit Richard Everson came with me. I started on the Christmas Tree, but I was keen to try other areas in case I was missing something, and when two fish crashed out during the night at the other end of the lake, I packed up and was on my way round soon after first light.

I had learnt the value of following jumping fish during previous visits to this and other lakes and was waiting for the fish to show again, but they didn't. Feeling like a stroll, the next morning I went to see a bloke I knew who was fishing opposite the point, and he mentioned in passing that he'd heard a fish jump in the night. "It was like a cow falling in," he said, but he'd hardly got the words out when I started giving him an ear-bending for not saying something sooner.

l was round there like a shot and fished the point for the rest of the session. It felt like a good area, and I decided to put most of my effort into it on the next couple of trips. When the next two trips were blank I began to wonder if I'd done the right thing. The weather wasn't right, I wasn't sure I was in the right area, and the nights were getting longer. The only good thing was that the lake was becoming quieter as the cold, wet weather and short hours of daylight started to put anglers off. Often I was the only angler there.

It was half way through October when I decided it was time for one last effort before fishing became really unpleasant and my chances disappeared. All or nothing, I'd go for the big hit – three weeks of solid fishing. I knew it was my last chance of the fish that year. I arrived on October 12th for the long session and went to the point swim. Richard appeared soon after and set up nearby. The weather was good – neither warm nor cold – and I found myself looking forward to casting out, which is always a good sign.

Nothing happened on Friday night, but on Saturday morning at 11.30am Richard landed the golden 23lb fish I had had a few weeks before, and things were looking better all the time. On Saturday night I couldn't sleep. It may sound funny, but I get a feeling that something is about to happen and I can't relax. I lie awake looking out across the lake, expecting one of the buzzers to go off at any minute. It's a bit like being a kid on Christmas Eve, unable to sleep because you know something great is going to happen the next day.

I was surprised when Sunday morning dawned and I hadn't had a run, but there was still an electric atmosphere around the lake – as if everything was holding its breath. I was tired, not having shut my eyes all night, and I fell into a light doze during the morning. At lunchtime Richard, living locally, went home for his Sunday lunch. Either he didn't share my feeling of expectation, or the temptation of leg of lamb and roast potatoes, a few beers and a kip on the sofa was too much for him. I was invited, but it would have been like switching off a whodunnit?-film without finding out if it was the butler or not. I stayed put, and opened a tin of beans and sausages.

At 6pm two friends of mine appeared, Geoff and Wendy; it was to be a visit they would never forget. I was glad of the company as it took my mind off thoughts of roast potatoes and a sizzling leg of lamb. I made them a cup of tea each and we were chatting when it happened.

At 7pm I had a run. I picked up the rod and as soon as I struck I knew what I had hooked. The fish started moving slowly, steadily and powerfully away from the island where it had picked up my bait, and I said to Geoff: "Reel that other rod in. This is the one."

There was only one snag to overcome and that was between me and the fish. As the fish kited parallel to the bank, I pulled it towards the snag and, like most fish you hook, it responded to the pressure by swimming in the opposite direction and into open water.

From then on steady pressure with 8lb line brought it slowly towards me, and in under five minutes it was ready for the net. No one had said a word until then, and I broke the

During the four-day session I had a 28lb 4oz mirror from the back of the Christmas Tree.

silence to ask Geoff to pass me the landing net. He said: "You're standing on it." In all my concentration I had not noticed the mesh under my feet. A few seconds later she was mine.

Geoff read the scales and announced 47lb 4oz, which, with a quick calculation of minus 1lb 8oz for the Old Man's weigh bag, left a weight of 45lb 12oz.

Until then I had just wanted to catch a 40lb carp. I soon realized I had done quite a bit more; in the sack was the second heaviest carp ever landed in Britain. I went round to Richard's house to use his phone and found Yvonne and the kids round there, which was perfect. I rang the Old Man and told him next and he was overjoyed as well. Then I rang Rod and, after hearing his congratulations, I asked if he would get hold of Bob Jones and come down the next morning with the cameras.

I had just wanted to catch a 40lb carp, but I soon realized I had done quite a bit more; in the sack was the second heaviest carp ever landed in Britain and possibly the largest one alive anywhere in the UK at the time.

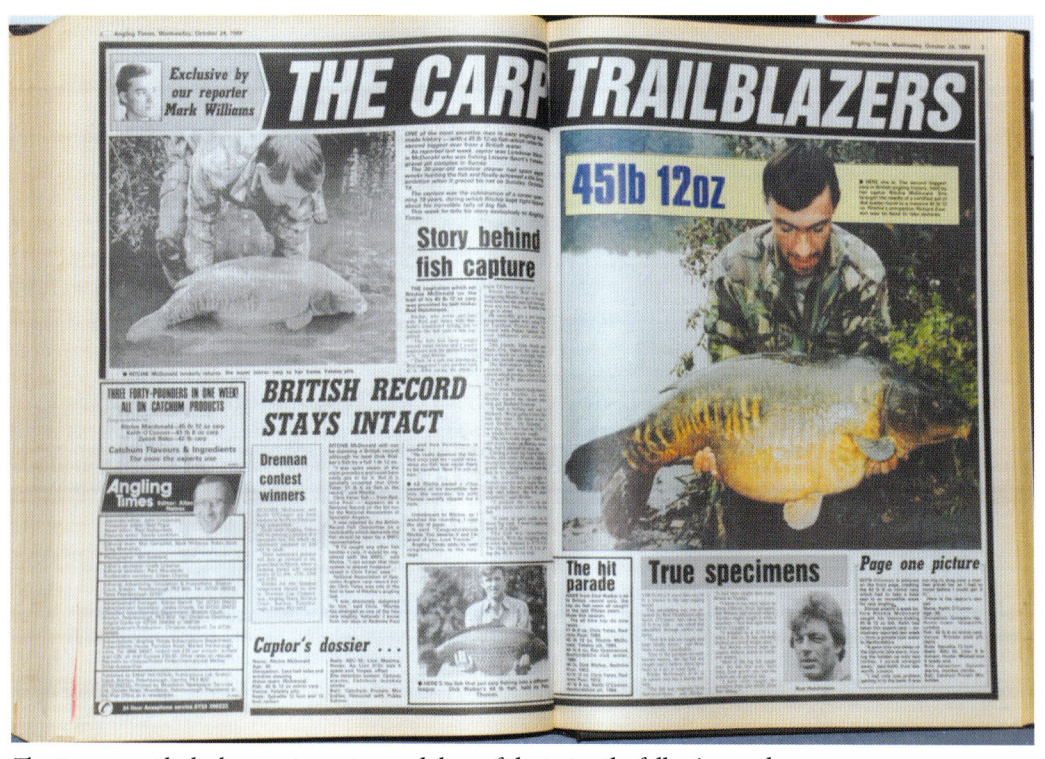

The story was splashed across pages two and three of the paper the following week.

A moment to savour.

One of the lads bought me a strip-o-gram to celebrate.

I went back to the lake that night, but I couldn't sleep. Fish were crashing out in front of me, but I didn't cast out. I was content with what I had caught and I wasn't interested in catching anything else.

The next morning everyone arrived. We took the photos and even a video and then it was down to the Fisheries pub, near Savay, for a pint and to organise a celebration. It was all arranged for Monday night. An evening in the pub, a meal in the Tandoori House and then back to Rod's bivvy at Savay, where we talked into the night.

Rod rang the papers and *Angling Times* got the exclusive story and pictures, in line with the Drennan Cup exclusive rule. Mark Williams came down on Tuesday to get the details and pick up the films, and it was splashed across pages two and three of the paper the following week. Keith 'the Tooth' O'Connor's 43lb 8oz fish was on the front with the words "and there's a bigger one inside". Poor old Keith. You catch a 43lb carp and still don't get Fish of the Week!

I got to the final of the Angling Times Drennan Cup that year, and won Angling Times Specimen Hunter of the Year, but what meant most were the phone calls and messages of congratulation.

So that's that story – a slice of history. For the record, I was using Rod's Pukka Salmon, which had produced the goods for Pete Springate and me that time in the Colne Valley, with Rod's Protein Mix as a base. The reel line was 8lb Maxima tied to a 6lb hook length and a size 6 Au Lion D'Or spade-end hook, and the 2 oz lead was back-stopped with power-gum tied to the main line.

I got to the final of the *Angling Times* Drennan Cup that year and went to lunch with Peter Drennan, the other three finalists (Greg Buxton, Neville Fickling and Alastair Nicholson) and *Angling Times*. I was told I had come fourth, Greg being the overall winner in that first year of the competition, and though I was disappointed that the 45 and a 37lb 12oz fish caught at the beginning of the same season had not placed me higher, at least I got my name on the cup.

What meant more to me were the phone calls and messages of congratulation when I caught the fish. People I had never met wrote to me to say: "Well done!" and people packed into halls to hear my talks. A youngster who had read the story in the papers made me a beautiful bronze replica of the fish, which took pride of place in my living room.

People have been very kind, and I've wetted the head of that fish more than a few times since that day in 1984. It's made me realize that, as well as attracting some of the strangest people I've ever met, fishing also attracts some of the kindest.

Part One

Chapter Nine
Cassien – The Beginning

I've never had a lot of money. Whenever I've been weighed out a sizeable wedge it's slipped through my fingers like water through the mesh of a landing net. Every week another bit falls off my car and has to be stuck back on at great expense. There are always things to buy for the home and the family, and I get so many letters with the word 'Bill' on them that I'm thinking of changing my name. So when Lake Cassien hit the headlines as the nearest thing to heaven on earth for carp anglers, I was as keen to go as most people, but twice as broke. It seemed such a shame. Here I was wondering where the next challenge lay after the 45, and Cassien, with its world record potential, came along at just the right time – but it was out of the reach of my pocket.

I began to wonder if I could borrow the money, and started thinking who I'd done a few favours for recently, and then I had an idea.

Angling Times had been very grateful to get the exclusive story and pictures of the 45, so I was in their good books. Why not offer them another exclusive – my expedition to the now-famous South of France lake to try to break the world record in return for money up front? The more I thought about it, the more the idea appealed. There was just one snag – what if I caught nothing. I tried to put that out of my mind. I had to go to their offices and appear so confident that I was going to crack the record that they would have no worries about parting with the cash.

By the time I got to Peterborough I had convinced myself that an 80lb fish was possible. Wearing my best whistle and flute, I put the proposition to the then Editor, Allan Haines, and with a bit of help from Mark, who knew me through the story of the 45, they agreed. I left with the promise of a cheque for £150, the use of Mark for a week to write the words and take the pictures and, if all went well, the chance of becoming a household name in fishing circles. It felt good going back to Richmond that day, with their generous hospitality inside me and all the talk of record fish still going round in my head. I couldn't wait to get out there and at 'em. Little did I know that my problems were just beginning.

The next thing to decide was who to take with me. I had heard Johnny Allen, who I had fished with years ago at Savay, was keen to go, and when I rang him he jumped at the chance. The third person needed a bit more thought. We had heard the French were getting a bit fed up with English anglers breaking the rules by fishing at night and using too many rods. Hardly a week went by without someone having their tackle confiscated or a gun waved under their nose. I could see us travelling all the way there with the intention of staying for a month and losing our gear in the first few days, just because we couldn't read the small print on the licence.

We needed someone whose appearance overcame the language barrier and who was not afraid to help us defend our rights. You probably won't have heard of Bob Tyrell, known to his mates as 'The Animal'. He doesn't catch a lot of carp, but, to be fair, fishing has always been his second favourite hobby.

He's a cross between Grizzly Adams and the Incredible Hulk, and when I add that he was accepted into the American Hell's Angels – and they don't take just anybody – you'll get the picture. He's had more motorbike accidents than Barry Sheene, and when he hit a roundabout at full speed and was technically dead for a moment or two, before a passing nurse re-started his heart, he was left with little feeling in parts of his body. People hit him and he just grins at them.

Anyway, Bob seemed to fit the bill, and when I rang him up he was delighted. He said he knew someone who was getting a brand new Ford Transit in a couple of weeks and we could borrow that. Everything looked great.

The first blow came when Mark rang up from *Angling Times* to say he couldn't make it. The date clashed with a family holiday he had arranged, so one of the other reporters, Greg Meenehan, would come out for the week in his place. I didn't know Greg, but as long as there was someone there to cover the action it wouldn't make too much difference.

Getting the tackle and bait together was expensive. Rod was kind enough to supply the Protein Mix and flavourings for the trip, but the particles – five hundredweight sacks of prime peanuts – had to be bought. Berkley supplied us with Berkley Trilene line, so we were able to keep the rest of our money for ferry tickets, petrol and food for the month.

It was a Transit all right, but it was about fifty years old.

Part One

On the morning of our departure, John was the first to arrive and Bob appeared soon afterwards: I looked out into the street, but I couldn't see the new Transit he had promised. That's when he explained that the new one hadn't arrived and that we would have to make do with one that was a bit older.

It was a Transit all right, but it was about fifty years old. The doors didn't have handles, just padlocks, and the first bag of nuts we threw into the back went through the floor. The driver had just a rickety old seat, but I didn't mind as I wouldn't be doing much of the driving. That's when Bob told me he didn't own a licence!

I couldn't believe he would keep this to himself until we were loading up the van. Eventually we were ready and I started it up. As I tried to slip it into first gear Bob told me that it didn't have a first gear! Nothing would surprise me after that.

Bob Tyrell, known to his mates as 'The Animal' – a cross between Grizzly Adams and the Incredible Hulk.

Somehow we got to the ferry and things were looking up. We just wanted to get down there as quickly as possible, but somehow Bob's money-saving plan of taking the back roads and avoiding the expensive motorway tolls seemed to make sense, considering our limited supply of cash. That was our next mistake!

Most people took between fifteen and eighteen hours to get there, and the coaches, which had to travel more slowly and had a couple of stops, took twenty-five hours. We took three days. We went through some of the dingiest, dirtiest little places I have ever seen. If you were planning to put someone off France by driving them through all the warts on the face of that country you couldn't choose a better route than we did. The villages were full of wrinkled old women and three-legged dogs; I was afraid we would break down and be stranded in one.

Most people took fifteen to eighteen hours to get there – we took three days.

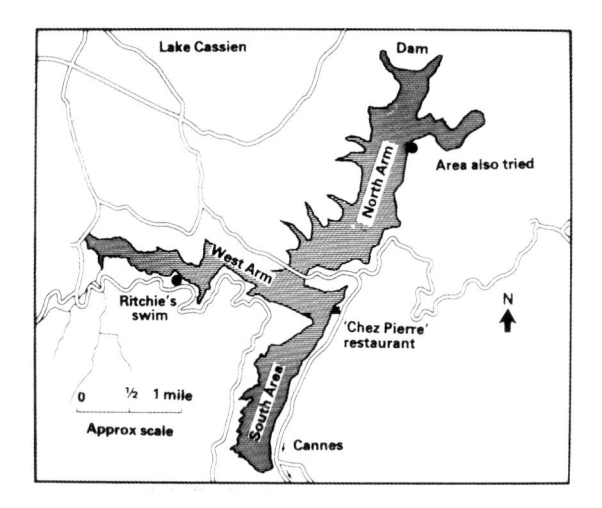

I should have been glad when we finally arrived, but my first glimpse of the lake confirmed my worst fears – it was massive. It took us ages to drive the length of the South Arm, and that was only a third of the total. There was no way it would be worth casting out in the first spot that took our fancy – that way we would take until Christmas to find the fish. We would have to find them before we started.

We were all very tired, but having seen the task that lay ahead and knowing that our money was very limited, I was determined to get started. I had a feeling, even then, that time might run out on us, so the first call was at Chez Pierre's restaurant, where we left the tackle in the van, hired a boat with an electric outboard motor for £16, and took to the water with snorkel at the ready.

If anything, the place looked bigger from the boat. My original plan was to explore the North Arm, which few anglers had fished. I thought this would be where the biggest fish lived, but I found out just how wrong you can be. The water was deep, so deep that you couldn't find the bottom. Even the strong South of France rays didn't penetrate that far – it was pitch black. Ideally we were looking for a plateau about thirty feet down, but the only areas like that in the North were covered in weed. Add that to the fact that we didn't see a single fish in all our explorations and it was time to cross the North Arm off our list.

We had just about made up our mind to go elsewhere when a plane flew low over the lake and as it came back round it started to get lower and lower and was heading for us. Suddenly it hit the water close by, travelled along on the surface just a few yards away and then took off again. Our tiny boat rocked violently in the wake of the disturbance and we began to realize how close that plane had come.

Later we found out that it had been gathering water to drop on one of the forest fires that they get every summer in that area, and the marker buoys that we had seen, but taken no notice of, were its runway! With our combined lack of skill at manoeuvring the boat, it had been a bit like taking a driving lesson on the runway at Heathrow. We couldn't get to the West Arm fast enough.

We spent that night in the van and the next day took a rowing boat for £5, to try to save money. Once again I thought Bob would come in handy; with arms like tree trunks I thought he was made for rowing, but I was wrong again. It turned out that he couldn't make a circular movement with his right arm. Okay, I thought, we'll each take one oar, but he was so strong the boat just went round in circles. In the end we had to row him, and it was like two cavemen dragging a dinosaur.

The effort was worth it when we got there, though. The West Arm was like a completely different lake. There were far more features, both in and out of the water, and I felt the old confidence begin to flow back again. We could see fish moving up ahead of us, so this had to be the place.

Part One

My first glimpse of the lake confirmed my worst fears – it was massive. This is just the North Arm.

On with the snorkel and over the side.

On with the snorkel and over the side, I found a beautiful plateau about twelve feet deep that dropped off into deeper water. We made up a marker with a lead, nylon line and polystyrene and measured the depth at the drop off. It was thirty feet – perfect! At last we had found what we were looking for: peace, fish and a perfectly proportioned swim. We could forget how big the lake was and concentrate on that one small corner.

The two days spent trying to find the right spot were very unpleasant. There were times when we wondered if we had come one thousand miles for nothing, and thought we might go back without even seeing a fish, let alone catching one, but by not giving in to the temptation to just cast out, sit back and wait, we had shortened the odds of catching what we had come for. "First find your fish" is a golden rule at home and abroad.

We baited up around markers using the boat, cast out, and within half an hour of placing the baits I had the first Cassien run. I don't know why, but I expected the runs to be generally slow tricklers or trundlers. I wasn't expecting the line to fly off the spool and the fish to have covered a lot of ground by the time I lifted the rod. Thinking about it now, it's not surprising that they move fast – the combination of clear water (you wouldn't run very fast if you couldn't see where you were going) and the fact that the fish had never been hooked before was bound to make them go like express trains. French anglers, who even then were still using raw potatoes for bait, killed and ate everything they caught, so the fish that were in the lake had never felt a hook, unless they had been played and lost.

That fish was on for a few seconds and then everything went solid. In the end I had to pull for a break. It wasn't long before we realized the bed of the lake was littered with snags. A lot of the time, when we picked up the rod to reel in and change the bait we found the tackle snagged, or we hit a snag on the way in.

It wasn't until later that we found out that the valley was once completely covered in trees, and before they flooded it they cut down all the ones that would be below the water line, leaving the stumps in the ground. Sometimes it seemed as if they had left whole trees down there!

I found a clear area, after much casting and retrieving, and at the cost of a few leads and rigs. When the next run came, sending the monkey climber into a blur, I was ready, and played and landed our first Cassien carp – all 26lb of it.

I thought I had cracked it. Find a clear area and don't let them take any more line than you have to. To say I was disappointed when the next fish became snagged is an understatement. Time for a rethink. It seemed to me that the leads were the most likely thing to snag, and so if I attached them by weak links – strong enough to stay together on the retrieve, but weak enough to break when snagged by a fish – I would solve the problem. The only drawback was the number of leads we would get through, and this is what made us take to the boat. We hoped that by getting above the fish we would keep the line well away from the stumps and we would be able to fight the fish in clear water. It worked.

It seemed that Cassien was all problems and answers. We were learning as we went along, finding out how different foreign fish are from our English ones and having to think out every problem logically. So far all the action had been to my rods, though I don't know why because I wasn't doing anything different from the others, but at last John had a run. He had begun to think the indicators were glued to their sticks, but he was at his rods in a flash. The battle lasted just a few seconds, and then back came the terminal tackle with a partly straightened hook.

Part One

We'd brought sacks of peanuts for baiting up, which we prepared on the bank.

Boilie making was one of the daily chores.

Several boilies on a hair made a bait shaped like a crayfish tail.

113

The next run sent the monkey climber into a blur.

Part One

Ready for action.

Playing a fish from a boat is very different. Any sudden change of direction by the fish can spin the boat around.

A hard-fighting 23lb 12oz fish goes back.

Part One

A new hook, another cast to the marker and... the same thing happened again. Two runs and two lost fish. John kept saying he couldn't remember the last time a British fish had bent a hook of his, and now it had happened twice in succession in France. He kept tying line to different parts of the hook and pulling it against a spring balance to try to test the strength of the wire. But the cause of the problem wasn't his tackle, it was the mouths of the fish.

Feeding on crayfish, the carp had mouths like old boots, and anything less than a very powerful strike didn't pull the hook in over the barb. If a hook doesn't go in fully it takes very little effort to bend it and make it spring out. Thankfully I hit my fish hard anyway, but I should have said something when I tried to get the hook out of my 26lb fish. It was like trying to get a hook out of the sole of your shoe.

It was at about that time that Greg Meenehan from *Angling Times* came out to get the words and pictures for the series. He got a lift with the coach party to the lake run by Paul Regent in early September, and tracked us down a couple of days after we had moved to the West Arm.

Each morning of his stay he motored out to meet us at dawn, and you could tell it was Greg because he was the only person around wearing a shirt. Everyone else was stripped to the waist and getting more bronzed by the day, but if Greg felt a bit hot he rolled the sleeves of his shirt up to the elbow – not forgetting to dab some suntan oil on his forearms – before retreating under the umbrella.

When I tried to get the hook out of my 26lb fish, it was like trying to get a hook out of the sole of your shoe.

Carp fishing in the South of France, a world away from English angling.

Part One

John's personal best 41lb fish almost had us in the water twice.

He would leave just before dark each day and if we got any fish when the light was poor, or before he got there in the morning, we kept them in sacks for him to photograph. That was what happened with John's personal best. The light was dim when he had the run and hooked something slow and powerful.

Into the boat to play it and what a fight it was! The fish almost had us in the water twice. Playing a fish from a boat is very different. You are trying to pull a fish up instead of leading it towards you; it can see the 'enemy' quite clearly, and a sudden change of direction can spin the boat around if you don't give line quickly enough. I was glad to see all 41lb of it in the folds of the net.

My fish kicked up a stink when I lifted the sack out the next morning.

Weighing my 37lb 8oz mirror.

Part One

If the fish are tired when you land them, though, a night in a sack does wonders for their fighting spirit and they are like caged tigers by the morning. My best fish of that early spell, a 37lb 8oz mirror, had a fit when I lifted the sack out the next morning, and when I held the fish to be photographed it hit me in the stomach with its tail so hard that I was winded.

As the shoreline of the lake is rocky, we had to use a padded rod holdall to protect the fish in case we had to lay them down between photographs. Even the early morning sun was too strong for their liking, so it was a couple of quick shots and then back in the water with them. That was all we needed, though, as the light was perfect for photography.

When Greg left each evening we retreated into the bushes for the night. The first job before turning in was to inspect your sleeping bag. In England we find earwigs, ants and flies a nuisance; in France if something crawls up your trouser leg it could be a snake, a scorpion or a poisonous spider. If any of those bite you, you'll need courage not to panic and a very good friend to suck the poison out.

We found a couple of scorpions in our food-bag one day, but we saw them before they saw us. A snake slithered by near John one day, but thankfully it didn't give him a second glance. But the closest I came to a head-to-head encounter was with something a little larger – a wild boar. And I was answering the call of nature in the bushes at the time.

If you haven't met a wild boar, they're like large, dark hairy pigs with tusks, I think, because I didn't stop to take a close look. I don't know who was more surprised, me or the boar, but we both reacted in the same way. I ran one way, he scampered off in the other and the toilet roll was left to roll down the shore like an advert for Andrex.

A powerhouse of a carp, and a real handful on the bank.

But that came later. In the meantime a few changes were taking place. Greg, having turned his forearms light brown and having filled his camera bag with used rolls of film and his notebook with shorthand, left to catch the Regent coach back to England. His stay had been short but entertaining. We'd particularly miss the way he motored through John's carefully positioned lines when he left each evening – or at least I would miss it. On the final night, as a special treat he took John's marker as well.

Bob announced that he had had enough of roughing it and was going to Cannes for a couple of days to drink, eat and make merry. We hadn't had much action from the fish for a few days and we began to think they might have moved to another part of the lake. It was a big decision after our early success in the West Arm, but we agreed it was time to cut our losses and try elsewhere, and with that we packed our gear and headed for the North.

I think we had forgotten what it was like, but it didn't take long for the memories to come flooding back – not a fish in sight. We were not far from Chez Pierre's, so with thoughts of French beer and friendly faces we headed for the jetty.

The first shock was to hear that Bob hadn't gone to Cannes. In fact he'd cadged a lift with the Regent coach and was back in England by then. He hadn't left us empty handed, though. That was the second shock; he left us his bill for several day's boat hire!

But what you lose on the swings you gain on the roundabouts. While we were reading Bob's farewell note, we met another English angler, Geoff Shaw. Geoff had been at the lake for a couple of days but had yet to see a fish. Our tales of screaming runs and big fish had him on the edge of his bar stool. He'd come to catch a 'thirty', which would be a personal best, and in his excitement at the number of fish we had seen and the number of runs we had had, he made us realize the rest of the lake wasn't fishing half as well as our hotspot.

We downed our beers and were back on the lake in double-quick time, destination: the West Arm. Within twenty-four hours John would hook a fish that was beyond belief. People use the phrase "a fish of a lifetime" rather a lot, but in this case it was the only way to describe his catch. It is still the largest coarse fish ever landed by an Englishman, and sometimes, even now, I think of that day in October and still can hardly believe what happened.

A scrub-up, Cassien style.

Part One

Chapter Ten
Cassien – Success at the Second Attempt

The monkey climber on one of John's rods lifted two inches and he was out of his bedchair in a second. He struck, but felt no resistance. As he reeled his rig into shallow water, he saw a silvery flash and swung in a 2oz bream – the cause of the tiny bite.

Giving the bream, which had his size 4 hook in its mouth, its freedom, John re-cast, re-set the bobbin and settled back in the sun again. It wasn't many minutes later that the bobbin moved two inches again, this time a drop. For a second he thought: "Shall I or shan't I?" but he decided to, just in case, and when he whipped the rod back over his shoulder, this time it hooped into a fierce bend. Out in deep water a powerful fish headed off in a run that signalled the start of John's epic ninety-minute battle with a truly monstrous creature

A lot has been written about the massive catfish that John hooked, played and brought ashore on October 3, 1985. Pictures of the seven-foot six-inch long fish made eyes widen and jaws drop all over the country when they were published in *Angling Times* and projected at slide shows on Cassien around the country.

The first bite came from a 2 oz bream.

Cassien - Success at the Second Attempt

At seven foot six inches long, the catfish took two people to hold it.

Helping the estimated 200lb fish recover after the ninety minute battle.

Part One

John told how he was playing the fish from the boat in the midday sun for so long that he began to hallucinate and imagine he was back home. A mosquito bite on his right bicep made his arm swell up with the continuous pressure of holding a carp rod doubled up for one and a half hours.

John told how he held his breath every time the portion of his 17lb line that was badly worn came through the rod rings, making a terrible grating noise, and how Geoff, who was in the boat with him and who has what could be called a 'natural suntan', went white at the first sight of the huge, horrible head rising towards him from the depths.

The struggle to net it was half comedy, half horror movie. John prayed that the hook would hold, Geoff jumped in after it but jumped out when it came towards him, and I shouted "cut the line" from the safety of dry land. I wanted nothing to do with it – I don't like catfish or eels of any size, and so you can imagine how I felt about one that was bigger than me – and if it hadn't been for Geoff and his nifty work with the landing net and a rod holdall, it would never have been landed.

The fish took the 112lb scales down to the bottom and 17lb beyond, at which point we took it off before it broke them. All three of us are used to lifting weights in the course of our work, and I would say a reasonable estimate would be 200lb. The only way of knowing for sure would have been to have killed it, and we all agreed that no fish deserved to die for the sake of a name in a record book. It took a long time for Geoff and John to nurse the fish back to strength, but they stayed with her in the water until she swam off.

I take my hat off to John for the way he played and landed the fish against almost impossible odds. Other people have tangled with huge fish at Cassien and never known what was responsible. Rod played a huge fish from a boat there and watched day turn to night with little headway having been made on the fish. Alone and a long way from where he had hooked it, shivering in the cold, strengthening wind and dressed for sunbathing not night fishing, he was forced to let it go. Another angler played an unseen fish for several hours from both shore and boat. When day turned to night he handed the rod to a friend while he went to get some warm clothes, but by the time he got back it was all over. The fish had swam under Chez Pierre's boat jetty, round the securing chain and the line had broken. I wonder what surprises the lake still has in store.

After the catfish, the burning question was "What happens next?" A fish that size charging up and down in the swim could have frightened every carp to the other end of the lake. John was still trying to rest his aching right arm, so he was glad when it was the turn of Geoff and me to do battle.

Geoff, like many English anglers, had come to Cassien to catch a personal best carp. Back home he had caught 'twenties', but had yet to land a 'thirty', and this was his target. "No problem," I said, confidently. "Stick with us and you'll catch a 'thirty'."

The first fish Geoff landed was a small common, but the second felt bigger and he played it very carefully. Not knowing if the line would wrap itself around a tree stump at any moment made Geoff tense, and I could feel him willing the fish towards the boat as I waited with the net. It was a good job it was safely in the folds at the first attempt; I don't think Geoff could have held his breath long enough for a second go. I held up the scales and we read off the dial – 30lb exactly, the fish he had come to France to catch.

I hooked a very powerful fish that took a long time to tire.

It's always nice to be there when someone catches a personal best. John had done it with his 41, as well as the catfish, and now Geoff had achieved his aim, too. Was it too much to hope for a hat-trick? Thoughts of big carp were mixed with thoughts of money as our cash supply began to dwindle. We'd half starved ourselves to keep going as long as we could, but now things were looking pretty serious. We decided to hold on for a few more days in the hope that the monster we were after would find our baits and we could call it a day before we were down to just our petrol money for the journey home.

When I hooked a very powerful fish that took a long time to tire, it crossed my mind that this could be the one we had been waiting for. When I got a glimpse of it in the clear water before it saw the boat and dived, I knew it was no eighty-pounder, but it could be bigger than my 45lb 12oz personal best.

When it came over the net I thought it might beat that weight, but it was not to be, though at 43lb it was my best from the lake so far. Perhaps it was in an advance party leading an army of big 'uns. We sat tight. Every day took us nearer to the time when we would have to leave. Then John had a run and a small common. We landed a couple of smaller fish, then I lost a good one and landed one of 26lb. The fish pyramid, whereby the middleweights pushed the flyweights off the dining table and then were pushed off by the heavyweights, was beginning. It was just a question of time.

But time was what we didn't have. There was enough bait to last for another week or more, but we were down to our last feed and water. We had enough cash to settle our boat bill, get us home and provide a bite to eat on the way, but only just. The time came when we had to call a halt.

I thought the fish could be bigger than my 45lb 12oz personal best.

Our final fish, at 26lb. We just didn't have enough food and money to wait for the heavyweights to arrive.

A group of English anglers who had just arrived saw us off. There was no point in carting the peanuts back to Britain, so we gave them to the lads, offered them our swims and even left our markers out for them. We wished them well, though really we wished we could have stayed out there for longer.

It was pleasant to get home. After a couple of weeks of sleeping rough, eating sausage rolls and drinking mineral water, it was great to climb into a proper bed and eat real food. Almost the first thing I said to Yvonne was "put the kettle on" because for someone who likes a cup of tea as much as I do, going without one for weeks was almost unbearable.

I think I was on my twentieth cup and we had not long unpacked the van when *Angling Times* rang up. They had a message from the lads whom we had met out in France: "Thanks for the peanuts. The 58lb 12oz fish we caught from the swim was just what we were looking for." They had also had a few 'twenties' and a couple of upper 'thirties', all in the time it had taken us to drive back.

I felt numb. If only we had had a few quid extra to tide us over. That lake owed us those fish, and I vowed, there and then, that somehow I would get back out there and make amends. When I want something badly, I'll work very hard to get it. By pulling a few strings, doing a few deals and explaining the situation to a few friends, I was back on the shore of Lake Cassien within three weeks. This time I only had a week, so if time was short before, it was doubly precious now.

No messing. Straight down the West Arm to the swim I had left when John and Geoff had been with me. There's a saying in life that you should never go back, and I found out

Part One

why when I got to the famous spot. The shore where we had landed that massive catfish, pulled out two personal bests between three of us and celebrated in the scorching sun was now cold and empty. No carp tails waved to me as I approached. In fact nothing moved, and the sun, which had been so welcome before, had lost its heat as autumn began to turn into winter.

So convinced was I that the 'golden' swim would turn up trumps again that I sat there for three days. It took that amount of time spent shivering and watching the motionless bobbins to make me realize that I was in the wrong place. A distance of one thousand miles is a long way to go to waste almost half of your fishing time, but nothing could turn the clock back; I had to pack up, move on and make the most of the four days left.

Bad memories of the North Arm ruled that out, which left just the South. It was an area I had avoided because it was the first part of the lake everyone arriving on the Cannes road saw and, as a result, it got most of the pressure from anglers, windsurfers, swimmers and people in pedal boats. When I called at Chez Pierre's, which is on the way, who should roll up but Rod Hutchinson and Roger Smith. After three days alone, and without even a sniff of a fish, seeing them was like having been marooned on a desert island and being rescued by your next-door neighbour.

A chat with them picked my spirits up and I was ready for action, aware that I had a very short time in which to do it. We all had our eyes on the same area. While I bought enough food to last the rest of the trip, Rod and Roger headed for the spot they fancied. Rod has always been able to pinpoint the best place on a lake just by looking at it, and Roger's no novice. They are not often wrong, and this time was no exception.

Bad memories of the North Arm ruled that out, which left just the South.

I had another run and, after a short battle, in came a mirror of 43lb.

Part One

By the time I got back, Roger was playing a fish, which weighed 18lb, and before I could get my rod rests into the ground he was into another carp that, by the look of it, was a better one. While I got my gear ready, Rod slipped the net under a 45lb mirror for Roger, and while I positioned markers and set up my rods he had another three chances. If only I had come here instead of the West Arm.

There was plenty of action, though. I was in half a mind not to sit down, I was so confident that the buzzers would sound as soon as I had placed my baits. I'm glad I took to the bed-chair. I was just one hundred and fifty yards from my friends, but it was two days before I got my first chance. When you've been sitting and waiting, hour after hour, for that line to move, it comes as a shock when it happens. You wonder if you are dreaming or if something else is responsible – a bird or a dog in the water.

By the time I had convinced myself that it really was a run, it was too late. I struck, the fish was on, and then I felt that all-too-familiar grating 'noise' through the rod as the line was wrapped around a snag and the fish (I wish I knew how they did it) transferred the hook to something solid. It was inevitable that it would take my first run to bring back the lessons I had learnt on the first outing. Even though I was alone, I had to be in that boat and out into the lake within a very short space of time of that fish feeling the hook if I was to stand a chance of securing it.

I worked out a system so that I knew exactly what to do and could carry it out smoothly and swiftly. I was determined that the next fish I hooked would be put on the bank. I had not seen the fish I had lost, and for all I knew that could have been the personal best I wanted to provide the fairy-tale ending.

There were two days to go and I refused to believe that the lost fish would be my last chance. It wasn't! Not long after I had another run and, after a short battle, in came a mirror of 43lb. Magic! Almost as heavy as my best from the lake so far and a sure sign that the big 'uns were about. The question was whether or not to put more bait in.

I suppose I was thinking of that when I had the next run. I was only a second or two slower than I had been for the 43, but the fish found a snag and it was all over. I had hardly got back to the bank when off went the other rod and the same happened again. I re-baited the rods, re-cast and off went the first rod again, and again the fish was too quick for me. I don't know which was more depressing, getting no runs or getting runs but losing the fish. To beat those you had to be faster on the draw than a Wild West gunslinger.

There were just one and a half days left and a decision about baiting up had to be made. Things had been quiet since that trio of lost fish, and I wondered whether the others had been spooked. A hooked fish doesn't always scatter the shoal, but a lost one can leave the swim at top speed and take the others with it. With three fish of unknown size bolting out of the area in quick succession, it was odds on that the rest had gone with them. That quiet spell could have been caused by just one or two very big fish feeding in the swim. You often get that lull just before a big fish picks up your bait, at home and abroad, because big carp are solitary feeders – they have to be to find enough food to keep up their weight.

If there were no fish in the swim, putting bait in might attract some, but that was a long term investment. If, on the other hand, there was a big fish down there, I didn't want to risk spooking it by raining 25lb of peanuts down on its head.

Rod and Roger were not piling in the bait. It seemed, from where I was sitting, that they had decreased their amount of loosefeed, and it made me wonder. Rod knew his stuff; maybe I should follow suit.

The final day dawned and I decided to hedge my bets by putting in the customary 2lb of boilies, but the peanuts stayed on the bank. At 6am I had a run, and my heart started pounding as I wondered if this was what I had been waiting for. Whatever it was, I lost it. I tried not to think that that might be my last chance before 5pm, when I had to head for home.

At 9am the line started to peel slowly and steadily off my reel. I hadn't had a run like it all the time I had been at Cassien, and when I struck it was with all the controlled power I could muster, knowing that if I didn't make a success of this one I would always wonder what had been on the other end.

With line being taken under heavy pressure I made for the boat. I had pushed it out while playing a fish a fair few times that week, but this time I made a mess of it. The boat wouldn't budge, and then when it did I grounded it on a bar close by. Cursing and trying to concentrate on the fish and the boat at the same time, I suddenly had the feeling that I would not land this fish. It felt so different that I desperately wanted to see what it was, but somehow I could imagine myself on the road home still wondering just what I had hooked.

I gritted my teeth and pushed hard on the boat while keeping the rod bent and trying not to let too much line off the reel. Suddenly the boat came free. My struggles must have been more desperate than I thought because Rod and Roger noticed what was happening and Rod came over to help, I was too caught up in what I was doing to notice. With steady pressure I got the fish near the top and stared at the spot where my line pointed into the water, waiting for the lead and hooklength to appear. Slowly they came into view and, seconds later, I saw the fish, a massive red/brown flank of the biggest carp I have ever seen.

It was well hooked, but I was determined to make no mistake with the net, despite having to manoeuvre the boat as well as the landing net and the rod. When the head broke the surface I kept her coming, and the huge fish slid gracefully over the rim and into the folds of my net.

I tried to lift the fish over the side into the boat, but the weight was just too great. I shouted to Rod and Roger and it was only then that I saw Rod standing on the shore. The excitement of the moment must have pumped me full of adrenalin, because without thinking I took the net in both hands and hoisted the fish on board.

On the shore the scales went down to 58lb, which without the sack meant the fish weighed 57lb exactly. It was the carp I had driven a total of four thousand miles to catch. I had spent all the money I had and a lot of money I didn't have trying to get out there; it had taken a season of planning, preparation and saving to put the trip together, and it had taken weeks of searching for swims, baiting up and waiting, while living rough and eating next to nothing, but it was worth it.

It was the carp I had driven a total of four thousand miles to catch.

It was worth it for that moment when I put the fish in a sack and turned to shake hands with Rod and Roger; it was worth it when I got back to England and the people I knew wanted to hear how that final week had gone; and it was worth it when the series came out in *Angling Times* and that final twist in the tail gave those articles the ending they needed, and *Angling Times* what they had paid for.

A lot of people read those six weekly episodes in October, November and December 1985. Matchmen, sea-fishermen, even non-anglers read it and went out of their way to say how much they enjoyed it. Perhaps it was the way that I had gritted my teeth and gone back, not just to catch that carp, but to prove what can be done if you want something badly enough. Maybe that was what caught their imagination, and it didn't matter that it was carp, and not cod, I was after. I had climbed the mountain, and the view from the top was great.

Part One

Chapter Eleven
Big is Beautiful

There comes a time in everyone's life when you have to look back on what you have done to see what you should do in the future. If you look over your shoulder at the way you've come, either by accident or intent, you will see a pattern that tells you what your next move should be. Often it is as easy as matching up the patterns on two pieces of wallpaper.

When I looked back on my years of fishing I found that big was beautiful. Medium-sized carp were fun to catch and after a long spell without a run one such fish could make the day, but every time I put a rod together and threaded up the line, it was with a big fish in mind.

I believe this influenced my approach to fishing in that I started trying to catch particular fish, learning their habits and their haunts and going prepared for a long wait for the one I wanted to catch. It isn't easy to tell someone how you go about sorting out the bigger fish; sometimes it involves nothing more complicated than finding out where the fish was last caught, or where it has been seen sunning itself.

Patience is the biggest problem — some people just can't resist the temptation to creep away and stalk a few small fish basking in the shallows further up the lake. It's really a question of being asked to choose between a fleet of family saloon cars or one fast sports car. The sports car will cost you a lot in petrol just as big fish hunting costs a lot in long, lonely hours on hard waters, while others are getting action all the way at a lake full of smaller fish down the road. But if you've got true big-fish blood in your veins, you'll put up with the problems of perseverance in return for the pleasure of the gold at the end of the rainbow.

When I flicked through my fishing diary, which I have kept since I first started carp fishing seriously, I counted six fish of 35lb and over. The first came from Longfield in June 1979, and was a mirror of 35lb exactly, the one that was camera shy and leapt out of my arms and back into the water, as I described earlier.

In 1981 I started the season at Longfield with another one of exactly 35lb, my reward for a baiting-up programme that lasted from February until June, and then the following month I landed another mirror from that water, the 38lb 4oz one that made my mate Keith's eyes stick out like organ stops, once again, both described earlier. These are the stories of the other three fish.

Winter fishing was shown to be worthwhile in about 1970 when the man of the moment was Jim Gibbinson, who ventured out with carp gear in hand when other anglers were talked into helping with the Christmas shopping.

Starting the season in style at Longfield with a 35.

Part One

A month later Keith's eyes were sticking out like organ stops.

While many were searching for something suitable to give Aunt Agnes come the festive season, Jim was proving that winter carp fishing could be just as productive as summertime sessions and it could produce bigger fish. So, the following year, when Jack Frost was putting in a regular appearance, instead of stowing our gear away and opting for slippers and a seat by the fire, the Old Man and I took a leaf out of Jim's book and went fishing.

We used to go to Cut Mill, which was pretty heavily stocked with small 'doubles' and 'singles', and although we didn't do the long sessions that today's blokes do, dressed like Eskimos and stopping only to celebrate Christmas Day with the family, we gave it a good try.

People still believed most carp hid in the mud and became dormant in the winter, so we were experimenting, but it soon became a big part of the season for me, and for many others. The winter of '73 was the turning point. We went to the water on Friday night, to fish through until Sunday, but on Saturday night the lake froze over. All the lines were trapped under a thick sheet of ice with the tops pointing under the water. The lake took on the appearance of a painting – motionless trees, motionless water and, tucked up in bed, motionless anglers. By 10am we had had enough – it's amazing how much you can look forward to a warm room, a hot drink and a favourite chair from which you can toast your toes in front of the fire.

I reeled in the first rod and was about to do the same with the second when I saw it shake in the rests. I picked it up, struck under the ice and was amazed to find myself attached to a fish. John said I had no chance of landing it but, thankfully, the ice was thin in the margins and we smashed a big enough hole to get the landing net in. The fish didn't put up much of a fight, and soon a 14lb mirror was on the bank, played out with much of the rod under the water. I've been winter carp fishing ever since.

If someone had arrived with a pair of made-to-measure straight-jackets, I would have been hard pressed to explain how we found this torture enjoyable.

"Hang loose, Moose. Everything comes to he who waits."

If ever there was a year to go fishing in winter it was 1981. The summer had been so special that if the back door had been blocked with snow I would have dug my way out, rod in hand and bag on back. As it turned out it was too cold for snow.

At the end of November I waved goodbye to the warm front room for a weekend and went to Longfield. It was bitterly cold and I spent most of the two days wrapped up in bed. The largest spell out of the sack was when, reluctantly, I dragged myself out to hit a run and land a 20lb 4oz common. What I needed was some company to keep my mind off the temperature, so when planning the next trip I gave Bruce 'The Moose' Ashby a ring and he agreed (the fool) to come with me.

I arrived on Thursday and set up in what we call the Middle Swim, and when the Moose arrived on Friday he went into the Birches a few yards further on. If I'd thought it was cold on the previous outing it was because I hadn't been out in the sub-zero temperatures that greeted us this time. Bruce said: "We must be mad!" and if someone had arrived with a pair of made-to-measure straight-jackets, I must admit I would have been hard pressed to explain how we found this torture enjoyable.

I wouldn't even get out of the bag to rustle-up a steaming pan of beans and sausages, but I'm not one for going home early, unless disaster strikes, so I said over the sound of Bruce's teeth chattering: "Hang loose, Moose. Everything comes to he who waits. I had one, last week – we might be lucky." He mumbled something about no longer caring.

There was no movement anywhere. The margins of the lake were frozen to the bank, the birds were frozen to the trees and, for all we knew, the fish could be frozen to the bed of the lake. It was Saturday morning when it happened. I was in the sack with only the bits of me needed to keep up a conversation – mouth and ears – exposed to the air. If I could have got the rest of my face under cover while leaving the necessary bits outside, I would have done so. Bruce was making the tea and trying to turn his hands back from blue to pink, which took most of the heat from the Camping Gaz and left little for the kettle.

Suddenly I was away. We both jumped up in surprise because, to be honest, neither of us expected anything to happen. Although the run was fairly fast, as soon as I struck, the fish stopped and came in like a sack. Another 'twenty' was a very welcome reward for braving the cold weather; we were both amazed when the fish that appeared and slid gracefully over the waiting net was a good deal bigger. It was a leather, and the scales registered 35lb 5oz!

Bruce had to do all the work, I'm afraid. I couldn't believe the size of the fish, and I just stood and stared as he organised the weighing and photography. It was then, and still is, the biggest fish I have caught in winter, and proof that a bit of discomfort can produce rich rewards – even if you do spend most of your time in the bag.

A little success can produce a lot of enthusiasm, and after the big 'un I spent most of January at the lake – without a single run. On the last session of the month – again, the sort of weather you wouldn't let a dog sleep out in for fear of getting into trouble with the RSPCA – I had just got set up and not even turned the buzzers on when I heard a thumping noise. I looked around towards the rods and one of the indicators was in the butt ring. The fish responsible was a mirror of 29lb 4oz, and Clive Diedrich came out to photograph it for me.

Three-day sessions throughout March produced nothing, but then the pattern of no runs for ages and then a sudden spurt of activity repeated itself when I had a fish of 9lb from one swim and then, when I was able to get the swim I wanted, a 20lb 4oz mirror. Then, to cap it all, the next fish was a familiar face – the 35-pounder I had caught in December, now weighing 34lb. I'm always pleased to see old friends.

So, drawing conclusions from a successful winter on the bank, I would say you should be prepared for long waits between short spells of action, but don't worry too much if it's brass-monkey-climber weather. Buy a good bag that'll keep you as warm as toast and dream about the big fish that weigh more and are easier to land at this time of year than at any other. And as far as baits are concern, smelly ones are better in winter. The last two of those fish fell for Pukka Salmon, and the others to Cheese (or was it sweaty-feet?) flavour.

There's a saying that success is two-thirds skill and one-third luck. People say you only get out in achievement what you put in in hard work, and usually that's true, but there's nothing like succeeding by accident now and then to make you smile.

I couldn't believe the size of the fish, and I just stood and stared.

I looked around towards the rods and one of the indicators was in the butt ring.

I'm always pleased to see old friends.

Anyone who is honest with himself will admit he has caught fish that he hasn't fully deserved. Maybe he was somewhere he hadn't intended to be, fishing a water he didn't know and had only just cast out when it happened. When all three are rolled into one story, even the most image-conscious angler has to admit the fish caught him and not the other way around. That's what happened to me one day in June 1982.

I was at Wraysbury – a good place to go for sunbathing and sleep but not for easy fishing. I was fishing the south side and although I wasn't bubbling with confidence, I felt I might get a chance. That all changed when Ken Hodder strolled around the corner. Now, I value Ken's opinions on carp fishing in general and Wraysbury in particular. Anyone who can catch fish there either lives on the banks or knows a thing or two about fishing.

When Ken said he hadn't seen a carp on the south side all year, my face fell faster than a lead balloon. But only a fool ignores local knowledge; I packed my gear, loaded it into the car, and took a stroll round to the other side. In the couple of hours I spent chatting to Ken, neither of us saw a sign of a fish, and when enough tea had been drunk and we had wagged chins for long enough, we went our separate ways, leaving Wraysbury to the waterfowl and wildlife.

I decided to take a look at Longfield on the way home, it being good fish-spotting weather, but when I got there, the fair-weather fishermen were already out in force and the car park looked like Wembley way on Cup Final day. I left the car by the side of the road and walked round the lined banks of the lake until I met someone I knew, Longfield regular Terry Disdale. More tea and talking followed and then who should appear but Ken Hodder. Who was following who?

Neither of us fancied squeezing onto the overcrowded lake, so we went our separate ways once again, Ken for a final stroll round and me to the car to drive home. I was about to start the engine when I remembered Kingsmead, which is at the back of Wraysbury. The Previous October, rumours of a 35lb fish from there had gone the rounds. It was certainly worth a look, so instead of turning right for home, I took a left.

The water is only a small one, about three acres, but it has a lot of charm, and when I didn't come across a single person on my walk round, it went up even further in my estimation. I decided to give it a go and, as is often the best plan on new waters, I set up in a swim halfway down the lake that provided me with the best view of the rest of the water. That way if I was in the wrong place I should find out quickly and would know where to go.

I had just set up when who should appear but... you've guessed it, Kenny Hodder. Talk about me and my shadow! "We can't keep meeting like this, Ken," I said. "People will talk." Neither of us had fished the water before, so sport was going to be slow. I was glad, then, when Ken dropped in next to me, for he's always good company.

I was still finding my mallet to knock the buzzer bars in when I heard a couple of plops and bleeps, which meant Ken was ready for action. Now, I'm not saying he was telling porky pies, but I have known him for quite a long time and fished a few waters in his company. Both of us know that when you arrive at a new water you don't put all your eggs in one basket – or, as in this case, all your baits in the margins.

Grinning from ear to ear I put it to him that he had not been entirely straight with me, but he still denied he had been there before. He had put all three rods close in, and

Part One

about twenty loose baits around each hookbait. Within an hour he had a good 'double' on the bank. It presented me with yet more evidence in support of my theory; I felt like Perry Mason in those old black-and-white films and I had to fight the urge to say: "I rest my case, m'Lud."

I had put one rod at sixty yards, one at about thirty yards and one a rod-length out, and scattered about one hundred baits around the three areas. About an hour after his fish, I was in action and landed a mirror of 19lb 9oz – on the close-in rod, would you believe?

It was getting dark fast, so we supped our final cup of tea and settled down for the night. At 2am I had a very slow, steady run on the long-range rod. I was out of the bag in a trice and gave the rod a wallop. Solid resistance. Either a snag was involved or I had hooked something special. I gave Ken a shout and he appeared out the darkness. "If that big 'un really is in here," I said "I think I've got it on."

Talk about me and my shadow!

On the close-in rod, would you believe?

It was moving very slowly and had reached one of the many weedbeds in the lake by the time I had put the hook home. Steady pressure was the only answer I could offer for the moment. It didn't make any mad dashes, probably because some of the weed had slid down the line onto it, but the fish knew what it was doing and as I tried to steer it around the two thick beds between it and me, the fish fought its way into each one in turn. By the time I coaxed it out of them it seemed as though I had more weed than fish on the end, but it kept coming in steadily. I slid down the steep bank, landing net in hand, and at the first attempt the ball of green and grey was mine.

What happened next I can't fully explain. I looked into the mess in the net and even wearing a toga of weed the fish looked very big. I suddenly thought of how I had almost gone home after Longfield, how I had never even seen the water before, how I had thought about reeling in my distance rods and dropped them in the margins. The road to this fish had been steered entirely by luck; I hadn't even been looking out of the windscreen. Then I started laughing.

I laughed and laughed, quietly at first and then loudly, and then I had to sit down before I fell down, I was laughing so much. Ken had to do the honours with the fish (where have you heard that before?) and it scaled 36lb 8oz – a beautiful mirror. Ken was pleased for me, but he couldn't see what was making me roll around on the floor clutching my sides and laughing like a hyena.

I will always argue, and have done lots of times, that luck plays a big part in fishing. Luck will never make a bad angler consistently good, but it can make a good angler seem superhuman on occasions.

I laughed so much I had to sit down before I fell down.

I knew from the spring in his step that Rod had some good news.

Part One

After an introduction like that, how could I fail to fall in love with Kingsmead. I spent the rest of the season at Savay, but in the Close Season I got in touch with the owners and talked them into letting us form a syndicate on the water, and Rod, Clive Diedrich and Malcolm Winkworth came in with me. Clive and Malcolm fancied the bigger lake next door, which we also had the use of, so it looked like Rod and I would have the place to ourselves. Savay took up a lot of my fishing time in 1983, but Rod had a few goes at Kingsmead. One day in January I had the chance to fish there with Rod, but I chose Savay, as much for the crack as the fishing. That big fish was keeping Rod awake at nights, though, so it came as no surprise to hear he would still be going.

There were three or four of us standing around my bivvy when I saw Rod trotting round the lake towards us. I knew from the spring in his step that he had some good news, and when he arrived I just said: "How big is it?" It was 38lb 4oz.

Roger Smith and Bob Jones came with Rod and me to get the fish photographed, and to say Rod was a happy man is an understatement. Just as the lake had worked its magic for me, it had done the same for Rod, and he went on to catch almost every fish in there.

What impressed everyone who saw the fish, apart from its size, was how young and well proportioned it was. We all agreed it had plenty of potential to reach 40lb by June, and I decided to have another go for it in the hope that it would be over the magic figure.

I did my homework in the Close Season, and each time I saw the fish it looked bigger than ever. At the start of the season I was able to have the place to myself, and when I arrived on June 15, the sun was up, the fish were out and within ten minutes I had every fish in the lake taking floater. I had the place to myself and I was sure the scene was set for a fish of over 40lb in the morning.

The next day, June 16, there wasn't a fish to be seen. It was as if they had a calendar. The tench were in a feeding mood and sucking and blowing at my baits, but the carp had vanished. The next day, Monday, I lost a fish that could have been a tench, but on Tuesday a few carp started moving and gave the first indication that they were willing to feed again. Why fish disappear and reappear again, as suddenly as a light being switched off and then on, is a mystery as old as angling itself. We just have to wait for them to come back in their own time.

The only surface activity I could see was in a small bay on the other side of the lake. Picking up a rod, some floater and a landing net, I went round for a closer look. You've heard how some people say you can't buy beer or beef dripping that tastes as good as it used to do years ago, well I can't get floater as good as the stuff Rod used to make and sell. It came in several flavours, but the salmon was best. Talk about "melts in the mouth but not in the hand," it was very hard when you put a hook in, but when it had been in the water for a few seconds it was as soft as marshmallow. If fish had tongues they'd have licked their lips. Unfortunately you can't get it now, and although I've tried making it, I've never found the secret.

When it comes to end-tackle for floater fishing I don't believe in messing about. I like a big hook, about size 1/0 or 2/0, and I push just one piece over the point and barb and round the bend to the shank. As soon as the fish closes its mouth – I'm in!

I started catapulting the floater out and very soon several fish were having it. Others came to see what the fuss was about and soon there were about fifteen fish in the swim, including the big 'un. With them all feeding confidently I cast out, but the secret of catching fish on floater is to put the rod down and keep feeding, because as soon as you stop, so will they and you will be hard pushed to start them off again. Greed is only a stronger instinct than caution while there is plenty of food and plenty of competition for it.

I was trying to keep my eye on the big 'un, keep the bait going in and watch the line, all at the same time. It was inevitable that something would happen while my eyes were in the bait bag instead of on the water. I looked up to see a swirl and the line shooting across the surface. The last fish I had seen around my bait had been the one I had come to catch. This was it!

In my eagerness and surprise I struck a bit too hard and pulled out. The shock of what I had just done was eased when I got a clear sight of a fish of about 18lb bolting out of the area. It hadn't been the big 'un after all. I thought it would spook the rest, but they seemed more interested in mopping up the free offerings. I kept myself busy with the catapult, and at the same time tried to work out the path that the big fish was taking. I worked out the best spot to put the bait in its path and flicked it out at what I thought was the right moment. Three times I did this, and every time it came up to the bait and nosed it or knocked it, as if it knew something was not right. At the fourth attempt the mouth opened and my bait was gone. At exactly the same moment a young lad appeared behind me and said: "Any good, mister?" I almost lost my concentration – almost, but not quite. The hook went home, the fish powered off and the boy didn't need an answer.

The battle lasted no more than three or four minutes, but once I had netted it and carried it up the bank, I knew it would not make 40lb. In fact it weighed 37lb 12oz. I was disappointed that it hadn't made the mark, but you should have seen that lad's face. It was like Christmas had come early as I folded back the landing-net mesh.

I believe the fish did reach 40lb one year later. Rod caught it in June and after being sacked for an hour-and-a-half to get suitable scales, the heavily spawn-laden fish weighed 39lb 12oz.

So that was my tally of big fish as it stood at that time. I was then, more than ever, determined to break the 40lb barrier. There was one other incident, though, which I will tell you about, just for good measure. Fishing is about mysteries – problems that puzzle us and the satisfaction we get from solving them. Until the scientists show us how to communicate with fish, we will always be scratching our heads, but how can we even start to fathom out what makes a fish tick when we sometimes can't understand our own actions.

It was February, a month that has produced very little for me, at Longfield or any other water. It was raining when I got there, raining as I set-up, and there was a stage when I wondered if it was ever going to stop.

By Friday it only rained for most of each hour instead of all of it, yet quite a few people arrived to huddle beneath brollies for the weekend. An old friend, Dave Campbell, came strolling past, a timely arrival because the fishing was looking to be about as exciting as watching the grass grow. I had set up in what we call the Noddy swim, which is really two swims, but they are so close together you need to know the other angler well to get two anglers in there. I invited him to join me, and he accepted. Another friend from Savay, Pete Ridley, appeared and set up in the Bar swim, a good way away.

Part One

The next morning at 2.30am, with rain coming down like stair-rods, I got a steaming run. There's a law of carp fishing that says the faster the line is leaving the spool, the greater the hurry you will be in to reach the rods. I was about to hit the run when I heard: "Don't strike! I'm in!" come from across the lake. I stood there, poised over the rod and dressed only in a thin shirt, trousers and slippers, while the rain soaked through to my skin.

I put my fingers against the spool and could feel the line still running out. I was convinced he couldn't be across me from where he was fishing. I called out to Dave, but there was no reply. I couldn't wait any longer, so I cupped the spool and struck. The fish was on, and it didn't feel as if anyone else was involved. Dave appeared, to see what all the shouting was about, and I got him to play the fish while I put my coat on. I said to him: "Does that feel funny to you?" and he said it didn't.

I still wasn't happy, and wanted to go around to see the bloke on the other bank, but Dave insisted on giving me the rod back. When I had played it into the margin I could see it was a fish I had caught before, so I think I may have lost interest a bit. I piled on the pressure, too much as it happened, and as the fish approached the landing net the hook came flying out and over my shoulder. I lifted the landing net to pull it back out of the water and it wouldn't budge. There in the folds of the net, shining in the torchlight, was the fish.

It was like Christmas had come early.

I carried the net up the bank, but then came the strange discovery — in the mesh of the net was a hook with about six inches of line, and it didn't belong to me. I looked at my rod and the hook was still attached.

Dave said the fish was definitely mine, but not having taken my hook out of its mouth I felt I couldn't claim it. I picked up the net, carried it to the water and released the fish without weighing or photographing it. Looking at my diaries, I saw that the fish had weighed 35lb 5oz back in December, when The Moose had been with me, and I caught it again in March at 34lb, so if it was down to me it weighed something between these two weights.

But what of the other angler. I went round to see him and said I had had a fish and it might have been his. I showed him the hook and when I asked him if it was his he said it wasn't, and that his was still on his rod, but when he reeled in, it was gone.

Dave said I was mad, but I decided not to claim the fish because it wasn't one hundred per cent. I don't know to this day what happened, but whenever I hear someone shout: "Don't strike! I'm in!" I think of the night when confusion reigned and we all got wet.

Chapter Twelve
The Famous Four

Great carp anglers are like Liquorice Allsorts - they come in lots of different shapes and sizes, but they all leave you with a pleasant taste after they've gone. If you stood Chris Yates, Rod Hutchinson, Bill Quinlan and Jack Hilton side by side they'd look less like the cream of one of the country's most popular sports than the cast of Emmerdale Farm. Yet, those four are largely responsible for making carp fishing what it is today.

Dick Walker, of course, had the greatest influence on the shape of modern day fishing, and were he alive today I'm sure he would still be doing so. The many thousands of words he wrote in books, magazines and papers will be read by future generations who, like us, will be dazzled by his wisdom and his foresight.

But equally worthy of note are the dedicated anglers we meet regularly on the bank — the thinking anglers who have practised and persevered at their pastime until they have become experts. They don't succeed by selfishness or secrecy – they will help anyone, especially youngsters, and still catch more fish than most.

I would like to mention a few names at this point, but the one sure thing that happens is that someone who should be there gets left out. So, first I'll apologise in advance to the people I've missed out, but it was necessary to keep this list very brief.

There's Pete Springate, who you read about earlier and who, along with Kenny Hodder, has caught fish on waters so hard they have caused anglers to give up the sport. Then there's John 'The Bolt' Holt, a bloke who likes to fish for the big 'uns (where have you heard that before), Ian Booker, Dennis Davis, John 'The Business' Walker, Len Arbery, Johnny 'The Cat' Allen and Bruce 'The Moose' Ashby. I've fished a lot with all of them at one time or another and, having watched them in action, I know they've got what it takes.

But what of those household names mentioned at the start – men whose catches and contributions to the development of carp fishing have brought thousands of anglers into the sport. One of the earliest influences on my fishing was Jack Hilton. He would spend all of his time trying to catch just one big fish, something that I have always identified with more than going for lots of runs from fish further down the size scale. Only by comparing our strengths to those of the people we admire can we gain confidence.

I don't read many books, but I read and then re-read *Quest for Carp* and I would recommend it to anyone starting out today. Going to Redmire was a dream come true for me because I was able to set up in the swims where Jack had once sat waiting for the line to move and battle to begin. I fished with people he had fished with – Len Arbery, Bill Quinlan and Tom Mintram – and after long evenings talking with them about him, I felt as if I knew him. He was single minded about his fishing.

Jack Hilton's biggest ever carp.

He would set himself a target and go to great lengths to achieve what he had set out to do. I have tried to do the same. I have heard some people say he was a greedy angler who didn't like anyone fishing near him in case they caught fish he had drawn towards his swim, but I do not mind who is 'next door' to me and I wonder if this was true of Jack. If my neighbour hooks the fish I'm after they will still have to show skill to land it, and if they manage to do that I'll shake hands with them, congratulate them and come back for the fish another day.

One year at Redmire he changed, so I'm told. The man who lived for carp fishing suddenly decided all his spare time had to be spent working for the church, and he became a Jehovah's Witness. He still mixed with anglers occasionally, and when I got into Redmire and was helping with the swim clearing, he appeared one weekend and I was introduced.

He had a very dry sense of humour, and when he was trying to talk to me about religion and I was trying to get him back onto fishing, he would use every trick he knew to keep the conversation going his way. In the end I gave up and just listened, after all, I was interested to hear how someone as talented and dedicated as Jack, who once wrote a regular column for *Angling Times*, and went fishing all the time, came to give up everything.

He told me he felt it was wrong to go fishing because all sports were sinful. He had to spend all his spare time working for the church and trying to convert people. One day I heard he was planning to go to a gathering at Twickenham, just down the road from me, and I offered to put him up. The day before, I took him down to the local lake and he did finally admit that being in those surroundings again made him itch to go fishing, but then the conversation moved on and I knew he would never come back to the sport. At other times he wouldn't talk about it, and I think now the reason he kept changing the subject was because he missed fishing like mad.

Part One

Jack with an 18lb 12oz mirror hooked on maggots.    *Returning the 22lb mirror.*

Jack Hilton with a 22lb 8oz fish, accompanied by Ron Barnet.

The Famous Four

Bill Quinlan – the Compleat Angler.

Bill with a Redmire common.

Bill Quinlan with a 20lb 4oz Redmire mirror caught on legered chrysalis and maggot on June 16.

Part One

Although I never fished with him, I looked up to Jack as an angler. The tips he passed on taught me a lot and whenever I think about cupping my hand over the front of the spool of a reel before striking, I think that it was Jack who showed me how. I also used to have problems with knots, until Jack gave me a watchmakers' eyeglass to see if the turns were neat and the nylon undamaged. I've kept it to this day. I still can't understand why someone would have to give up the hobby they love, no matter how strong their beliefs, but Jack couldn't, or wouldn't, be persuaded.

One of his friends and fishing partners from the early days of Redmire was another of my 'Famous Four', Bill Quinlan. There are anglers who have caught bigger fish, and others who have caught more fish, but I would say Bill was the most complete all-rounder I have met – the original Compleat Angler.

He was an expert at finding fish, he knew how to arrange free offerings in a swim to attract any fish in the area, and he played fish cleverly, knowing what to do to fool them into going where he wanted them to go. Yet he didn't expect his methods to always be right just because he had caught a lot of fish, the sign of all good anglers. He was always prepared to change, and always trying to improve his skills, discover new techniques and solve problems. He never forgot the old ways, though. With the arrival of bolt rigs and 2 oz or 3 oz leads, anglers often forget the importance of a stealthy approach to the water, but not Bill. He still sometimes put up a camouflage screen when he was fishing in the margins, to keep himself hidden at all times.

But the test of a truly good angler is when he is called upon to do two things at once. Playing a good fish in a weedy swim while watched by a gallery and when you've got other urgent matters on your mind is a true test of skill. It's rather like walking down stairs wearing a blindfold and chewing gum at the same time.

The water was a Colne Valley lake well known for its big tench, and I was fishing alongside Bill and Len Arbery. Bill liked to have the odd forty winks, especially after meals, and when he did so he took his teeth out.

Now on this occasion we had more visitors than usual, and as one after another turned up on the off-chance of a chat and a cup of tea, the swim began to look more like Piccadilly Circus, but Bill slept through it all. Then, suddenly, his buzzer sounded. He was awake in an instant and out of his bivvy like a shot. Over with the bail arm, back with the rod and he was in business.

Bill always dropped on to one

A brace of fish taken at night by Bill – 23lb 2oz and 10lb 6oz.

knee when playing fish, to gain more control and to get out of the fish's field of vision. I went across to get a closer look, and when he heard me coming he turned his head slightly and by his look of surprise you could tell he didn't know the gallery was there. Still controlling the fish expertly, he whispered to me: "Can you getsh my teethsh for me? They're in the bivvshy."

Bill was a great friend, and I would swim the length of the lake to help him, but you have to draw the line somewhere, and for me it's dipping your hand in a mug of Steradent to fetch someone's gnashers. In my rule book, there are parts of the body that are to be handled only by their owners, and that goes for 'syrup-o-figs' (wigs) as well. There's no way I would pick up his teeth, or anybody else's for that matter.

But I couldn't be seen to let him down, so I went into his bivvy, rummaged around for a bit and pretended I couldn't find them. All credit to Bill, he played the fish, landed it, weighed it and returned it, watched by a dozen people, and it all went without a hitch, despite his turning round every few minutes to ask: "Havsh you shfound them yetsh?"

I suppose Bill was experienced enough to be able to play a fish well without having to concentrate fully, but that only comes after a lot of years of fishing. He would be the first to agree that playing a fish means being in control of it rather than it being in control of you. You need to be one step ahead, watching what it is heading for, anticipating danger and taking the right course of action. Using brute force is not playing fish, for often the harder you pull, the harder the fish will pull back. A real expert can trick a fish into the net before it is exhausted, and you will see the water lashed to a foam when the angry catch realizes its mistake, too late.

Imagine, for instance, you have been lassoed around the waist and are being pulled by a rope. The harder you are pulled, the more you will struggle to make the shelter of that building across the street. But, if the pull suddenly comes from the direction of the building, you will think twice about running in the direction in which the rope wants you to go That is why you will see the good anglers moving around while they are playing fish, holding the rod horizontal to apply sidestrain and leading the fish first from one side and then the other. The angler who stands with his rod held vertically and hooped over while cranking the fish in will lose as many as he lands.

How often have you heard anglers on your local water talking about the fish they have lost, and have you noticed that the bloke who seems to catch more than most rarely loses a fish? Skilful playing can often be the main difference between the expert and the also-ran.

Sometimes while playing fish you have to take chances. When Chris Yates was playing his 51lb 8oz fish at Redmire it was steaming straight towards him and the safety of a willow tree. He knew he couldn't stop it so he pulled it towards the tree, and the fish stopped in its tracks!

I once hooked a fish in a very weedy swim, and the only route through was a direct line between me and the fish – a straight path through thick cabbages. The only thing I could think of was to pull alternately from left and right, swapping over time and time again until the fish didn't know which way the pull was coming from and I led it more or less straight down the line. Nine times out of ten this won't work, but as a last resort in a seemingly impossible situation, it put a fish on the bank and made the capture all the more satisfying.

But the best place of all to play a fish from, if you fancy confusing it, is a tree top. When the pull is from above, the fish will go down, and when it gets to the bottom and has run out of room it will wonder what to do next. I saw a bloke hook a fish on a floater from high up in a tree once, and with no sideways pressure it couldn't tell which bank it was being led towards. When it was in the margins he could pull it towards the bank or back out towards the middle of the lake with his 12 ft rod. The fish just rolled over and over, wanting to swim away but not knowing where the danger was coming from, and very soon a 'mid-twenty' was netted by a friend on the ground. I'm not saying it would always work, and you certainly need the help of someone on the ground, but it was a success that time.

The 23lb fish steered left and right.

A winter mirror for Rod. A day of watching him fish is a day well spent.

Rod Hutchinson is one of the scruffiest anglers I have ever met, but he is also one of the best. He catches carp like Jimmy White pots reds, and if you are lucky enough to be on the same water as Rod, a day of watching him fish is a day well spent.

To see him in action is to realize why he is so successful. He just knows where the fish are and what they will be doing – it's almost as if he was a fish in a previous life. We mere mortals have to work out wind direction and water temperature and get last year's diary out for clues, but to Rod it is a natural instinct to be able to read a water straight away. He seems to find fish in a lake as easily as we find the car in the car park!

Rod will always get more chances than other anglers – the odds just seem to be stacked in his favour. When Rod walks on to a lake, people move into the swims around him because they know that if the fish are not already there, he will attract them like a magnet, and it won't be long before someone's buzzer is sounding. I know there are times when anglers fishing close-by have spoilt his fishing, but he accepts that this is unavoidable when you make a living from the sport and your face has become known. He still manages to get his share of the action, even with people fishing his swim from the far bank.

But although Rod attracts large numbers of carp, he doesn't seem to hook the big 'uns. Whether it is a conscious thing, wanting to get lots of runs rather than wait days for one chance, I don't know, but it could be that if there are smaller fish in a swim, the bigger ones feed elsewhere or get spooked more quickly.

Whatever the explanation, Rod began to wonder if he was ever going to catch a very big fish, and after a couple of near misses just before he landed the 38lb 12oz mirror described earlier, he was desperate to put a lunker on the bank.

Part One

I remember the day at Savay when the conversation turned to big fish, and Rod said he felt he would probably never land a big one. I told him that was rubbish and added that the only reason he hadn't put one on the bank already was because he was not fishing for them. He said he didn't have the patience, but I thought that if he knew the fish was there he would find the patience.

"I will take you to a water that holds a very big fish," I promised, and arranged a visit to Kingsmead. I could see what he meant about patience, though. We had only been there for about six or seven hours, fishing from a causeway that separates one lake from another, when he saw a mirror swimming along the margins of the lake behind. It looked to be about 3lb and had only one eye and a couple of fins, yet he reeled in, turned around and cast to it!

I told him at the time, that big fish could have been just about to pick up his bait when he reeled in. I wouldn't have done it, and the one-eyed fish didn't think much of it either because it kept on swimming, but everyone is different, I suppose. Rod does like to have his string pulled.

It was the second trip when he finally hooked the big 'un. I was in the swim, having a chat, when the buzzer went off. It had to be that one by the fight because it took a full twenty minutes to bring it close in. Rod was a happy man and he was just about to tell me how there's no need to sit for days on end to catch big fish when the hook pulled out, just a few yards from the net.

I don't think I've seen Rod as disappointed as he was that day, before or since. He must have believed even more in his prediction that he would never catch a really big fish – as if he had some sort of jinx. I made us a cup of tea without saying a word and after a couple of mouthfuls Rod looked at me and said: "What did I do wrong?"

I said he had done nothing wrong and that he had played it well. Sometimes they just fall off and it isn't the angler's fault. I could see him thinking that it would never be, but I told him he only needed to stick at it and success would follow. One week later he was back at the lake and he hooked and landed it at 38lb 12oz. He even had it again at 39lb 4oz and he's never mentioned jinxes from that day to this.

Rod just knows where the fish are and what they will be doing.

The Famous Four

Chris Yates is unique. In over twenty years of carp fishing I have never met anyone remotely like him. He has a number of qualities which make him special: his kind and gentle approach to life and people, his love of fishing with antique tackle, his undoubted fishing skill, his wonderful conversation (ask him about his evil eye next time you see him) and his feeling for the sixth sense that anglers often have that something is about to happen. We used to talk long into the night at Redmire, sitting bathed in moonlight beside the rods, discussing the times when we have felt a change in the atmosphere at a lake, as distinct as if distant music had suddenly stopped, and a memorable capture had followed. This was a couple of years before Chris dreamed of catching a record carp, went fishing and did just that the very next day.

Chris Yates' Redmire "crock of gold", at 43lb 12oz.

Part One

Chris Yates is unique. In over twenty years of carp fishing I have never met anyone remotely like him.

I like Chris because he is skilful. Everything he does is done with care and capability and you get the feeling that, like the others in this chapter, if he had been a film star or a footballer he would still have fulfilled these roles with the same excellent end result. Gifted people are born that way. Chris achieves his success with tackle a lot less easy to handle than modern equipment — to my way of thinking. He is a perfect example of the saying that you should never judge an angler by the appearance of his gear.

But perhaps what I like most about Chris is his ability to be silly without being embarrassed. Being able to put up with looking foolish is part of being successful, and when you can laugh at yourself you can laugh at anything.

One day at Redmire he told me about the small pool at the end of the lake that is not visited much by anglers. When I said I hadn't seen it, he offered to take me, and so we made our way there and crept round looking for fish. Chris was on all fours, because he is so tall, when we came across a fish in the margins without it seeing us.

We decided that he would creep up to it while I watched from a tree. The fish was about twenty feet from us, tight in against the bank, and Chris wanted to see how close he could get before it was spooked. He inched forward like a cat stalking a mouse and we both waited, expecting the fish to bolt at any moment. Suddenly Chris jumped up and roared with laughter. The fish we had been carefully stalking was a log – but it had fooled both of us completely.

It's an easy mistake to make. I did it at Yeoveney when I came across a fish in this thick weedbed. I could see this big back sticking out of the water and I tried casting all sorts of baits at it for a couple of days. I must admit I wondered why it was always in roughly the same position; so when curiosity got the better of me I pulled off my shoes, socks and trousers and went in after it.

As I waded across, up to my hips in murky water and thick weed, I could see even more clearly the scales on its back that had made me sure it was a fish. By the time I reached it I was up to my neck, but I had to know what it was. I'd never have guessed – it was a tyre! Mind you, it could have been worse. I know a bloke who kept leaving his swim for a few hours to stalk a fish he had seen in some lily pads further down the lake. It turned out that the fish he had been after was dead!

So these are the anglers I admire most in carp fishing – past and present – but what of the future? Who will have the skill, dedication and new ideas to lead the way in years to come, and will the world ever see an all-round angler and writer of the calibre of Dick Walker again? I like to think that whoever takes carp fishing into the next century will still find time to help the youngsters just joining the sport. A weekend spent helping them, perhaps as part of a prize in a competition, is two days they will never forget as long as they live – a small sacrifice to make to help dreams come true and guarantee the future of the sport we all love.

Part One

Chapter Thirteen
One Last Cast

So, that's the story so far. I wish I could write the next chapter of my life now, and make all my dreams come true, but I've left my magic wand at home and, no matter how hard I peer into my crystal ball, I can't get a clear view of what lies around the next corner.

I know what I would like from life, but writing it down is a bit like telling Santa what you would like for Christmas – you soon realize it's a pointless exercise. I'd rather lay plans than make predictions.

Where will the sport of angling be by the turn of the century? Will we all be fishing for 80lb carp with machines that tell you the number and size of the fish in your swim at the press of a button from the comfort of your bed-chair? If so, I for one will either join a club that has banned the use of fish-finding equipment, or else take up tiddlywinks.

But there will never be another sport quite like fishing, no matter what changes it undergoes. How many other pastimes take you away from the roar of the crowd to the peace of the waterside, but with no less excitement? How many others provide one or two moments in time that will live in your mind forever, the occasions when your wildest dreams came true?

How many other sports allow you to rub shoulders with the country's best? The anglers you read about week after week in the papers are out on the waters that are open to anyone and, unlike in my day when a question to an adult would often be answered with a grunt, these people are very approachable. You can't say that about football or snooker.

There's also a lot more tolerance within the sport. Matchmen now realize that specimen hunters are not just chuck-it-and-chance-it people, and specimen hunters are paying more attention to presentation and realising they can learn a lot from matchmen. We are all specialist anglers, it is about time we understood each other better. But what parts of the sport could be improved?

Sometimes I wish the people who make the fishery rules understood the anglers better. I feel I am not fishing at full potential unless I have got three rods out, yet lots of waters restrict you to two. Why? Is it because the pike anglers spread their rods out along the bank and fish die from deep hooking? If so, keep an eye on the pike men and penalise the offenders, but don't make us all pay the penalty for a crime committed by the few.

I wish youngsters didn't buy expensive gear until they had tried carp fishing for a while. They might get bored with it and then they will have wasted their parents' money. They are told too many times that they need this rod or that reel, while we know that many of the best and biggest catches ever made were on tackle I wouldn't give a tenner for. Watercraft, that skill learnt in the school holidays spent trotting a home-made float down the village stream for dace and bleak, has always been and will always be the thing that puts fish on the bank. The best carp anglers began their apprenticeship fishing for anything with fins.

I think I've led a full fishing life so far, mainly by saying "yes" to most things. Difficult challenges, hard work and the demands of time and money – you have to say "yes" to them all. Only you can decide the moment you must turn away and leave the fish for another day, but I can recall quite a few fish that have been caught on days when I almost opted out and went home.

Fishing should be a pleasure, not a pain, and when cold weather or long hours turn it into a feat of endurance you must consider calling a halt, but how much more enjoyable it is to then catch yourself a fish after deciding to give the water a little while longer.

I've known some very good anglers who have caught a lot of fish, including some huge ones, but they made the mistake of living for angling and angling alone. Nothing else seemed important and they sacrificed everything else. They had to be beside the water, to the extent that they practically lived on the bank.

As a result they burnt themselves out by overdosing on fishing, and for them the sport lost its appeal. They've sold their gear and they will probably never hold a rod again.
Enjoy your fishing. Be like that boy in the first chapter of this book, quick to learn, eager to share your knowledge and ready to enjoy the company of other anglers; and when the day dawns that provides you with more chances than you ever thought possible, think of me, and smile.

Work hard, play hard, give everything your best shot, and if you get to paradise before me, tell 'em Ritchie will have his usual.

Part One

Glossary of Ritchiesms

This book contains a number of phrases that people who live north of Watford and do not watch Eastenders or listen to Chas & Dave records may not be familiar with.

Referred to while you are reading this book, the following may prove useful in helping to overcome the language barrier and so increase your understanding and enjoyment of this volume:

Diabolical liberty:
Conduct which greatly displeases one, like seeing someone's lead land in your swim.

Right hump:
Angry reaction to the above, often resulting in the having of words with the offender. No connection with Quasimodo.

Leave it out:
Insistence that the other party is joking or at least is not making a suggestion which can be taken seriously, such as recommending that the captor of a single-figure carp buys everyone on the lake a celebratory beer.

Upstairs for thinking, downstairs for dancing:
Motto referring to streetwise shrewdness or, sarcastically, to one who demonstrates a lack of common sense. Used most often on people who offer to make the tea for Ritchie and then slop boiling water into his tea caddy.

What is occurring:
Expression of bemusement used when things are not what they should be. Most commonly used on the angler's return from a local hostelry when he tries, by the light of the moon, to cast out four rods and place them in eight rests and decide which of his bivvies to sleep in.

Stone bonk needle:
Used by one who is upset to refer to the mood they are in. Often reserved for fellow anglers who play with their buzzers every ten minutes of the day.

Out of order:
Informs someone that they are in the wrong or have overstepped the mark. Reference to friends as being as bald as a billiard ball, having a nose like a toucan or a face like the back of a bus come into this category.

Glossary of Ritchiesms

That's handy, Harry:
Refers to something useful or clever. A device that makes the tea, wakes you up, mixes and rolls baits and can fit into a standard matchbox could warrant this description. First used by Frank Bruno.

Guarrn, my son!:
Words of encouragement to, for instance, one who gets a run while Ritchie is visiting their swim and he recommends that they get up and strike. No parenthood is implied.

Never normal:
Describes one who behaves oddly. Used in the past to describe anglers who eat boilies for breakfast, keep potties under their bedchairs and like catching catfish.

Cyclepath:
Term used to describe a dangerously unbalanced person given to sudden, irrational behaviour. Famous carp-angling joke: First angler: "There's a cyclepath to see you"; Second angler: "Tell him to get on his bike". First used by Alfred Hitchcock.

I'm gutted:
A feeling of intense disappointment reserved for that moment when the hook pulls out of the fish of one's dreams, when swear words fail you. Often accompanied by an overwhelming desire to snap one's carp rod over one's knee – often followed by a desire to visit the casualty department of a hospital.

Do a runner:
Depart at speed, knowing that one has been 'rumbled'. Often associated with leaving one's tackle behind in the haste to escape. Those most often engaged in this activity tend to be thin and green, rather like the bean of the same name.

Magic!:
Expression of delight used by those who have just achieved success. Often accompanied by repeated punching of the air and childish skipping around the swim and, occasionally, the shout of: "Everyone to the pub! The drinks are on me!"

Do a Mike Tyson:
To use brute force and/or aggression to achieve ends. Most often used during pre-season swim clearing to extract stubborn fallen trees from favourite swims and then on June 16th to extract stubborn early-rising anglers from the same favourite swims.

Get down (verb):
To listen to Tony Blackburn's soul-music programme on Radio London from one's bivvy.

Get down! (order):
Command used with raised voice when Ritchie's Staffordshire Bull Terrier jumps on his Lafuma bed.

Muller it down:
To eat quickly. Most often associated with eating habits during near starvation in winter or eating contests between bored anglers on very hard waters. Not recommended when curry is involved.

Fannie McCraddock:
Affectionate name for Ritchie coined by starving anglers offered one of Ritchie's famous curries.

Right result:
Describes success beyond the angler's wildest dreams. Has been known to be used by pools winners, captors of fish of over 40lb and people who are about to write the final word of their first book.

Picture courtesy Chris Ball.

PART TWO
THE WHOLE STORY

Foreword 1
by Chris Ball

There will be few who open this book and have any kind of interest in carp fishing that will not have heard of Ritchie McDonald; top carp angler of his day, outspoken, opinionated, brash, loud, yet in the same breath passionate, committed, funny and possessing a mind-set for big carp that can take your breath away.

I've been lucky to know Ritchie through his 'all conquering carp years' when it seemed he was simply unstoppable in his quest for big carp.

Back in the early 1970s when I first ran into him after I started the Surrey/Middlesex region of the British Carp Study Group, Ritchie and a host other young super-keen carp anglers, including Pete Springate, John Carver, Chris Seager, Chris Yates, Joe Jarman, Mike Starkey, Ken Hodder, Dave Goy, Colin Claydon, Andy Holland plus many others, used to meet on a monthly basis at a pub outside Staines town centre called the Crooked Billet. These meetings lasted for many years and got busier as membership increased. Many

Chris and Ritchie at the May 1987 Carp Society Conference at Hatfield with Andy Little and Len Arbery.

exciting things happened at these get-togethers – like the time eminent carp catcher Tom Mintram, who lived close to Epsom Racecourse, was accompanied by the mighty Jack Hilton when Tom occasionally arranged some work for Jack in the area. At a guess this was the first time Ritchie and many of the BCSG regional members had met Jack Hilton, and in Ritchie's case it was to lead him to fish the mightiest carp lake in the land – Redmire Pool.

It seemed there was never enough time to talk about carp fishing at these meetings, and several times after leaving the Crooked Billet a group of us would retire to a nearby house to continue the discussions into the night. This house was in Richmond and it belonged to Ritchie McDonald.

It was here in the mid-1970s that I saw Ritchie and the late Chris Seager poring over a bait tin with what turned out to be Strawberry flavoured red-dyed sweetcorn inside, a special version of the flavour that Chris Seager had sourced.

Once in a while, members from other regions would attend our meetings. When Kent BCSG people came – the likes of Bruce Ashby, Mike Harris and particularly Roy Johnson – everyone listened. I can remember one time being in Ritchie's front room when Roy Johnson spoke and the place went quiet. Also a number of years later, in the Close Season of 1980, this time in Ritchie's kitchen, was the time I first heard the name of somewhere called Savay Lake mentioned, and details concerning the formation of a carp syndicate.

Years later when Tim Paisley, Kev Clifford and myself started the weekly carp news magazine Carp-Talk, I became a serious journalist intent on getting the best stories and pictures of big carp captures for the mag. Of course, someone who had provided an almost constant source of newsworthy carp stories in the past was Ritchie, and I was glad to get an exclusive concerning his famous capture of the Penn Pond, Richmond Park biggie on the last day of the 1994/5 season.

But that's only part of the story, for many is the time I've bumped into Ritchie at notable lakes such as Longfield. Once as I was about to walk onto the fishery, Chris Seager rushed up and said: "For Christ's sake don't go near Ritchie! A 30lb-plus carp has just jumped out of his hands and back into the drink before any pictures were taken! He's fuming!" Taking note it was with some trepidation that I approached Ritchie's 'lot'. But he was okay about it all, and though a little subdued, he soon told me about the capture.

I also found Ritchie in March 1991 on the Car Park Lake at Yateley, just after one of his most outrageous catches of two highly prized Yateley inhabitants, both over 40lb, captured from different lakes within the space of a week – Christ, the man was on fire!

I've also written about Ritchie's exploits a number times over the years for various publications, and remember well the time I helped him with a winter carp fishing chapter for a Carp Society book. Once the text had been completed I returned to his house having asked him to sort through and find suitable pictures to illustrated the chapter. When I arrived and after we'd agreed on the text, I asked about the pictures. "Oh, I've sorted that Chris." A few moments later he returned with a bulging plastic carrier bag. "There you go, sort that lot."

Peering inside there was a mass of photographic prints, slides and such like.

"Blimey, Ritchie! What am I supposed to do with this lot?"

Quick as a flash he said: "No worries. You know what you're looking for. You know more about me than I do...!"

But it all got done in the end and later when I returned the carrier bag Ritchie let me keep some rare and important prints of notable big carp for my trouble.

Ritchie's belief in being able to catch big carp was extraordinary – the only thing I can think of that might give you an idea of what I'm talking about is the fact that he'd caught these fish (in his mind, anyway) before he'd even got to the water in question.

Perhaps one of the greatest legacies Ritchie has left in carp fishing is the motivation created by the capture of Yateley's Bazil in October 1984. This one capture fired the imagination of so many, some of whom have stated that it started them on the road to chasing big carp.

Make no mistake, Ritchie is a resourceful, accomplished and very successful angler whose resolve to outwit monster carp is an inspiration to all who know him.

And finally, when Ritchie faded from the limelight some years back, an article I'd written about a famous capture of his ended with: "If you ever read this, Ritchie, give me a call, mate." And you know what... he did! Welcome back, Ritchie.

Chris Ball

Foreword 2
by Mike Starkey

Well, what do you say about Ritchie? – a larger than life character. I use the word 'character' loosely. I know of so many tales and incidents, but alas most of them cannot be told.

I first came across him in 1973, when at the age of nineteen he was fishing in the winter with John Walker at the Tarn Pond, Cut Mill. They were bivvied up every Friday night until Saturday in the Big Double. I was top rod on the water due to my early use of trout pellet paste and arrived to fish every Saturday morning throughout that winter. I should perhaps add that at the time very few carp anglers fished nights in the winter, so they were pretty hardy.

As a bailiff on the water I soon got to know them both, I believe they were quietly catching one or two and as I was a member of the British Carp Study Group it was not long before I recommended them for membership.

Mike Starkey and Reddingvale Hazel.

Mike with a 29lb fish from Sway Lakes, in Hampshire.

My house at the time was quite close to The Tarn, at Seale, near Farnham, and I owned a Fiat 127, bought from new, which was the worst car I have ever had the misfortune to own. One of the many faults was that a cam follower had broken off inside the engine. Servicing I could do, but this sort of repair – NO!

Ritchie promptly offered to undertake the repair and came down from Richmond, started dismantling and soon had the carb off and the cylinder head. No doubt he saved me a lot of money, but sadly the car managed to burn out a clutch every year thereafter – of all the cars I have owned, it was the only one I have ever needed a clutch repaired on!

I went on to better things when I became a member of the Redmire syndicate in 1975 and moved to Herefordshire. At the time I recommended Ritchie for membership of Ashlea Pool, and still remember the iconic photo of him holding a thirty from there.

When I left Redmire after the 1976 season I gave up fishing for a while to concentrate of renovating the derelict smallholding I had purchased, but kept in touch with Ritchie. The advice I gave him as to how to gain a place in Redmire was well used, and along with several other members he came to see me on one of the days they had been viewing the Pool. Another piece of history.

Foreword 2

I moved back to Guildford in about 1983 and having started fishing again, the first person I looked up for advice on the current scene was Ritchie. As usual he was only too happy to help, even though his catches and fame had far outweighed mine. I later dropped in to see him when he was fishing the Copse at Yateley, and fished with him on the Pads Lake. He was about to hit the headlines once again.

One thing I had to admire him for was on a baiting-up session on Stanstead Abbotts during the Close Season. We had taken my inflatable along and I rowed around the lake as Ritchie's little helper, passing him bait whilst he swam around looking for features and putting in boilies. He had on a wetsuit, but the water was COLD and he was swimming around for a couple of hours or more. Unusually, one of his failures, as he never caught the forty from there.

Something I will say about 'the man', he values his friends and remains true to them, and if you work it out it was forty years ago our paths crossed. His advice is always freely given, even to those he does not know. He may not be the best writer around, he would be the first to admit it, but his stories and successes are bloody interesting.

Mike Starkey
Westonzoyland, Somerset
2014

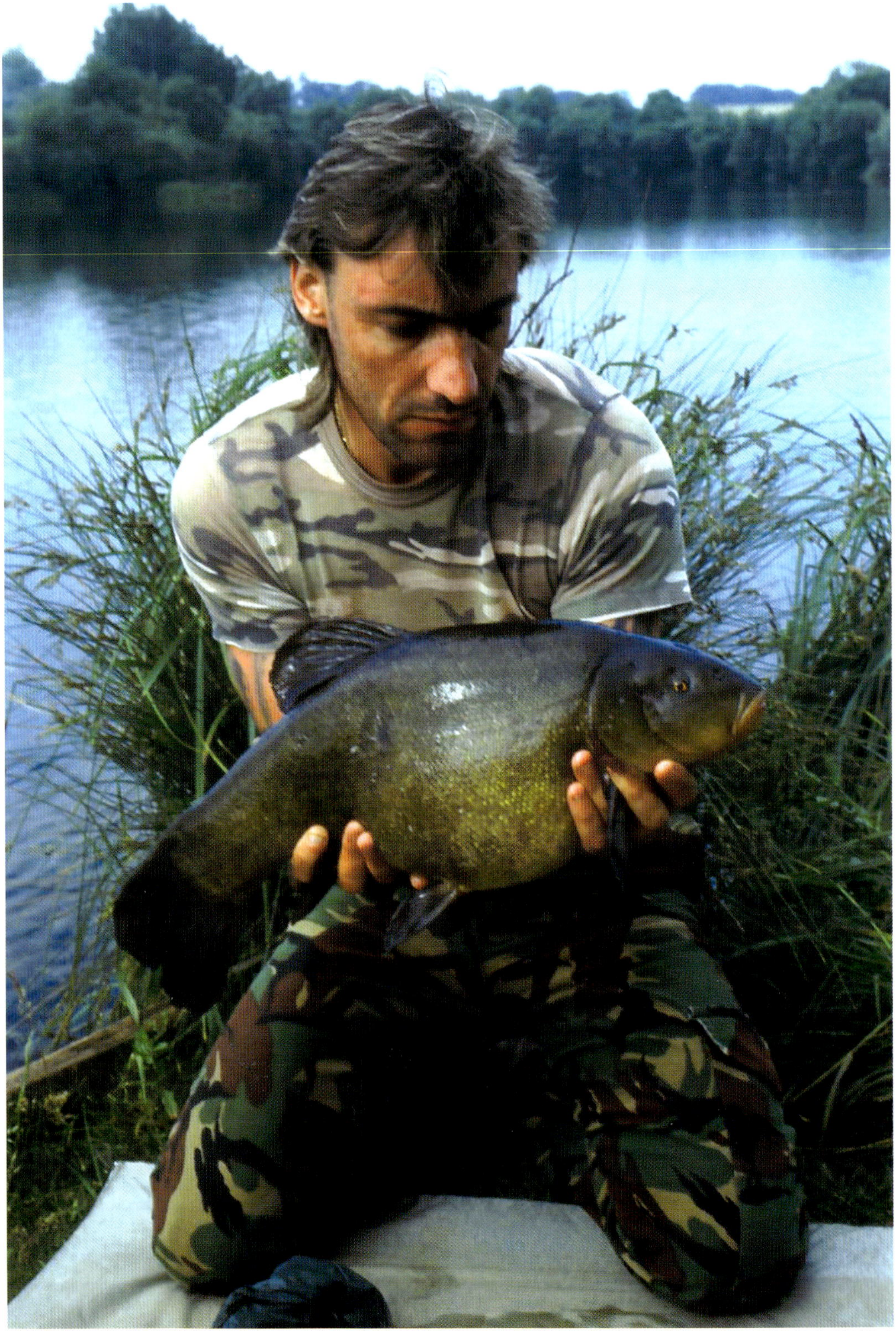

Part Two

Chapter One
Finding a Forty

Wherever I've fished, I've always had one aim and that's to catch the biggest carp in the lake. But after I'd had the 45-12 from Yateley North Lake in 1984 I knew I wasn't going to get a bigger one in this country because one didn't exist, so that's why I went to Cassien in 1985.

When I came back from Cassien I needed to find a new challenge, and while I was working out where to go I joined Len Arbery and Bill Quinlan on Longlife, just around the corner from Savay, in the Colne Valley, to try to catch myself some big tench.

It was good to step back from the big carp scene for a while and consider my options, and Len and Bill were great company. I used to visit them when I was fishing close by for carp on the Cons, and I fancied spending some time with them.

Len Arbery and Bob Buteux tench fishing at Longlife.

Bill was the best angler I ever fished with, and he was my angling idol. He was a master of all types of fishing, very stealthy in his approach and as good on rivers as he was on lakes. He could turn his hand to catching any species that he felt like fishing for.

Although he was after tench and wasn't actively carp fishing any longer, you could tell he still got the itch when he saw one in his swim.

I was fishing there one day and Len came along for a chat from where he was fishing above me and asked me if I'd seen Bill first thing in the mornings.

Bill was fishing the bottom bank and I had to get right out of my bivvy to see him, so I hadn't spotted it, but Len said have a look next time because he keeps getting his big specimen net out and trying to catch one of the carp.

Longlife was known for its very big tench, but for some reason the carp anglers left it alone. It didn't hold many, but I saw one or two splosh out that would have put a very healthy bend in the strongest carp rod. I was surprised that we didn't catch more of them considering we were using boilies.

Even later in life, Bill still had the old magic.

I went round to Bill's for a cup of tea later on and while I was there these carp came round in front of his swim about 20 yards out.

He said to me: "Do you reckon you can catch one of them?"

I said: "Easy!"

He didn't think I could, so I went home and made up some bait with Pukka Salmon. I didn't even roll them, just cut them into squares and came back with about half a pound and my carp rod and reel.

Anyway, I cast out and within five minutes I had a 28lb fish on the bank. It was the only carp I caught that year, but it was made extra special because it was done in front of my hero, and it's a capture I won't ever forget.

That Pukka Salmon was so good it worked no matter where you went with it. Fish just couldn't resist it. I wish I had never let it out of the bag when I'd reported my catches. I was the first one ever to get it. It was back in 1976, when I joined the Ashlea syndicate and Dave Powell was one of the members. He used to work for international flavour and fragrance company Bush Boake Allen, and during the Close Season I was at a meeting when he brought down a sheet with all these different flavours listed on it and passed it around to see if anyone would like to buy some.

While I was working out where to go next I decided to catch some tench.

A proud moment – the 28lb fish caught in front of Bill.

Finding a Forty

This was back in the days when you couldn't just go into a tackle shop and buy stuff off the shelf. You had to get your bait ingredients from someone with contacts in the food industry, and everyone was on the look-out for something that the carp couldn't get enough of, and which would take waters apart wherever you went. Back then, bait was an enormous edge over other anglers because it was a struggle to find anything decent to use, so if you found something that the fish loved, you were laughing.

I told Dave I'd have some, and I went down the list and picked out several flavours that were quite cheap, at £2.50 each. But then I saw one that was £9 for a 500 ml bottle and it was just called Salmon Oil.

I ordered all of them and they turned up at the next meeting. I started going through them and giving them a sniff, like you do. I came to a nice dark brown bottle labeled Salmon Oil and when I opened it and smelt it, it made me jerk my head back as soon as I got a whiff. I thought: "Urrgh, that's disgusting!" It smelt just like beetroot. So I did the top back up and when I got home I put it at the back of the bait cupboard because I wasn't interested.

26lb 4oz from the Con club, round the corner from Longlife. I had thirteen and Pete had nine.

Part Two

From 1978, Clive Diedrich, Malcolm Winkworth and myself were doing ever so well on Cheese and Maple flavours, but in 1981 a geezer on a lake I was fishing found one of my baits that had fallen on the bank and he copied it.

I was fishing dead opposite him one night and he caught three fish and I didn't get a bite, and our baits were just a few feet away from each other. So I went round there while he was playing a fish and when he landed it I grabbed the bait. I gave it a sniff and it was just like my Cheese, which was my winter bait that I had been baiting with since the summer.

We had serious words, but I knew then that I had to introduce another bait, and so I decided it would be worth trying that bottle of Salmon.

I didn't have much heart in it and the season was coming to an end, so I shelved the idea again for a while. I had been doing very well on the Con Club on Maple and it was only when the action had started to slacken off that I finally got round to trying the Salmon.

I decided to introduce a new bait to see if that would gee things up a bit, and I cast a Maple bait out onto a nice bar where there were fish, and then did the same with the Salmon. Before I could even get the indicator on it was away.

I started fishing with it regularly and I was smashing everything apart with it. I took Pete Springate over there one day and the lake was full. The fishing was hard with so much pressure on the fish. The only two people to catch anything on there that day were Pete and me. I had thirteen and Pete had nine!

It was just an immense bait, and everywhere I went with it I would smash the place to pieces with it.

The first person I gave it to was Bob Baker, because I was working for him, and he copied it and brought it out. But by now I was running out of the original and didn't know how to get it again, so when I started fishing with Rod I gave it to him to copy and he put it on the market, which is how Pukka Salmon was born.

No one could ever match baits exactly the same as the original, but wherever I used it, Pukka Salmon still did the business for me and the difference was only very slight.

It caught me fish wherever I went with it, on hard waters such as Wraysbury, Fox Pool and Savay, and on the Con Club and Harrow Waltonians. At Longfield I had a season when I caught thirty 20s, which had never been done before, and of course I had the North Lake fish on Pukka Salmon, which was the biggest carp in the country at the time.

Incidentally, in Kevin Nash's recent book he said he was fishing Silver End at a time when I was there in the early 1980s and that I lost a big fish and he wondered whether I had been on the same bait as him, which would account for his lack of runs after that.

He's right in that I did hook and lose a fish there. I don't know if it was the one he was after, which he eventually caught in 1985, though it did feel like quite a good one because it was slow and dogged and then it came off.

But for the record, Kevin, my notes say I was using both Cheese and Maple-flavoured boilies but not Salmon, so I don't think we were on the same bait.

I usually like to have a look at a place before I fish it, but It was a bad journey up there to Essex from Richmond so I turned up to fish without having set eyes on the place and was I in for a shock when I did? What a shit-hole it turned out to be! I like big fish, but you've got to have some sort of surroundings to sit in or you just go mental.

My thirtieth 20-pounder of the season.

The first thing I saw was a great big metal pipe in the water in front of me, like you'd find at some sewage outfall at the seaside. I made the mistake of not fishing it that summer and it was a horrible place to be in the winter. There was mud everywhere and there was nothing pleasant about being there at all.

But I just wanted to catch that big fish because there wasn't anywhere else I knew that held a 'forty'. I'd only see an odd guy there because it was winter, but I knew that on a small water it only takes a few people on it to make the job a lot harder, so when things began to get more busy I decided to give it a miss.

If it had been at Yateley I would have carried on fishing it, but it wasn't long before I thought: "I can't be doing with this any more," and I gave it the big heave ho.

I did intend to go back there one day, but I never really got the opportunity because I had other things to do.

Anyway, back to fishing with Len and Bill on Longlife in 1986. They were using home-made swingtip rods for the tench, so I decided to make myself a set as well. I was working in

Stu Arnold's shop in Waltham Cross, in Hertfordshire, at the time and when I set eyes on the top-two kits of the match poles on display, I knew I'd found what I was looking for.
There were always a few breakages when people were trying gear out, especially when it came to tackle demonstrations and a bit of competition crept in between me and Ivan Marks.

Stu had come up with the idea of asking Ivan and me to serve in the shop for two days every week, to get people through his doors rather than anyone else's, and it certainly worked for a while because the shop was packed with people who wanted to come and talk to us.

He rang me up and said: "Stick with me and you'll never have to work again. I want you to design some rods for me," which we did, on Tri-Cast blanks, with my name on the butt, and we sold a fair few.

I was sceptical at first, because I have been taken for a mug when it comes to working in fishing over the years, but I said to him I'd serve in the shop on Fridays and Saturdays for £270 a week, which wasn't bad money then, and it turned out to be a good job while it lasted. We were in the shop one day and we had a bit of an audience and Ivan was casting this tiny bomb into a beer glass at the end of the other end of the shop.

Ivan turned to me and said: "Do you reckon you can do that?"

Now, I like to think I'm a decent caster, but I'm no Ivan Marks when it comes to little leads and leger rods, but I'm not one to back down from a challenge, either.

I said: "Easy! Give us it here."

When I got the bomb in my hand I bit it off and tied on a 3 oz lead. I took aim, gave it a flick and smashed the glass!

Ivan was a great bloke to work with, and we had a really good time together. We served all the best anglers at the time. Bob Nudd used to come in every week, and I was never dismissed by the match anglers.

We used to stay open late on a Friday night for people coming round after work, and have a right good chat. The match anglers who came to see Ivan were interested in what I was doing, and I was keen to learn from them. I've always said you will always learn something from a match angler, but you won't always learn from a carp angler, because a lot of carp anglers just sit in a bivvy reading a book, and you aren't going to learn anything from them.

One thing that made Ivan so good was that he was a thinking angler. He took good ideas and made them even better. When I first started there in 1985 he said: "You're just the man I want to talk to. I want to get into flavours for my maggots."

He said one day: "This hair-rig works really well for you specimen fellas. I've been wondering if I can make it work with a maggot." He was experimenting with imitation baits and using a small piece of shammy leather on a hair to see if it would work like a maggot.

I went to watch him on a match on the Thames at Richmond and he wouldn't even be looking at his float but he'd still catch a fish every cast. He'd just cast out and count and then lift the rod and hook a dace.

I worked at Arnold's Rods & Tackle with Ivan for two or three years, and we were certainly attracting other shops' customers because another big carp shop just around the corner was really hit by it.

Stu used to get his gear from Holland for silly money and sell it over here and make loads on it. He'd have a briefcase with £50,000 in it that he used to give me to look after for him, and he was driving a Porsche and having trips to the casino.

But it was a journey and a half for me to Enfield each time, and I was offered the chance to work for Mike Davis of Penge Angling at his Basildon and South London stores for two or three days a week, so I took it.

I understand Stu Arnold moved down to Brighton when the shop closed down and he's now got a boat that he takes people out in for sea fishing.

I was working for Mike when I wrote my first book, so I agreed to let him publish it. I think he printed several thousand copies and sold most of them, though I wonder if I could have earned more publishing it myself.

The last few copies were bought up by Kevin Maddocks when he still had his Beekay company, and it's been out of print ever since. If you look on the internet you'll see copies changing hands for £90 each, whereas the cover price in 1989 was £15.95. That's part of the reason for writing this updated version, to give people who haven't got that sort of dough a chance to read it and find out how things were done back in the pioneering days of carp fishing, before you could buy a packet of hair-rigs and a bag of boilies off the shelf and kit yourself out with carp rods, reels and bite alarms just by walking into the nearest tackle shop.

From Penge I went to work at Hounslow Angling Centre, but having had a season of tench fishing and caught them to 9lb 2oz from Longlife (I never did manage a double), I was ready to return to carp fishing and I wanted to add to my tally of 40s.

At that time I was the only angler to have caught seven carp of over 35lb. But 40lb carp were rare creatures back then, and it was a case of investigating a rumour and trying to sort out the truth from the bullshit before mounting a campaign to put the target fish on the bank.

For every genuine 'lump' there were plenty of red herrings, and fish that were supposed to be in one water would turn out to have come from somewhere on the other side of the world.

Martin Gay was in the weekly papers at that time with a 40lb common that he swore he'd caught from Essex. I remember going to the NASA Conference that year and the fish had caused an uproar because everyone was talking about it.

He said it was in the Lea Valley, and because I knew him I believed him, but I was on a wild goose chase. I went round the Met Lake and all over the area trying to find the water, but found nothing. There are 40s there now, but not back then.

If you catch a fish that's one of the biggest in the country at the time, in the end you are going to tell someone the whole story, but he never did. I'm convinced that fish came from Canada. I could be wrong, but we'll probably never know for sure.

And then there was Stanstead Abbotts, the hardest lake I've ever fished, but where at least I managed to get my target fish on the end of my line, though the day I did is still one that gives me nightmares when I think about it.

It all started when a geezer came in the shop and showed me a photo of this 'forty' and said: "I can't tell you where it is."

You can imagine my reaction. I wasn't best pleased and said to him: "Look, don't bring photos in to show me of fish that I can't fish for!"

He looked a bit embarrassed and then he said it was from Stanstead Abbotts, just past Enfield, in Hertfordshire.

Part Two

It was a vast lake and it held mainly tench. There weren't many carp in there, and it turned out to be even harder than Longfield in the early days. If there had been a fair few fish in there of a decent size I would probably have carried on fishing it. It was a fair old drive, and I did a lot of time there, but struggled to find the fish I was looking for, which had come out for the first time at 42lb.

I remember almost losing Sabie, my Staffordshire bull terrier, there one time, when she was being drowned by a swan.

She used to chase the birds off, and this swan was in the water and she ran up to the edge to chase it away and she slipped and went in. The swan started to beat her up and I had to run up there and grab her or she wouldn't have got out alive.

I caught quite a few tench while I was there, including fish to over 7lb, but they weren't as big as they were in Longlife.

One day I was fishing on this island with Alf Engers and Terry Glebioska. Alf used to leave at 3am to bait up and he'd hang plastic loops from beer cans on the trees to give him a path to follow to find his way back to his swim in the dark.

This was too good a chance to miss, so when he'd gone one time, me and Terry put a crayfish in his slipper, swapped all his spools over on his reels and changed his pathway so he would be walking round in circles.

Nothing happened until about 4am when all of a sudden we could hear all this shouting about what he was going to do to us.

Then it went quiet for a bit, and then there was all this shouting and swearing again and then another pause before he was calling us bastards again.

The first noise was about what we'd done to the path, then it was when he'd put his slippers on, and then it was when he tried to cast out. He took it well, I thought!

I used to walk round the lake looking for the fish, but could never see it and couldn't work out why. There was one place that I used to give a miss to because it was hard to get to. I was walking past it one day and I glanced over and there it was, in the one place that I'd ignored.

It just goes to show how you should never take anything for granted, or ignore any areas just because they're difficult to get to.

It was in this bay where you could just get two rods in and a bedchair, but that was it. So I put a bit of bait out and got the rods out just as it was getting dark.

The next thing I knew it started raining. Great! I didn't even have a brolly. It pissed down all night and all I had was my sleeping bag. I had Sabie with me, and she hid under the sleeping bag as well, laying on my chest.

I opened the bag at dawn the next morning and the steam was unbelievable. I even weighed the bag later to see what it went and it weighed 70lb! I had to drag that all the way back to the van.

But as I opened the bag I looked at the water and I could see it rocking right in front of me, so I knew the fish was back in there. I put my finger to my lips and said "Sshh!" to Sabie and she never made a sound. She was ever so good like that, and amazing at understanding what you wanted her to do.

When the water is rocking like that in that depth of water it means the fish is upending and the tail is making the water move, so I had a feeling that a good fish was feeding, though I didn't know at that stage which fish it was.

Where the pads were there was a branch going into the water, and all of a sudden the indicator was up and I was in.

I hooked it and was holding on to it on such a tight line to stop it getting under this branch that it came up to the top of the water. I saw it and I slackened off for a second and as I did it jumped over the branch, which was just a few inches above the water. The line went tight across the bough of the tree as the fish crashed back in and the line snapped.

I'd seen it as plain as day, and it was the 'forty'. I was really gutted about that because that would have been a proper fish. It would have been well earned with the stalking I had done and after sitting there all night in the rain I felt I'd deserved it.

When I'm determined, nothing will stop me, but after that I thought: "How long before I get another chance?" I felt that I'd had my one opportunity after all that effort and then it had gone forever, so once I'd lost the fish I pulled off.

By now I was looking for something a bit closer to home, so when Micky Gray and Jock White both told me about a fish that looked every bit of 50lb in the Copse lake at Yateley, I was very keen to take a look.

They called it the Pineapple, because of its yellowy orange flank, and I started doing some serious time for it.

At 50lb it would have been bigger than my North Lake fish, and when I eventually saw it, from up a tree, I thought: "There it is! And they're right about the weight! It looks massive!"

I stayed in the tree for a long time, looking down at it among the sunken branches and working out a plan of attack.

There were fish in the channel in front of me.

The water was about 5ft deep and I had a choice of holding it tight and netting it in the tree or letting it run and going in after it, swimming round a bush and on to the bank to net it.

I decided to make the fish head away from me by pulling it towards me hard and then swim through the tree to play and land it from the bank. You could walk out on the branch to a certain point, but then you had to get in the water, but I could push the rod though and then swim through with it.

I went back to my swim, found some worms (when you are fishing from a tree, a worm is a good bait to use, rather then try sticking a boilie on a carp's head), and I was going to lower one down from the tree with a float above it.

I was watching the fish and it looked big and yellow and chunky, but then all of a sudden it righted itself and I realized that it had been lying on its flank and feeding on its side, which is why it looked so massive. I realized that it was a fish called the Parrot, and what looked like its width was actually its depth.

I was disappointed that I'd spent all this time fishing for a carp with a dodgy mouth that wasn't as big as a fish that I'd caught already, but I thought I'm here now so I'm going to catch it. And the best place to catch it was from up this tree, because it was in the snags and obviously didn't want to come out.

I climbed down and I put my landing net on the other side of the bush, ready, got what I needed and then I got in position back in the tree. I took the lead off the line, which in hindsight may have been a mistake, but I thought it might have spooked it, and lowered the worm down to it.

To my amazement the float hadn't even touched the water when the fish came up and took the worm. I struck and hooked it and gave it a bit of welly, but the fish came towards me, and had I brought my landing net into the tree with me I could have netted it easily because it was just coming up and up, and all I had to do was scoop it.

I had to really give it some for it to turn and go away from me, and it didn't swim away very fast. As it went to go out of the swim I slackened off, but I could still feel a bit of tugging from the other end. I got in the water and followed the line down to check on the fish and found that it had thrown the hook into a branch and all I was getting was the branch tugging backwards and forwards when I pulled it.

I'd made the wrong decision. If I'd done it the other way, the fish would have been on the bank.

Another time I was sitting in my bivvy looking at the water when I saw this fin show above the surface heading towards this shallow bar. I got up quickly and sure enough it was the same fish.

It was coming into another bay along the bank and the way it was mooching about near this bar I thought I was going to have it. It looked like it was going down on some of the free offerings I had put out there, so I put another couple out there and it didn't spook off, but it swam off slowly.

I ran back to get my gear, and when I got back the bait was still there, but the fish didn't come back. And those were the only two times that I saw it. I felt that I'd been unlucky with that fish, but at least I can say that I did hook it.

If I'd caught every big fish that I'd hooked, I'd be able to fill another book with all the stories, and maybe could have made my fortune out of angling and retired to a place in the sun by now.

28lb 2oz from the Copse.

One day on the Copse I turned up and my car was the only one in the car park. A car pulled in behind me and this guy got out as I was unloading my gear and said: "Hello, Ritchie. How you doing?"

I didn't know the geezer, but he said: "Do you want a hand round with your gear?" and he picked up the holdall, which, let's just say, had something in it that I shouldn't have had.

As we got to the lake I dropped my bag off my back and he put the holdall down. I said: "Are you down here for long?" and he said he'd got a day off.

I asked him what he did do for a living and he said: "I'm a Copper."

Obviously I couldn't open the holdall, so I got all the tea making gear out and he said: "Aren't you setting up, like?"

I said: "Nah, I'll set up a bit later, when I've got my bivvy up." But the bivvy was in the holdall as well.

So I made him a cup of tea, which he seemed to take an age to drink, and then I said I might have a walk round and get up a few trees, but I had no intention of doing that because I knew exactly where I wanted to be.

Finally he left and I got my gear out as quickly as I could and had two rods on the bank and two more set up in my holdall, with the holdall lying down on the bank so close to the water that you couldn't see the lines between coming out of it and into the water.

All of a sudden this bailiff turns up and I thought: "That's all I need."

There were fish in the channel in front of me so I didn't even offer him a cup of tea because I just wanted him to leave.

He looked like he was dying for me to offer him a cuppa, and it took him about ten minutes to realize he wasn't going to get one. Luckily I didn't get a run on one of the 'snides' in the holdall or I'd have been in trouble.

I did have a fish on one on the Pads Lake, and that nearly got me in trouble. I had two rods out and one rod cast out and broken in half and put in the rod holdall with those plastic car door protectors on the top of the zip, so that the line couldn't break or fray on it and it would get a nice smooth run, which worked a treat.

Then the bailiff came along and was chatting away. He left after a few minutes and he hadn't got more than five yards away when I heard this "Zzzz!" of the reel going.

I jumped up and a bloke called Big Nose Keith was coming towards me. I said: "Reel one of those rods in for me would you," in case the bailiff turned round and saw me with a rod in my hand. The line was still running out so I put it together and struck into it and landed a 24lb fish.

On the Car Park Lake one time I had an inflatable boat for looking around, but I could only get out in it now and again because it was always too busy.

One time I was baiting up with oats on this bar about 40 yards away and taking a big bag out with me and laying it all around the bar and then placing my baits on the bar by swimming them out. All I ever caught from there was tench, which was a lot of work for a few green things.

It took a lot of time and effort to pump up so I certainly wasn't going to let it down again when I'd finished, so I just hid it in the bushes where people wouldn't be looking unless they were going for a dump.

This one went 30lb 10oz.

It's another string to your bow, but you couldn't use it blatantly because if you did, everyone would be using them, which is why they are banned, but as long as you are discreet about it.

When I did my slide shows I used to say: "You must find out about your quarry before you go for it, otherwise you are wasting your time." That's why I used to get in the water sometimes and was always up and down trees.

I used to say: "If you were game hunters, a lot of you would be dead, because you'd be set up in the wrong spot, sitting in the lair. The lions would come back and think: 'Here's another kill!'"

If a fish has come into an area, I want to know why. Is it coming in there to feed or to hide because it has been spooked? All these things take work. I don't think anybody has got up a tree more than me on any lake that I've fished when I've been on there.

I've been in every lake that I've fished for a big fish. About the only lake that I've fished that I haven't got in is Redmire, apart from the time I fell in. But even there I've been out in the punt and up the trees.

On the Copse Lake I even got an air bottle so that I could go underwater to have a good look round. What I didn't bargain for was the amount of weed, and not long after I got in I was back on the bank again because I didn't like that at all. You hear about people not being able to untangle themselves from weed when it's really dense, and I didn't fancy ending my days that way.

At Wraysbury in 1981 I got hold of a proper boat, though it wasn't strictly mine. I was fishing with Pete Springate and we were rowing our baits out, or rather I was, because Pete can't swim.

White Scar at 30lb. No one else was on the lake to take a picture of me with it.

When I'd first got there I'd seen this fish jump out at about one hundred and twenty yards and I thought: "That's a bit of a cast!" So when Pete came I told him and as he had a little boat I said let's put our baits out there.

When there are other anglers around I don't think you can use a boat, but we were the only ones on that side of the lake so we weren't getting in any other anglers' way.

I hadn't really thought about what it would involve, though. I had to row all the baits out and I could only take two at a time, with the leads in my mouth and the hooks in my clothing, to make sure they didn't tangle.

We had eight rods between us and we had eleven chances that weekend so you can imagine what I felt like by the time we'd finished. I was back and forth like a seaside donkey and thinking about entering for the Olympics by the end.

But I had a 28-pounder and Pete had a 24, though we kept getting cut off by fish running over the bar. The boat wasn't any great shakes, so I said to Pete: "I know where there's a proper boat."

At the back of Longfield there was this old fibreglass one that had been there for years. We went and got it and thought while we are there we'd take a load of bait with us and bait up at the same time, because I thought no one would be fishing, and having gone in the back way we wouldn't be seen.

As we were rowing back to the car park, baiting up as we went, unbeknown to us Terry Disdale was fishing there.

At about 2am he came up to me back at Wraysbury and said: "I've got a big fish on. Can I borrow your boat?"

I said: "I haven't got a boat."

He said: "Yes you have. I've just seen you going across Longfield in it!"

So we lent it to him and he went back and the fish was still on, but it was weeded and it eventually got off.

I only fished Wraysbury a couple of times, but I did well there considering how little time I put in.

But then, having spent time searching far and wide for another 'forty' to add to my name, without a result, I ended up finding two just a couple of hundred yards apart, and in one memorable week in March I managed to create a little piece of history.

"I haven't got a boat."

Chapter Two
Two in a Week

I remember telling Yvonne as I left the house on June 15th 1990 to go to Yateley's Pads Lake that I wouldn't be away long. The fish I was after, which became known as Jumbo, had every chance of being over 40lb, and between January and March of the previous season I'd caught three carp from the lake, at 25lb, 29lb and 36lb 8oz. I thought I'd got it sussed. I should have known by now that you can never count your chickens before they are hatched.

June slipped by without success. I gave it a couple more weekends, but at the end of these Tony Moore hooked something special, and when the fish rolled over his landing net it was the big 'un at 38lb.

Now, you may have thought I'd be gutted when the fish I'm after was drawn over the rim of someone else's landing net, but not so. I was after a 'forty', and when the scales stopped short of the magic number, I had a feeling that I wasn't meant to catch it. Not yet, anyway. My main chance would be at the back end of the season.

So what should I do? The fish that I wanted was weighing in at less than 40lb and was holed up somewhere recovering from the fight and vowing never to touch another boilie. When this has happened before, I've packed my bags and legged it back indoors for a few weeks to enjoy a few home comforts while the big 'un gets its appetite back. However, at the back end of the previous season, when I'd been fishing the Pads Lake, I'd heard walloping great crashes on the lake behind me and I'd nipped across and noted the spots.

Those of you who know this part of the Yateley complex will be aware that the Pads Lake and Car Park Lake are separated by just a narrow strip of land.

They are so close that it would be possible, if you were daft enough, to cast a bait in each water and fish with rods pointing in opposite directions, though every passer-by would have to climb over you to get past. I hadn't anticipated fishing the Car Park Lake for Heather the Leather until later in the season, but things being what they were, this seemed an ideal time to start.

When I got a glimpse of Heather, I knew I'd made the right decision. She was huge, maybe over 45lb.

The weather was glorious, ideal for fish spotting, and I must admit I thought she was there for the taking. Perhaps I was overconfident, but whatever the reason, I ended up spending the rest of the summer up and down trees more often than I want to be at my age, watching Heather, hearing Heather, casting to Heather, in fact doing everything short of putting her on the bank, which is always good news because you learn something every time you see the fish you are after.

I dropped baits in her path and saw her ignore them, and I even bumped into her when clearing some weed, which was worse than I've known it, but still she refused to be caught. I watched her after I'd spooked her, and when she thought I'd gone she came straight back, which told me that the spot she'd returned to was rather special. Perhaps this was one of the larders that the fish visit, with rich supplies of bloodworm or snails, testing them to see which ones are ripe for harvesting.

In action with the 36lb 8oz.

36lb 8oz – I thought I'd got it sussed.

Two in a Week

Finding somewhere dry to photograph it was a nightmare.

25lb – one step closer.

29lb – just a matter of time.

I didn't mind spooking her. I believe you have to be where the fish are to learn about them, and there are going to be times when you overstep the mark and are spotted. I'm sure they know we are there ninety per cent of the time. It's their home and they know everything that goes on in it. Having said that, I reckon it's harder to put feeding fish off their food than we think. If I was hungry and I'd just sat down to dinner, it'd take a lot of disturbance to make me leave my grub. However, I couldn't understand why I hadn't had a chance at her yet. It wasn't like her to be so anti-social. The previous season she'd paid a visit to the lads on the bank in October at 40lb 10oz, 39lb in September of that year and three tunes in 1988, at 34lb 13oz, 38lb 4oz and 39lb. So what was I doing wrong? I made a cup of tea and had a ponder.

The more I look back on my fishing, the more I realized that success, for me at least, comes when I'm in tune with the water and its inhabitants. It may sound a bit strange to some, but it's a question of getting your head together. Some of the lads were probably laughing and shaking their heads, saying: "Old Ritchie will be lighting joss sticks and sitting cross-legged in front of his bivvy soon, chanting mantras and raising the palms of his hands to the sky. What is occurring?" But, they say that wisdom comes with age, and I found myself getting more philosophical in my approach to fishing than back when I couldn't get my bait in the water quick enough.

I need to feel in tune with a water, because when I'm on form and everything's just right, I don't miss a thing. When I'm feeling right, if I see a bubble that looks out of place I'm on to it, the cast is accurate and the strike and the fight perfectly controlled. If anyone could achieve that state of mind all of the time, the fish wouldn't stand a chance, but it's just not possible to keep that sort of awareness going indefinitely. All you can do is realize it's happening and make the most of the situation.

I just needed to be patient and to try to blend in, but things were destined to go very wrong before they finally came right.

The first set-back came when I got another look at Heather (we can't keep meeting like this) and she looked much smaller. Fish this big vary so much in size. In June they can be huge with one or two years' spawn inside them, then in July they can be down to their lowest weight. I think September to March is the best time for the genuine weight. There was no mistaking Heather's drop in size.

Then there was the problem of the tench. Don't get me wrong, I like tench. I've spent many a long session fishing for a big 'un, and a hefty male can give you the sort of scrap that you won't forget in a hurry, but the sort I was catching were females of about 4lb. Every time the buzzer went, my heart gave a jump, and every time there was a short, plucky fight and another green-flanked baby got lost in the folds of my carp-sized landing net.

Not that catching tench is a bad thing when you're alter carp. They are far more finicky feeders than carp, and if you're catching them, there can't be much wrong with your baits and rigs. Also, when you get them going, they create an attractive feeding area. The tench will stir up clouds from the bottom of the lake as they pick up the free offerings, and this in turn will attract carp. I would be much more confident of catching a carp if four or five tench were milling around the baits than if the fish I was after came across them alone.

As for hooked fish spooking the shoal and so scaring the carp, I learnt a long time ago from a matchman that if you strike sideways you pull the fish through the shoal, not up above it, and provided you lead it carefully, without applying too much pressure (the harder you pull, the harder they will pull back) they will come along without disturbing the others.

Then there was the fact that I'd told them at work at Hounslow Angling Centre how close I was coming to catching Heather, and begged a couple of extra days off because I thought it was going to happen at any moment. It seemed like it was, too, but despite everything pointing towards action, the moment I was waiting for just wouldn't come, and it looked as if I'd have to face them without the capture I'd predicted.

Then I began to lose it with the tench. I missed a run and I lost a fish when it ran through weed and the hook pulled. I had been using a rig shown to me by Tony Moore, who used it to catch his fish of 45lb and 38lb, and I couldn't resist giving it a try. He went out and freed the line, but the fish had gone. I'd broken one of my golden rules, which is not to try things for the first time on hard waters. But the rig was excellent, and I decided that when I'd put it through its paces on smaller fish I would bringing it into the front line for my serious fishing.

To cap it all, after a sleepless night stalking Heather, I went to bed at dawn and had been akip only half an hour when I had a steaming run. I felt like Arnold Schwarzenegger in *Total Recall*. I was awake and sitting bolt upright on my bed but my brain was missing. For what seemed like ages I didn't know where I was, and by the time I'd got my head together, my slippers on and the rod in my hand, the line was lying limp on the surface. Looking back now, I've got a sneaking feeling that a swan was responsible. There was one skulking around not far away, looking sheepish – if that's possible – and that was the only screaming run I had, from carp or tench.

It's not unusual for me to be mooching around at night and asleep during the day. I swap information with the other lads on the lake, so if I've got my eyes and ears open at night and they're on the look out during the day, we've got a round-the-clock watch going. If you're asleep and you hear a crash, you'll never know if it was a fish jumping to clear its gills of silt and giving away its whereabouts, or a goose trying to get onto an island. However, if you're in tune, you'll know straight away when it's a carp. One disadvantage at this time was the number of anglers on the lake. A few years ago you could have gone down to Yateley in mid-week and almost had the place to yourself, but not now. Sometimes it feels as if the world and his wife are down there, which makes the fishing that much harder. Add to that the fact that Heather was now making herself scarce during my regular visits and you begin to get the picture.

Never mind, though. There was a storm forecast – that would be sure to stir things up. I've usually found that if there's a storm while fish are active, it can bring things to a halt, but if things have gone quiet, as they certainly had at this time, it will liven the fish up. However, this would have been all well and good if the weathermen hadn't got it round their necks. Every day they said it was on its way, but for all we saw of a storm, it may as well have been Scotch mist.

In August I spotted six fish feeding in a bay into which the wind was blowing. With just a gentle ripple, the conditions were ideal for getting them going on floaters, but anyone who's ever tried the method on Yateley will know it's a waste of time and energy. You only have to whisper the word floater and every coot, swan, tuftie, goose and seagull – in fact anything with wings and a beak – will make your swim look like a corner of Trafalgar Square. You name it, they're there, squawking, flapping and fighting to mop up your free offerings.

You can hold some of them back by stretching a line across the mouth of a quiet bay. Swans and geese, for instance, won't go through line intentionally, but seagulls don't give a damn. In fact, they seem to take a particular pleasure in getting where they are not wanted (I know a few human beings who behave like that). If it weren't for the bird life, catching fish at Yateley would be easy. As it is, we'll have to wait until the seagulls go back to the sea, where they belong, before we can expect some good floater fishing. What I would say, though, is that however much birdlife frustrates me, there's no way I would kill one, or put up with anyone else doing so, because they have more right to be there than we do.

Anyway, I tried my luck with the six fish in the bay, casting as far away from them as I could and reeling back in to avoid spooking them. I watched them drift around for a while, just asking for a bit of floater, and then swim slowly out of the bay and away. And as if all this wasn't enough, one week later I finally found Heather, mooching about over a clear patch with another fish. I fetched the rod, cast in a little way along and straight away she came across to the bait. The float slid under, but I could see she was in mid-water and had touched the line. I sat there all night, gazing at the isotope (I always have one on the float in case daylight fishing turns into night fishing) and six times the float bobbed under and back up as she gave me line bites just a rod-length out.

What did I have to do? I found out later she was taking fry and pond-skaters, which covered the surface in their thousands, and in their preoccupation the fish wouldn't look at my floater I'd rigged up with a worm wriggling enticingly in the middle.

The following week I was back again, and the first two captures were tufties (what was I telling you about the birdlife?). But this time I was determined to succeed. That fish had my name on it, and I'd get her in the landing net or go mad trying. I gave it all I had. I stayed awake all night, I changed my rigs, I changed my bait. I even waded in and cleared out some weed to improve my chances. What was the result? The heavens opened and down came the rain, making me cold, wet, frustrated and fed-up.

The last straw came in October. I found a couple of her mates rolling in the weed, so I nipped around with my float rod, which I always have at the ready, set up with a waggler, and put out a bait. Keith Sullivan was behind me while I was fishing, and it was just as I turned to speak to him that his eyes bulged and he said: "Your float's gone under."

I turned back and struck, and there was a big fish on the end. But I knew almost at once that something wasn't right, and when she came towards me belly first, I knew what it was. She was foulhooked. I netted the fish, gave the rod and landing net to Keith and said: "Sort that out for me, I'm too gutted!" and walked away. One by one the lads came around to my swim that afternoon to offer me their condolences. I felt that they were genuinely very sorry that I had foulhooked a big carp, which turned out to be the Big Orange.

When the weather turned cold in December, I gave it a rest. I believe in perseverance, but when the lake's frozen solid and the weather's diabolical, even I draw the line, especially when we're talking fewer than one fish per acre. I'm certainly not going to sit there and wait for the ice to thaw. I may be dedicated, but I'm not daft.

Someone did venture out and two fish were caught, one on Boxing Day and one the day after, but I came home, had a Merry Christmas and a Happy New Year, and was back at the end of February.

I had something up my sleeve when I returned, and it wasn't a present from Father Christmas. At the end of the previous season I had spoken to a bloke who'd had three runs at the far end of the Pads Lake, and when I'd had a look around I noticed that the frogs had been spawning. Now, I know from my Redmire days that carp feel about frogspawn the way kids feel about sweets – you just can't keep them apart. They were eating so much of it at one time that Chris Seager tried out tapioca and caught a couple of the famous lake's fish on it. For while a carp that's on frogspawn won't stop for a boilie. If your bait is in there with the eggs, I believe that a fish will mop up the lot.

Never one to pass up an opportunity, I got on the blower to London Zoo and found out that the little fellas in lakes lay the stuff about one week after their friends in garden ponds do, so I kept my eyes peeled, and when I came back in February I headed straight for the rushes at the far end. As it turned out, I wasn't there long enough for the free groundbaiting to begin.

There was no sign of frogspawn or carp, so I fished the birdfood boilies over a couple of gravel bars I had found about 25 yards out from the far bank. I'd got to know the water by plumbing it pretty extensively the previous season, and found a clear patch that I can only describe by saying that it felt like I was dragging the lead over a billiard table and then I hit the balls. Whatever it was made of, it was rough and lumpy and different from the rest, and the first time I put a bait there I caught a fish.

It was on the second session, when I had been there just three days, that it happened. At 3pm on March 5, I was having an afternoon nap when there was a single bleep. I looked out and saw the rod tip bounce down, but the line hadn't been pulled out of the clip (I use a circle of rubber tube pinned around the rod so that the trimmed ends form a 'V'). I climbed out of bed and as I did so, the line dropped back. I struck and felt a little kick a long way out, just like the tench were giving me.

The fish kited straight across the lake, and it was only when I put pressure on to bring it around a bush that I realized it wasn't a tench. It hadn't fought until then, but suddenly it surged away and got me in trouble. The line started to go through the branches of a fallen tree, and I had to release the pressure to avoid damaging it. I called a couple of the lads around and I put on their waders and tried to get the line free, but the water was too deep. I knew it was either the big 'un or her 36lb mate, so I decided to go in after it.

I think I lasted about ten seconds before I had to come out. It may have been March, but it wasn't long after the thaw and that water was cold enough to turn an Eskimo's nose blue. People were saying I should throw a brick in, but that could have damaged the fish or the line, or both.

This is where I have to say a big thank-you to the chap who saved my bacon, Keith Sullivan, who's been a friend for about ten years. Without a moment's hesitation he fetched his lilo (a handy piece of equipment for resting fish on when photographing them, as well as for kipping on), stripped down to his tee-shirt and shreddies and paddled out to the end of the tree. He must have had his Ready Brek that morning because he only said: "Bloody 'ell, it's cold!" just the once.

First he tried to free the line by breaking branches while on the lilo, but he couldn't break enough off. So, in an act worthy of a bravery medal, he plunged in up to his neck, took the rod from me and swam around the tree and back in to the bank so that I could play the fish from the other side. What can I say? A greater love hath no man than to whip off his Bill Grundies and wade out into an icy lake for a friend. That's one I owe you, Keith.

On the other side, the fish was still snagged in some pads, but gentle pressure got her out and then I kept in front of her, steering her left and right until she was where I wanted her to be. Then she rolled, and the big 'un was mine.

The scales were ready and waiting, and on them she pulled the needle down to 41lb 9oz – the fish I wanted at the weight I'd hoped for. It didn't matter what happened after that; I'd done what I'd set out to do and I could go home happy.

I was having an afternoon nap when there was a single bleep.

41lb 9oz – that's one I owe you, Keith.

Two in a Week

Needless to say, there wasn't much fishing done for the next few hours as pictures were taken, people were informed and we wet the big 'un's head with a beer or two. People started asking what I was going to do for what was left of the season, and at first I just wanted to catch a few easy fish. But when the dust settled and I was alone with my thoughts, it seemed too good an opportunity to miss not to spend the last few days trying for Heather. I'd planned to be on the complex until the last day, and considering how close I'd come to catching her and how much I'd learnt about good areas, it seemed a waste to go home. I had a pretty good idea where she would be.

When I'd been fishing the Pads I'd heard her crashing out behind me and I'd said to Rob Maylin and Kevin Maddocks to give it a go. Now with the job done on the Pads lake, it was too good an opportunity to miss.

So, at 4am (I'd just woken up after the previous afternoon's celebration) I moved on to the point of the Car Park Lake, an area where it is shallower and warmer than the rest and there is plenty of cover, and put baits out on an area of gravel over which I'd seen her earlier in the year.

I could have set up where I'd heard her crash out, which was just a twenty-yard lob out from the bank. But the swim was in full view of people arriving at the fishery and I knew there was a good chance that someone would set up alongside me. So instead, I opted for the long chuck from the point on the other side, back into the swim, which took three or four goes every time to get it just right.

Ideally, I like to anticipate the fish's movements and lay my ambush ready for their arrival. A planned surprise attack is far more effective than stumbling on your quarry and having a go. With this in mind, I put a line of baits across the channel, to draw fish to where my critically balanced Richworth Tropicana pop-up was waiting.

The Car Park Lake – too good an opportunity to miss.

I moved on to the point of the Car Park Lake, an area where it is shallower and warmer than the rest.

Things started, as always, with tench, and then more tench, and then more tench! It got so I was dreaming about tench. It also meant that I was getting through a fair bit of bait, because when I catch a fish I like to put out some free offerings. The hookbait is likely to be the last one out there, and it's probably been in and out of several mouths without anyone knowing about it.

The weather was getting better all the time. It would rain all night but then ease off in the morning, and the sun would come out to dry the ground and warm the lake, giving everything a fresh, newly polished sparkle and lifting the water temperature by the hour. I still fish hard when the weather is bad, for someone, somewhere has caught a fish in those conditions, but there's nothing like the right weather for getting the juices flowing

The feeling of expectancy was electric. Something just had to happen. On March 10, 1991, at 6pm, it did. There was a bleep, the rod top started bouncing, and the line was pulled out of the clip. I tugged on my boots and was ready for action, like a fireman answering a call. This was it. This was the one I'd been waiting for. By the time I got to the rod, the line was peeling off the spool. I cupped the front of the reel (that method was good enough for Jack Hilton, so it's good enough for me), struck, and hooked another 4lb tench. I don't mind a bit of action, but this was getting ridiculous.

And still they came, getting bigger all the time. At 9pm I landed a 5lb male, which gave a great fight, even on 8lb line, and would have been a real arm-acher on tench tackle. By the end of the evening I'd had twelve. The one consolation for me was that the anglers around me were not getting them. I reminded myself, as I slipped yet another of the little red-eyed creatures back into the lake, that success with the tench could only be a good sign.

Two in a Week

There was another tench in the early hours, and by breakfast time all this tench catching had made me hungry. I got some bacon and eggs off Keith and soon had them sizzling in the pan. I don't normally cook myself a breakfast, because fried food does my face in like a dartboard, but this morning my mouth was watering at the thought. I could almost feel the grease dribbling down my chin.

A young lad called Alan, who lives locally and spends as much time on the lake as off it, came around. I bet he turned out to be a great carp angler because he was always spotting fish and asking us questions. I thought how he'd know more about those lakes than anyone before he was much older. It was while I was talking to him and stirring my grub that the tip of the left-hand rod dropped back. l struck and straight away I knew it was a big fish, even though it was a long way away. When I felt that 'Donk!' down the line, I thought: "That'll do for me!"

It didn't do a lot at first, though there was a nice bend in the rod. Suddenly it hit a weedbed. I put as much pressure on the 8lb line and 6lb hook link as I dared, and she came out of it,

She registered 40lb 8oz, the first time she had been out for a year.

but instead of running away from the source of the pull, she ran towards me so that I couldn't apply any side-strain. I think it was when she did something as cunning as that, that I really knew what I had hooked. Her movements were slow and decisive, with long, strong pulls, as if she knew the situation and how to get out of it. She didn't go mad, like some people have said she does, but then I didn't play her heavily.

She tried to get among the overhanging trees to my left and I had to get into the water to stop her reaching them. This brought her along the bank in front of me, and when she rolled a little way out, I knew for certain. Here was Heather at last, and even after all the hard work and the near misses, I couldn't help thinking how lucky I'd been.

I gave a shout to Jock to get his video camera, and the next time she rolled she was in the net, with Alan looking on, just six days after the Pads Lake fish.

The leeches on her side and belly, which I relieved her of, showed she had been lying dormant for a while. I lowered Heather onto the scales and she registered 40lb 8oz, the first time she had been out for a year. Two 40lb fish in under a week had become a reality.

Two 40lb fish in under a week had become a reality.

Two in a Week

Two 'forties' in a week, and the first angler to have landed three 'forties'.

    As I watched her swim off after the photos, it struck me how much narrower she was compared with when I'd seen her in July. I can only wonder how much she'd weighed then.

    People asked me afterwards why I didn't go for the North Lake fish and try for a hat-trick of 'forties'. But that's a fish I've already caught once before, and it wasn't on my list of aims, so I didn't try for it. I will never know whether or not it would have come true in the remaining three days. To tell you the truth, I'm not really bothered. I did what I came to do and then went home. If Heather hadn't succumbed, I would have been back there on June 16 to try again.

    As it is, I could move on, to another water, another fish and, hopefully, another 'forty'.

Chapter Three
The Royal Forty

There I was, serving behind the counter of Hounslow Angling Centre, when Joey Kavanagh came in. He pulled a photograph out of his pocket, leant over the counter and said: "What do you think of that?"

It was a picture of him with a big Old English carp, which looked to me like a Leney strain fish, and he told me that it had weighed a few ounces over 40lb. I looked at it and thought that it was a lovely fish, so I said: "Where did you get it from?"

He smiled and said: "I can't tell you that."

It was like dangling an ice-cold beer in front of a thirsty man. I said: "You can't show me a fish and then tell me that I can't fish for it."

But he wouldn't tell, though that didn't stop me bringing the subject up every time he came into the shop. I kept pestering him until one day he came in and said he'd caught it a second time.

This time I sensed that he might be about to crack. I said: "Are you the only angler fishing this lake?" and he admitted that basically he was. He told me that one or two others were having a dabble, but that not many people knew about it, which told me that it was off the normal carp anglers' radar, and made it even more enticing.

I thought if I could find out where this lake was, I could have myself a fourth 40. So I kept on at him until one day I broke him and he said: "It's not far from where you live. It's Richmond Park."

They say that the best place to hide something from someone is under their nose, because they aren't looking for it there, and that was certainly true in my case. Richmond Park was the closest water to my house, and a lake I used to take my dog round when we went for a walk. Probably that was the reason I hadn't even thought of fishing it. The truth is, I didn't believe him at first. I knew it had carp in it, but I didn't think they would be of that size.

I said: "Leave it out," but already my mind was going into overdrive at the possibility of a 40lb carp within walking distance of my front door, right on my 'manor'.

I was later told that the lake below held a 37lb fish, which made his story all the more believable.

So I went there and on my first visit I saw Joey's fish and I knew it was true. I knew also that I wouldn't be able to rest until I'd put that fish on the bank.

So I started fishing there, and I must admit that at first I thought it would be a pushover. I lived so close that I could be there in minutes to fish or bait up, and I had little or no competition from other anglers. There didn't even seem to be many other fish to get in the way, just a few low 'twenties'. The fish wasn't shy of showing itself, either, so I was almost making room in my photo album for the catch picture already.

After all, Joey had caught it twice without even setting up. He'd been walking round with a rod, spotted the fish, dropped a bit of luncheon meat in front of it and it had taken it straight away.

It was summer 1991, four months after I'd caught the two 40s, and the perfect time to take a closer look at the lake without drawing too much attention to myself.

"We're going for a picnic," I told Yvonne and the kids, and I took them and Sabie, my faithful Staffordshire Bull Terrier, over there for the day.

I spent most of the time paddling round on my lilo with my dog swimming beside me. While I was playing the part of a dad with his family, cooling off on a sunny day with a refreshing dip in the lake, all the time I was looking down into the water and mentally mapping the bottom.

There weren't many features, just an island and a wall that divides the two lakes, and I fancied that because of all the snails and insects that would be attracted to it. By the time I came out of the water I knew that I'd found where I wanted to fish.

On my first proper fishing visit, I got my tackle down there and then drove back out of the car park and parked down in Ham, to keep a low profile, and then walked back and cast out. It was very late at night and I was laying on the bank on my bedchair without a sleeping bag when all of a sudden I heard this Land Rover coming along. Then I caught sight of the headlights and it pulled up right beside me.

All the time I was looking down into the water and mentally mapping the bottom.

A little bloke leaned out of the window and said: "What are you doing?"

It didn't take a genius to guess why I was sitting beside a lake with three carp rods, but I decided to humour him. "I'm fishing," I told him.

I had an idea what was going on but I also knew that on the permit I had bought it hadn't said anything about night fishing not being allowed. If you buy other Royal Parks permits they state on them that there is no night fishing allowed, but not on this one, so I thought that I was within my rights.

The little fella wasn't in the mood for a debate, though. He obviously decided that a more direct approach was needed: "You'll have to pack up!"

I told him: "I'm not packing up!"

In the background I could hear all these teenagers in the distance larking about in the dark and spooking the deer.

I said: "Listen, mate. There's people over there causing aggravation to the deer and you're doing nothing, and I'm sitting here minding my own business fishing and you're going throw me off."

Just for good measure I told him: "There's a sporting tradition in this park going back hundreds of years. Henry the Eighth used to hunt here for sport and no one told him that he couldn't, so I'm staying put."

With that he drove off, and half an hour later the same Land Rover reappeared, but this time with a massive Irishman inside who couldn't stop getting out of the cab.

He said: "You'll have to pack up!"

I took one look at him and thought he was probably right, judging by the size of him, and I was gonna have to pack up after all.

They started to try to help me but I said: "Don't touch my gear, mate. I'll do it."

They were kind enough to take me home, though I think they just wanted to know where I lived, so I didn't take them there. I got them to drop me at a place round the corner, and waited until they'd gone to head for home.

So, now the gloves were off. I've only ever fished one way, and that's on my terms. From now on when it got dark I would have to be out of sight.

On a walk round I saw the fish in shallow water close to the sanctuary and moved to where there was a big fallen tree that I could hide behind and not be seen from anywhere. It just needed a bit more camouflage.

Joey and his brother were coming over quite regularly to see me fishing at the lake during the day, and I got them chopping loads of fern up and throwing it over the fence to me so I could build a hide. The only trouble was that it died off quite quickly, and I knew that the rangers would spot it if it was a different colour from the rest and guess someone was hiding in there, so I had to keep replacing it with fresh stuff.

The main drawback to the fern swim was that I couldn't stand up. I had to be on my knees at all times, which if you've ever tried it is a right pain in the backside. I didn't even get a bite from there, so it was back to the drawing board.

I thought the fish I had seen close to the bank would have been making its way to the wall, which was a feature I really fancied, and the rig and bait presentation couldn't have been better. It was only 2.5 ft deep there so I could slide my lead down the wall and straighten my hook link out on the two rods and just plop some baits in beside them. Presentation doesn't get any better than that!

The Royal Forty

I thought it was a dead cert to get a fish, because I had seen a fish in the swim when I had been cutting the fern about twenty-five yards away, so even though it was very shallow there, I knew it was deep enough for the fish to come into. I did get a 19lb common from there, but after a week I knew I had to try a different area.

There was another area in the bird sanctuary with a swim that had been fished many times before. I hadn't seen anybody fishing it, but it had obviously had some attention. I thought this seemed like a good area, and it was opposite where I had been fishing before under the fallen tree, which meant I was familiar with the underwater contours.

It was a warm day, and I had been there only a few hours when I saw the fish I was after in the weed in front of me. I'd noticed that when the weather was warm it used to swim about with its dorsal out of the water, so you always knew where it was, which was handy, though strangely it never seemed to roll and I can't ever remember hearing it jump or crash out in the night.

Having put the rods out on a nice clear spot in the weed that I had found, I had to go for a pee, so I went behind the bush that my rods were in front of. I had been sitting right beside my rods, so I hadn't had my buzzers switched on, and even though I was away from them for only a minute, when I came back the indicator was in the butt ring and the line was tight.

I picked the rod up and there was a weight there, but the fish had weeded itself and it came adrift. Losing any fish is a big disappointment, but when you've had your bait in front of your target fish you know you've just made the job a whole lot harder, and it's gonna take longer than you thought.

If I was going to catch it, I was going to have to be geared up to spend the winter there, and that meant building a proper swim where I couldn't be seen, because you need more than just a sleeping bag to stay out throughout the winter. I decided that I would dig myself in like an SAS soldier.

I did think at one time that if I could get on the island, that would be the place to fish from, because I could just drop my baits in. The lake was very silty in places, which meant using long tails, but for some reason the silt didn't extend to near the island, except for one spot. I swam out there and in this one place I sank into the silt right up to my waist.

But the island was alive with geese and covered in goose shit, and desperate though I was to catch the fish, I thought I'm not fishing amongst that lot. You have to draw the line somewhere!

The birds probably would have spooked off there with me around, and I would have been seen during the day so it would have taken a lot of work to conceal myself. The rangers aren't stupid. The Police aren't around often enough to notice when something is different, but the rangers are there every day and would spot something out of place straight away.

So I went into the rhododendrons and made myself a hide by cutting a bivvy shape out of them from the inside. I had just about finished when I looked round at the water and saw there was an iron fence right in the way. The bars were flat but a couple of inches wide. I had no choice but to go home and come back at midnight with a hacksaw blade and a non-fishing friend, Rod, who offered to help me set up the bivvy.

After a cup of tea we set to work and I cut the fence through and bent it round the tree so that I could have access for my rods. If you've ever tried to cut through metal with a hacksaw you'll get some idea of what it's like, and I just had the blade and no handle, which is why it took me all night, but I was determined to fish there. I think it would have been easier to break out of prison by sawing through the bars because there would have been fewer of them than on this fence.

It took me until dawn the next day to get it the way I wanted it, but by the time we had finished I had everything you could ever want on a winter session in my bivvy and there was a feeling of satisfaction from a successful night's work.

Then on my first morning in my new 'home', I woke up just before dawn to the sound of hooves coming through the water. I couldn't work out what it was, so I took a torch out and there must have been a hundred deer coming towards my swim along the margins, heading straight for my rods!

I jumped up and down frantically waving the torch at them and they all turned round and ran off like stampeding cattle. Fortunately they didn't come back any more, but I was awake every morning just to make sure.

When I left I put all the fencing back the way it was and made sure it was firm enough to keep any deer out, short of getting some welding gear down to the lake. All that was left was a bivvy-shaped area in the bushes. I've been told that it's an official swim, now.

I planned to fish there every weekend for the rest of the season at night, and just before dawn I would come out and fish like a daytime angler.

Instead of taking a car down there I used to ride down on a pushbike, and then I'd throw it in the lake when I got there, to hide it from prying eyes, under the water in the shallows.

The only problem was that when I arrived in the dark I couldn't tell if it was completely invisible under the water. I came looking for it one morning, having thrown it in the lake the night before, leaving one of the handlebars sticking up out of the water so that I could find it again, and it was gone. The ranger must have come along just after dawn on his morning patrol with his searchlight and spotted it, thought he'd have that and put it in the back of his truck.

I knew they were looking for me because the patrol car used to come round every night to see if they could catch me out, but I was too well hidden. I'd taken the precaution of switching everything on one night – my gas lamp, my radio and my TV – and walking all the way round the lake with a pair of binoculars to see if I could see any light showing through the rhododendrons. I was pleased to find everything was so well camouflaged that I couldn't see a thing.

One time I heard the clop of a horse's hooves and a policeman on horseback rode no further than a couple of feet away from where I was. But under the rhododendrons I just lay there on my bedchair looking out at the water, and as the sound faded I humming to myself the Dionne Warwick track *Walk On By*.

Another time me and Yvonne were in my bivvy together when another angler, Dave Short, who was fishing there now and again with his son, climbed the tree above us to spot fish, completely unaware that we were right below him. He got to the point where if he'd climbed any higher he would have seen us, which is when I told him to… go away. I wasn't bothered about him seeing me, but let's say Yvonne wasn't exactly dressed for an audience. At least I knew the camouflage was working!

Every morning I would creep out before anyone was about and spend the day fishing the same area that I was baiting up every night, but from the point swim. Sometimes I wasn't there for weeks at a time, but when I was fishing I was there 24 hours a day.

This little lad called William used to come over and see me after school every day. He was very keen and used to sit there for hours talking about fishing. At that time he didn't know I was fishing at night in the rhododendrons, but as he became a regular daytime visitor I grew to trust him and let him in on my secret. It was a good job I did because he turned out to be a big help when it was most needed.

Quite a few people turned up for a chat, and there were always lots of dog walkers around during the day. One day I was sitting there with my mate, Rob, and Sabie, and all off a sudden we were surrounded by these five dogs going mental. I grabbed hold of her and shouted: "Who owns these f***ing dogs?"

This black geezer came along and said: "They're mine."

I said: "Well control 'em or I'll have to let her go because they're having a pop at her." She'd have ripped them to pieces given half a chance.

He got hold of his dogs and disappeared, and I thought that was it, but the next thing I knew the Old Bill turned up. I saw them coming and walked away leaving Rob sitting there, and Sabie came with me. They said to Rob: "Where's the bloke with the pit bull?"

I was behind the tree and I came out and said: "What are you on about a pit bull? It's a Staffordshire Bull Terrier."

They said: "We've just had a complaint about you."

I said: "The problem was caused by the five dogs jumping all over my gear. I had to grab hold of her to stop her fighting them and I shouted out and this black fella came along and said they were his and I told him to control them or I'd have to let here go. If I hadn't, one of those dogs wouldn't be here now." He agreed with me and nothing more was said.

But another time we were walking along and we were up wind of this bloke walking his greyhound and his dog could smell Sabie, but Sabie couldn't smell him and as we got level he bit into her side.

I got my hand in front of her mouth and told him to get his dog off or I wouldn't be able to stop her biting the greyhound. Fair play to him, he was kicking this greyhound hard to get it to let go, but it wouldn't give up. So much for a quiet bit of fishing on an unpressured water.

Another time I'm convinced that Sabie saved my life. We had been home and were walking back with a bag of sandwiches through all these ferns when all of a sudden this huge great stag appeared right in front of us. When you see what damage these things can do with their antlers to a car, and how they'll charge them and even chase them out of the park, I knew we were in real bother.

It wasn't happy with us, but Sabie reared up at it and I started waving the white sandwich bag around and shouting, and it ran off, but if I'd been on my own I think I'd have been in serious trouble. They are big old beasts and get one angry and it could rip you to pieces.

When other carp anglers got to hear that I was fishing there they would turn up. The likes of Dave Shilton, Terry Pethybridge and Terry Disdale, who lived just around the corner, came along for a chat.

Terry Pethybridge lived at the back of the park and he told me he had a boat with a fish-finder attached, which he said would show the features on the bottom and even the fish.

So one night we dragged his big inflatable dinghy all the way through the park. What he hadn't said was that it was bright yellow, and we'd chosen the night of the Full Moon, so if anybody had been about we'd have stood out like Santa Claus and his sleigh on top of a Christmas cake!

We gave it a go and even saw a few fish with it, but we couldn't tell how big they were.

They all looked the same size on the screen, and in the end I found the area that I wanted by casting out from the rhododendrons and fishing near the island.

When the birds were on the bait, it was only a matter of time before the fish were there as well. I did my baiting up at night to get through the seagulls, which were ravenous. They get a lot more bait than you think, and even dive under for baits, so when a lot of those are around it's a waste of time. I'd just done a sponsorship deal with Fisher Baits, so I was using their boilies, which the birds absolutely loved.

People used to come down to feed the ducks in one particular bay, and you would often see a fish have a swirl at a bit of crust or you'd see a duck spook and you knew there was a fish there. I could never get them to show any interested in taking surface baits, though, but they obviously liked a bit of bread.

One evening Terry Pethybridge was sitting beside me and I'd seen this duck spook and so I picked a rod up and went down there and there were several fish in the swim, the big one included. I flicked a bait out and the next thing Dave Short was there and he was about to cast in as well, standing just a couple a yards away from me.

I said: "What are you doing? I'm fishing here!"

We had a bit of an argument and he backed down and didn't fish, but he wasn't happy. If he'd got there first I wouldn't have just walked up and dropped a bait in his swim, any more than I would have gone round and cast out where his rods and gear were set up, but he didn't seem to see it that way.

The winter came and with it snow, which always makes things more difficult. One day I

A brief diversion to the Con Club in September produced this 26lb 8oz fish.

reeled in because the snow was settling and I decided to go home for the night rather than stick it out. I came out from my hiding place on the other side of the sanctuary, which leads onto a road, and I had planned to walk down into Ham, get in my van and drive home.

There aren't supposed to be any cars in there at night, unless they are Police cars, but after I walked across the open area and found where I could get under the fence, I'd just got under it and started walking along beside the road when all of a sudden this car came past. It got about 50 yards down from me and then put its brake lights on.

Before it had a chance to reverse up, I ran back to where I'd come out, dived into the bushes and waited there for a little while. From where I was I couldn't see or hear the car, so decided that rather than risk blowing all my hard work for the sake of a cosy night indoors, I would crawl on my belly across the snow in my thermals, to avoid being seen, get back to my bivvy, cast out and stay the night, which I did.

It may have been no one of any importance, but I knew I couldn't afford to get caught. Dressed in fishing gear on a freezing cold, snowy night, it would have taken all of my powers of persuasion to convince them that I had been sitting at home feeling bored and just come out for a stroll.

October, February and March are my favourite months for carp fishing, because the fish are in peak condition at those times of the year and look at their absolute best. In October they like to have a little feed up just before the first frosts, and March in particular is a great month, as the first hint of warmth creeps into the air and the fish feel it and starting to move around a bit more. And when a fish is moving, it's got to be feeding.

It was March 14 and I was out on the point in the daytime and this Copper suddenly appeared and came up to me and said: "Do you know Ritchie McDonald?"

I said: "No, mate."

He said: "Well, I know he's fishing here."

I had a feeling that the rangers had tipped the Coppers off to keep an eye out for me, and now I knew it was true.

I said: "Well, I haven't seen anybody and I've been here all day."

My heart was already pounding while he was there in case I got rumbled, but what happened next made it go into overdrive.

At 1.30pm suddenly one of my rods went off and I hooked into a fish. I knew straight away it was the big 'un. It was nice and slow and dogged, and I knew there was nothing else that would fight like that in the lake. When the fish eventually showed itself, the Copper couldn't believe the size of it. He made such a fuss, saying: "I've never seen anything as big as that before."

I couldn't resist saying to him: "That's why people like Ritchie McDonald fish here."

I netted it and weighed it at 40lb 8 oz and I sacked it up and walked out of earshot of the Old Bill to ring Chris Ball. I said to Chris: "Any chance of coming out and taking some photographs?"

He said: "No problem."

But I told him: "Whatever you do, though, when you arrive don't call me Ritchie if the Police are here."

He said: "All right."

Anyway, you probably know how enthusiastic Chris is about everything to do with carp.

"That's why people like Ritchie McDonald fish here." Picture courtesy Chris Ball.

As soon as he came down the lake he came rushing up to me saying: "Well done, Ritchie!"

I thought: "On no!" but either the Copper didn't hear it or he decided to let it pass. Either way he didn't do anything about it.

One of the hardest bits was getting my gear out when I'd packed up. It had started to snow and it was settling on the ground. I got all my gear to near the entrance of this overgrown tunnel and was waiting for the young lad, William, to act as a look-out. I thought: "I bet today of all days he doesn't come." That would have meant I would have had to wait until after dark, but with him as a look-out I could have my car in the car park.

Anyway he did turn up and keep look-out for me and when there was no one about I quickly ran out and dropped some gear down and then ran back and kept going in and out until he said there was someone coming and then I would have to stop. He'd just stand next to my gear and it would look like it was his.

I managed to get it all out and he helped me up to the car with it and I drove home a very happy man. I'd wanted that carp because it was such a beautiful fish and because it would be my fourth 'forty'. After being the only bloke to have caught three 'forties', to become the only bloke to have caught four was very special.

Since then it's been caught a good few times, including by Terry Pethybridge, and the lake has been opened up to night fishing now. I wonder if anglers who fish it these days realize what we went through to put a fish on the banks there. If they've read this, they do now.

Chris came rushing up to me saying: "Well done, Ritchie!" Picture courtesy Chris Ball.

Chapter Four
Plumbing the Depths

Now we come to the difficult bit. Lots of people have wondered what happened in the early 1990s to bring an end to my carp fishing. Word on the street was that I'd hung my rods up and turned my back on the sport. A lot of people have speculated as to why, and rumours have done the rounds, but the truth is that very few people know what really happened, until now.

For more years than I care to remember, the two greatest loves of my life have been carp fishing and the woman I married. But there's an old saying that you can never have two loves, and one will always win out over the other in the end.

My landing net was hardly dry after catching the Royal Forty when Yvonne told me that she wanted to split up. When I asked her why, she said it was the fishing, so I told her I wouldn't go any more, and I was true to my word.

I gave up the sport I loved because I thought it would win her back again, but I ended up losing both. It took me ten years to get over her, and by then carp fishing had moved on. So much changed in those ten years, in fish sizes, bait, tackle and techniques, that I'd been left behind, and now it's too late.

If I'd got over her in a year or two then I probably would have gone back to carp fishing and maybe I'd be making lots of money from it now like everybody else, but it's all too long ago, now.

I created my piece of angling history and I'll always be a name in carp fishing as long as it's alive in this country. But carp fishing doesn't bother me any more. I've got no carp tackle, except for a reel that was one of the first Baitrunners, which I use on my bait-dropper rod if I'm barbeling. I sold the rest for a lot less than it would have been worth now, along with all the rods I ever designed, and my fishing van for half what I paid for it.

For a long time after the break-up I was in a bad way. I knew there was more to it than just me spending too much time carp fishing. I had my suspicions, and all the guile and cunning I'd used to find and catch my target fish got channeled into getting to the truth about our split-up. If you wonder at some of the things I got up to, just imagine being in the same position and ask yourself honestly if you wouldn't do the same.

I'd moved out of the house and in with my Mum, but I was keeping an eye on the place, and when I saw this geezer shouting up at the window of our house, I waited until he'd walked off, ran round the corner, got in my car and caught up with him.

I was minicabing at the time, and had a smart silver Volvo 760 with leather seats. I pulled up alongside him, wound the window down and said: "Do you need a cab?"

He said he was going to Kensington, so I said: "Hop in."

Driving him to Kensington gave me plenty of time to persuaded him not to mess about with my missus, and by the time I'd dropped him off I reckon he'd got the message.

I was up this tree watching her where she was barmaiding in this pub and saw her talking to this geezer, and when she got in her car I followed her back to his place. They got out to walk to the house and they hadn't noticed me behind them until I said: "Not tonight, Josephine."

She turned round and went mental. I told him that I wanted to have a word with him and he invited me into his house.

I got him to open the back door because I knew what would happen next. What I hadn't expected was that his missus would be there, too, and when I looked across from his missus to mine you would have thought they were identical twins.

I'd only just told him not to carry on with my missus when I heard the clunk, clunk, clunk of car doors shutting and I knew the Old Bill had arrived, which is when I legged it, out of the back door and down the garden. I hadn't bargained for the 15 ft drop on the other side into a great big field, which hurt my leg, though luckily it didn't break it, and on the other side of the field I came out onto this road.

I saw a car coming so I got underneath this parked car to hide, but as the car got closer it slowed down and stopped right where I was. I thought I had been rumbled, but when the door opened I saw a pair of high heels and a woman's voice said: "How much do I owe you, cabbie?"

The road was a cul-de-sac so I knew he had to go up and turn round. I waited until she'd walked the other way and then I crawled out from under the other side of the car and flagged him down.

I said: "Listen, mate. I'm in a bit of bother here. Is there any chance you can get me to this nightclub I know where my mate is doing the doorwork?" I told him the story and he said: "No problem. Put your seat down." He was loving it. He thought he was in gangster world, and I got away.

I'd only got the Volvo back from her by using a bit of cunning. Her name was on the log, even though I'd paid for it, and she wasn't gonna let it go.

It was parked outside the house, so I went down to the main Volvo garage and said I needed a new key because I'd lost mine.

They came up with the goods and I went down while she was out at work, put the key in and it wouldn't open. So back I went for another set of keys and a few nights later, when she was out working again, I put the new key in and it worked, sweet as a nut.

When she came home she reported the car stolen, but by then I had it in my mate's lock-up, and when the police told her it was legally mine, she had to send me the log book.

When I'd started minicabing I'd fitted a good sound system in the car and with the volume whacked right up the punters could hear me coming for miles around. I'd pull up at a nightclub and everyone wanted to be in my cab because of the sounds.

I took a party up the West End one night and one of them asked me in to join 'em. I went back there when I'd finished at 3am and went clubbing with them for the rest of the night to unwind after work, and then brought them back home.

There were other bonuses, as well, like the women who took a shine to you and couldn't keep their hands to themselves. Let's just say some of the journeys took a lot longer than others.

But now I had my mind on other things, such as the truth about what had led to the break-up, and whether somebody had taken my place. One time when she went out clubbing with her sister-in-law I climbed up on the roof and got in a window to wait and see if she was with anyone, and another time I got into my house really late at night while she was akip and hid under all the washing by the back door, and still got away without her knowing.

But another time I let myself in to the house to hide, thinking she was out, and she was in. I told her I just wanted to know why, but the police were there in minutes. I heard them coming so I ran out the back door, jumped over the fence, ran through this alley, jumped up onto a flat roof and lay there until they gave up looking for me.

In the end I went inside for pestering her. She'd got a court order out on me and I got three months and did half of that, which was long enough in Wandsworth. It was the worst prison in Europe at the time, but I had to learn to cope with it.

I started off as a cleaner and worked my way up to number one on the hotplate with good behaviour, serving up the food to the other inmates. It's the best job in the jail.

I only had one run-in, when a bloke left his cell door open and then didn't like me looking in as I walked past when we were lining up to eat.

I grabbed hold of him and threatened to throw him over the railings. I told him not to leave his cell door open if he didn't want people to look in, and not to talk to me like that. You can't let them bully you or you'll get bullied all the time. He seemed to get the message.

This screw didn't like me and was giving me a bit of grief. He started talking about kick-boxing and I told him I used to do a bit of that and did he fancy coming over the gym and having a bit of a spar-out. Suddenly he didn't seem quite so keen on the idea.

When I was being released he tried to stop me getting out, but I was too quick for him. He thought I was on the first floor but I was on the fourth. And then they tried to make me sign a declaration saying I wouldn't ever own or discharge a firearm. I said: "I'm in here for totally different reasons that are nothing to do with guns. I'm not signing it."

So they said: "If you don't we won't let you out."

I said: "I don't care. I'll stay here, then." I did care, but they still let me out.

When I finally got to the bottom of what had been going on at home, I found out what I'd suspected for a long time, that one of my former best mates in carp fishing had been seeing Yvonne behind my back.

She told me something one night that only me and him knew and I thought: "Right, I've got you." So I rang him up and said: "I know now. I've known all the time, but I just needed proof, and now I've got it." Within a week he had moved house, family and all, and I've never spoken to him since.

His wife rang me up and said: "Why didn't you tell me?"

I said: "I couldn't put you through the same pain I was going through. I was hoping it would stop."

I had a ticket for Horton Church Lake at the time, but I couldn't fish, even though I tried. I'd turn up but I just couldn't concentrate.

By then I'd had enough, and I could see only one way out. I'm not normally a pub person, but I'd got in the habit of going into this boozer and there was a girl in there, who was also called Yvonne, who I'd got to know. Anyway, this night I got pissed in the pub and then went round to my sister's. She had cooked me dinner but I said I was going upstairs to have a kip and I took a glass of water with me. When I was up there I got all these Prozac pills and smashed them down my mouth.

I had a ticket for Horton Church Lake at the time, but I couldn't fish properly.

Yvonne noticed I'd left my jacket in the pub so she brought it round the house. My sister said: "He's gone for a sleep but he's only just gone up. Go and see him."

By now I was unconscious, so they phoned the ambulance and got me to the hospital, but I was dead on arrival. So they put one of those electric shock defibrillator machines on me, which has big pads that are giant electrodes that send a thousand volts through your body to restart your heart.

Now I pride myself on being able to take a bit of pain, but that really hurt. It's not so much what it feels like at the time, but the next day it's like you've had your chest caved in by an elephant.

They're a lot stronger than Tasers, which I can say from first-hand experience, having had a taste of both. My mate got one and he stuck it in my neck for a joke. It was one of the ones they stun cattle with that gives out a spark. It hurt like hell but if it came to a battle between someone with a Taser and someone with a defibrillator, I know who my money would be on. Bosh! Ave some of that!

People have asked me what it's like to be dead. Did I see the Pearly Gates or all my old friends and relatives beckoning me from the hereafter, or maybe a long tunnel with a bright light at the end? There's only one way to describe how it felt and that's by saying it was the best kip I've ever had. I went out like a light.

They pumped my stomach, but I didn't know anything until I woke up the next day. When I came round I had a piss bag attached to me and my chest felt like I'd been run over by a steamroller. My sister had phoned up my ex and she was there with you know who. She gave it the big fainting job when she saw me, as if she cared anything about me. One of my mates who knows a few naughty people was there, and when he told my former friend what would happen to him if I didn't pull through, he went as white as a sheet.

I did manage the Lady at 32lb, caught from a swim now called the Salt Circle. I woke up early and reached for a swig from an open carton of orange juice and as I took a gulp I felt something go down my throat. Later I found a slug crawling up the side and realised what I'd swallowed, so I sprinkled salt around my bivvy to keep them away.

I slowly got better, but had to take these tablets, which I wasn't getting on with, so a mate gave me something to… let's say… take the taste away. Half in the morning and half at night, and that did the job and with no side affects.

So I got through it without any lasting ill-effects, but mental scars take a lot longer to heal than physical ones.

Maybe we have to learn lessons the hard way, but I know now that I'll never live with a woman again. I wouldn't ever want to get hurt like that again. I'd rather not be in love than risk going through what I went through before. Besides, I've been on my own for so long now, I've got used to it. When I come home I can do what I want, and that's something I've never been able to do before.

People will say that carp fishing is a selfish sport, and I admit that I didn't compromise much when I was fishing. If it weren't for her I wouldn't have caught the fish I caught, because I wouldn't have been able to go as much if she'd been a different woman, so she did help me build a career, but she was the one to be unfaithful first.

When we were first married I used to work up the West End and I was really fit. I used to be able to leap up onto the window sills to clean the windows. I didn't need a ladder. Birds were forever tweaking me up the arse, and I never thought anything of it. But she made a mistake, when we'd been married five years, and I wasn't strong enough to handle it. I couldn't forgive her. It was only a one-night stand, and it would have been better if she hadn't told me. We would still be married today. I wouldn't have been unfaithful first.

But after that I had loads of affairs with all her best mates, just to get back at her. One of the birds I met even wanted to marry me. She thought the world of me and maybe if I had gone with her things would have been different, but now I'm not bothered.

Yvonne went through a bit of hell herself, but I think I went through more in the end. I think she got her own back.

She's doing all right now. She remarried and they've got a nice house about twenty minutes up the road from me. I haven't spoken to her since the divorce. I don't know what's going to happen if any of our kids get married.

But I'm not looking to cause trouble. I'm past all that, now. I'm happy for her. I'm not the jealous type. The kids still see her and she doesn't speak badly of me any more, as I don't of her. She knows that I'm quite happy that she's doing well because the kids tell her.

Stephen and Lindsay have dealt with it all okay, but Danny is the oldest and I think the older you are the more it hurts, because they understand a bit more about it.

There are people I know who have got young kids and have split up and their kids don't seem to have had such a hard time.

The worst thing is he has got a gift for fishing. He's a good fisherman and could be better than I was, but I think the divorce really got to him more than the others.

For me, the first ten years were a nightmare. I'd never lived on my own before. I went from my Mum's house to her house to live with her and her father and then we got married and I was with her for twenty-seven years, so when I got thrown out I didn't know what to do.

But I've been on the river bank most of my life, so I'm well happy with just a few possessions. I don't need all this posh stuff in the house.

The one thing I would like to have if I could is a big kitchen. If I won the Lottery tomorrow I'd have every single item you could ever use in a kitchen in there, even if I never used it.

I'm not a bad cook these days. Even on the bank it always had to be right for me to eat it, and what I cook at home is far better than anything I ever cooked on the bank. My spaghetti Bolognaise is better than anything you'll get in any Italian restaurant. It takes me a long time to prepare it, but everyone who has had it has said they have never had anything like it before in their life.

My stew is unbelievable, but someone has borrowed my big pot to cook up a load of bait in it, so that's off the menu for the time being. When I do it, though, I go down the butcher's to get the lamb chops and put all the veg I can get my hands on in it. Or for a little snack I put a load of butter in a pan and a load of garlic and cook a couple of those big mushrooms. Or another of my favourites is asparagus wrapped up in Parma ham.

My lad taught me to cook. When I got thrown out I had to start to fend for myself. Now I can do Christmas dinner at my sister's place for the whole family. But if I don't do it regularly I forget what to do, because I don't write any of it down.

Every spaghetti Bolognaise I do is different from the last, but they all get better than the one before. I can't be arsed to write down what I do. I don't like writing. I don't even like writing my autograph. I used to have a Dictaphone on the bank to record what was happening in my fishing.

A ride in a stunt plane in 1993 for my fortieth birthday.

When I was thinking of doing my first book I realized people would want me to sign it, I wondered if I could get a rubber stamp made with my autograph written perfectly on it and when someone asked me to sign one I could go – Bosh! But I don't think people would like that.

Biggest mistake I ever made was writing my full name when I started. Then I saw other people were signing books with just their initials. I should have just put Ritchie and left the McDonald bit out, or done just a squiggle. But you live and learn.

If I did win the Lottery, and it was a right fortune, I'd employ my mate to be my agent and financial advisor, because he's a right clever geezer, and we'd travel all over the world.

I'd definitely end up living in Thailand. I like the people and I like the heat. It's a dangerous place to be if you are a troublemaker, but if you are polite to them and don't take liberties with them, they won't take liberties with you.

With Len Arbery, Kevin Clifford and Bob James at BB's memorial in April 1991.

All the prostitutes try to take you for all your money, but after you've been there for a while you get wise to that stuff.

I do like the Thai women. I think they are lovely looking. But you go in a bar and you see all these lovely young girls sitting on the laps of guys who are 80 or 90 and I just feel disgusted with it. There's a very good book called *Private Dancer* that tells it like it is.

Back here I don't go out much and I've never been much of a pub person. I'm quite happy living the way I do. As long as I've got a TV to watch, that's all I'm worried about. I'm used to living in a bivvy, so my flat is like a palace to me. You don't get wet unless you're under the shower. I've been here twenty years now, so I must like it.

There's a lot to be said for living a simple life and not having to handle all the hassle. When people come round for a chat, they tell me all their troubles, and then as they're going they say: "I'll leave you in peace."

I tell them: "I get plenty of peace these days, since I became single again. There's no worries on that score."

Part Two

Chapter Five
Trouble and Strife

By the time you read this I'll have turned sixty. They say that wisdom comes with age, and that you're supposed to learn from your mistakes. If that's the case I ought to be a genius because I've made some bad ones in my time.

You'd think that looking back I'd be able to give younger anglers a bit of good advice on what to do and what not to do to be successful in carp fishing. But plotting the best route through the minefield of life is a tough one because it's different for everyone, but for what it's worth, here's my two-penneth.

When you look at how many carp anglers' marriages end in divorce, it makes you wonder whether it's possible to be successful and stay married.

When I started out I had the best fishing wife you could ask for. Before the kids were born it was great because she used to come to Longfield with me and John and Eileen Walker. She would fish for the bream with Eileen while I'd be fishing for carp with John.

When the kids were born I could still go fishing as and when I wanted, and it wasn't a problem. She never distrusted me, but I never did anything wrong, so it was good.

But everyone is different. I know of anglers who when their wives said they weren't going fishing, they didn't go.

It's down to the couple, and you do have to give and take in a relationship. I suppose with me and Yvonne I did tend to wear the trousers, because I did what I wanted to do, but I don't think that's the best way to go about it from the start. If I got in a relationship now I would do things differently, but I'm not interested. I'm too long in the tooth now. I've had a couple of birds who after a while have tried to change me and I've said: "Listen, mate! I'm not having it!" I am who I am.

It doesn't bother me being single, but if you are someone who still needs some female company from time to time, but you want plenty of time for fishing, the truth is you'd be better off paying for it. You'd probably have a better time and it wouldn't cost you as much as the housekeeping, and then you can do what you want at the end of the night.

And if you want to be successful as an angler, my advice is don't get married, especially these days, when there are so many carp anglers trying to catch the same known big fish.

If you're a young man today and fishing the way you have to fish to get to the top, you are on the banks for most of the week. If I were to start carp fishing again I would only come home every now and then to have a shower and stock up, and spend the rest of the time on the lake.

But when you've got other people to think about and a family to support, you need to work.

In the early days I was fishing three days a week and then going to work. She did more looking after the kids than I did, but she knew fishing was my life before we got engaged. She asked me to marry her, not the other way around. I've never asked anyone to marry me.

The ideal job for a carp angler is to work part time in a tackle shop, because you can be working when it's busy on Fridays and the weekend, which are the days when the lakes are crowded, but you can go off fishing on Monday morning when it's quiet.

And you can design products for the shop, like I did with my hooks and rods, my unhooking mats and the zip sack (which I still think is the best type of sack you can have). So you would be earning royalties from the tackle as well as getting wages from work, and if you could write a book you could also earn from that as well as making a name for yourself.

But I think if I were trying to make a name in carp fishing now, I wouldn't be fishing the lakes for the famous named fish. There are too many people doing that, and when one comes out now it's just another face holding the same carp. It's hard to stand out from the crowd. If I wanted to do something that would make a big splash when I hit the jackpot I'd fish for carp in the rivers.

There's a story that I've never made public knowledge, but which tells you all you need to know about the potential of the rivers. When I remember it now, it still makes me think what might have been. Like the time at Redmire when a record carp had my bait in its mouth, only this time the fish in front of me was even bigger.

Back when I'd just caught the Royal Forty I was wondering what to go for next when a mate of mine who owned a restaurant that backed onto the Thames at Kingston invited me down to have a look around.

He had a private garden that led down to the river and he told me he would often see these big carp when he wandered down to the water.

When I came and had a look I saw some good fish of around 30lb, and what I liked even more was that nobody else could fish there. I'd never fished for carp on a river before, but it was too good a chance to miss.

So I loaded him up with a lot of bait and said I wanted him to put half a bag in every morning about five yards out, where you could see the bottom. I told him that if there's no bait left in the evening, put another half a bag in then, but don't put any bait in if you can see any still there. And don't throw it any further than five yards out, where we'd seen the fish.

This went on for a while, and then I went down there myself after work one day with a bag of bait to have a look at what was happening.

I was watching the spot when all of a sudden I saw this huge fish that was well over 50lb, but probably in spawn because it was in early June. There were several other fish with it, so I threw in a handful of bait. Not one of them reached the bottom!

I thought, I've got it cracked here. It reminded me of Kingsmead, when I got the fish feeding and I was able to pick whichever one I wanted. I felt I could do the same here, and it was just a matter of time.

But then things went wrong for me in my home life and with one thing and another I never got back there.

If I'd caught that carp it would have been my fifth 40-plus. It was a massive common, and I'm convinced that if I'd landed that fish it would have been a record.

I told Albert Romp about it, and he was keen to have a go. He knows the potential of waters other than lakes to produce big carp. Many years before that he'd told me about a 37lb carp that

Part Two

had been caught from a canal near to where he lived in Slough, and he asked me if I wanted to go and have a look. But he didn't know that me and canals have a bit of history.

I told him I didn't care if it was 137lb, there was no way I was going to fish a canal for anything. I just don't like them. The first time I ever went fishing I was taken to a canal and I hated it. I've never fished a canal since and never will.

But the fish I saw in the Thames that day convinced me that the river has the potential to do a record, and if somebody catches it, for them it will be like winning the Lottery because even if no one has ever heard of them before, they will become famous overnight.

You can see the headlines now, and the scramble to sign up the captor and to know everything about him right down to his shoe size and what he had for breakfast. So if I did go back to doing a bit of carp fishing, that's where it would be, rather than going for the same, named fish that everyone else is chasing.

I've got nothing against those anglers who do that, and I admire their determination because they are fishing against other anglers as well as trying to outwit the fish they are after. But if you're going to gamble, you may as well play for the highest stakes, so that if your number comes up, you're made for life.

I think I could still catch the biggest fish in the well-known waters, but I don't think the achievement would be the same as back in my day. After all, there's no point in me fishing for a 'forty' again, so it would have to be a water with a 'fifty' in it, to give me a bit of encouragement.

But to earn a living from it again, that's a young man's game. I've worked outdoors all my life and I've got arthritis in both my hands now because of it, and my thumbs hurt from where I've broken them doing one thing or another. So climbing trees might be a no, no. I might not be able to hang on any more.

I fell in at Redmire last year.

I fell in at Redmire last year. I didn't have a change of clothes so I had to borrow one of John and Eileen's lads' spare clothes. They didn't fit at first, but I made them fit.

I did one of my thumbs last year when I rode into a car on my bike going home one night and hit the wing mirror. I went back the next morning to knock on the door of the house and offer to pay for it, until I saw the damage and realized I didn't have that kind of dough.

The other thumb I did when I was roofing. But even if I couldn't climb trees any more, I'd still have the ability to work out what was going on with the fish and to move at any time to be on them, because I'd fish a lot lighter than how I used to.

If I was carp fishing on lakes again I think I'd fish like I do on the rivers. I wouldn't have a full bivvy, just the sides. It's all according to the lake. If there are quite a few anglers all after the same fish, you have to move around quickly, so I would fish very light. But if it was a lake where you could just walk round and find your fish before fishing for them, I would be a bit less mobile, because you have got more time.

But more than catching carp, I'd like to earn a living out of fishing again, though it may be through fishing for barbel and chub. Being able to go for a few days at a time should give me a slight edge over other river anglers, and once I'd found my feet on the rivers I could start designing baits for barbel. I keep getting asked to design stuff for carp, because people know that if I put my name to something, it's definitely worth buying.

An ideal season would be to fish for tench at the start, through to August, because I don't really rate river fishing in the summer. You get a lot of people there who don't really know what they are doing and are just there for a day out, which is fine until they start messing up your fishing. So I would wait until September or October to go on the rivers and then fish right through, being there when the conditions are right.

It's funny how as you get older you realize how little you really need… in life and in fishing. Everything gets slimmed down to just the essentials, and there's a lot to be said for that simple approach, at home and on the bank.

Where once I had a wife and three kids and a whole load of fishing gear, now life's a lot more straight-forward.

Even, Sabie, my Staffy and my companion on the bank, has gone. She was seventeen when she died. I would never have any other kind of dog other than a Staffy.

She was so well trained, that when I was fishing if any bird life came near I would say: "See 'em off!" and she would run out and bark at them and they would all fly away, which saved me a job.

I never had her on a lead. She used to wander off around the lake, but she would never go away from the water. She used to catch her own food. She would bring a mouse back to the bivvy and lick the fur off it and then munch it.

And if we were out anywhere she would only go 25 yards in front of me before she'd look behind to make sure I was still following, because when she was a pup she'd run off and I'd shout: "Wait!" and she'd stop and look back, and after a few months of that she'd do it automatically.

When I did the slide shows she'd come with me, but she wouldn't settle until I'd taken something off and thrown it on the floor, even at someone's house. But once I'd done that she knew I wasn't going anywhere.

When I went to Hounslow Angling I didn't need to have her on a lead. I would tell her to wait until it was safe to cross the main road and when I said it was okay to cross with me she did.

Part Two

When we went to the Horse and Barge, next to Savay, it used to get chock a block with people and I wouldn't know where she was. But I always used to put my keys on the bar and as soon as I picked them up she'd be straight by my side. She was brilliant.

I'd had dogs before, but nothing like her. I used to have an Alsatian, but you can't take one of those fishing. A fishing dog has got to be a small dog and one that is obedient. You can't have it jumping in the water every five minutes. If you had a Labrador, the first thing it would do is leap straight in the lake and mess your fishing up straight away.

One thing you do need to be able to fish properly is a set of wheels and a driving licence. I've learnt that to my cost. I got nicked because I was home having a bit of a get together when my son's girlfriend rang up and decided she wanted to come around to join in.

Danny was going to fetch her but he wasn't fit to drive, so I said I'll have to drive him over there. Big mistake. I should have just let him go.

He'd just had new brake pads fitted to his car and you could smell them where they were rubbing. We got pulled over by the Police and when the Copper looked at Danny in the car he could see he was pissed. So he breathalised me. I'd only had two pints in the pub and two cans but I was just over.

I knew I would get a ban, but I didn't know whether I'd get prison because I'd had two driving bans before. I got stitched up a few years back when I was on a ban and the minute I pulled out onto the main road in front of my house I saw this Police car sitting in the side road and he came straight behind me. They knew I was on a ban before they stopped me. So I owned up to it, but I didn't realize until much later that it was my missus and my ex-carping friend who had grassed me up because they were plotting to get me put away.

Even Sabie, my Staffy and my companion on the bank, has gone.

I still go to Redmire for a weekend every year with John and his two boys.

I thought I could avoid prison this time because I know people who have had five, six and seven bans and never been to prison.

But the minute I walked into the court and saw this old woman magistrate I knew she was gonna stick me to the wall. My sister was in the public gallery and from the dock I gave her a sign that I would be going down.

But in the end I got a ten-year driving ban because I have been done twice before. I wish now that I'd gone for jail instead because it's taken ten years off my life when I couldn't really do what I wanted to do.

I'd been working for myself doing roofing, driving one of those little Suzuki flatback 'peanut' vans. You should have seen the ladders when they were on that, miles over the front and miles over the back, but I got around in it.

But after the ban I had two years with no work, until I found some work locally and could ride there on my bike.

I would go up on a roof in all weathers, even in the snow. I was the one who would do the stuff that no one else would try. They would tie a rope around my ankles and lower me down to fix the bit that the others couldn't reach. But your age catches up with you working outdoors, and every year it gets harder.

But fishing without your own wheels doesn't work. Friends offered to take me, but when people do you a favour you have to go when they have got the time, which may not be the best time to be on the bank. When I'm fishing seriously I know when it's the right time to be out there. You can look at the weather and just know they'll be having it. Sometimes it's in the middle of the night, but you can't expect people to stop what they're doing for you, so I just say thanks but I'll wait 'til I'm driving again.

I'd like to earn a living out of fishing again.

On the famous dam last September with Russell, John, Les and Simon.

But I still go to Redmire for a weekend every year with John and his two boys, just to have a dabble, which takes me back to the old days, and I enjoy having a chat with Les Bamford again. It reminds me of what carp fishing was like in my day. I'm not bothered whether I catch a fish or not; I just want the boys to catch.

And the other thing you need if you are going to make it to the top in fishing is a manager. I should have had Les as my manager. There are a lot of good things I've done that I haven't been recognized for. When the Carp Society wanted to buy Horseshoe Lake I raised thousands for that, and I started off the junior fish-ins. But when you get asked you give your time for nothing without ever thinking that you need to plan what you do carefully to make the most of your time in the spotlight

I wonder if I could have influenced the way that carp fishing has grown if I had still been involved, and if I'd still had a big voice in angling then maybe I could have persuaded people not to fish for imports

And maybe things would have been different for me, because it's no coincidence that they started going wrong in my life when I packed up. When I first started fishing, it was angling that kept me out of trouble. Maybe it has a positive influence right throughout our lives that we don't really appreciate.

It's only when we stop, and the focus of our attention on one goal of one big fish gets replaced by all the daily temptations and distractions, that we start to struggle to cope with life and all that it throws at us. That certainly seems to have happened with me.

Part Two

Chapter Six
The Good Old Days

I was outside the butcher's the other week, working out what I was going to buy, when this old fellow came along and nearly walked into me. I was just thinking there was something up with him when he said: "All right, Ritchie? How you doing?"

It must have been twenty years since I last saw him, back when I was working for Tony Bloomfield in Hounslow Angling Centre and he was a regular who used to come in the shop. We chatted for a bit and then he went on his way, but then when I was listening to *Fisherman's Blues* with Keith Arthur on TalkSport, the same bloke rang in to the programme.

He said he'd bumped into Ritchie McDonald in the week and one of the things that he remembered I'd said to him over the counter all those years ago was that carp fishing would be a totally different game in twenty years time. "I tell you what," he said. "He was dead right."

Carp fishing nowadays is barely recognisable from how it was when I started out. Things we could only dream of having are now second nature to modern carp anglers, and I still shake my head and wonder what we could have caught if we'd had those innovations back then that everyone now takes for granted.

The biggest step forward was undoubtedly the hair-rig. Imagine going carp fishing without that and wondering why you were getting lots of little plucks and twitches that you couldn't hit.

I was first shown the hair-rig by Dennis Davis and Colin Swaden when we were fishing Longfield. They were catching fish after fish and I wasn't hooking anything, but I was on fish and they took pity on me. I think they could see I wasn't just sitting in my bivvy all day, I was up and down trees casting to where fish were and my baiting was good. They must have thought I deserved to be in on it as well.

As soon as they showed it to me I could see straight away that it would work, but this was the early '80s and the days of absolute secrecy, so they said I couldn't tell anybody else.

As soon as I started using it I was away, and I annihilated Fox Pool the following year. I had been baiting up through the Close Season, so they were bang on the bait, and I was having fish all the time. That was the year I caught 30 'twenties', which had never been done before in one season.

But keeping it a secret was a big problem. The first week, Vic Gillings was there with the usual crowd and I caught this 25lb common, so everyone gathered round. Fortunately no one saw that the bait was wiggling about outside its mouth as I was netting it. I went down and took the hook out and put it in my bivvy, then got a photo of the fish and put it back. But what next?

One of the 30 'twenties' in a season.

The 25lb common I caught when everyone was gathered round, including Vic Gillings.

I thought I can't sit here with them in my swim and not cast out, because these people are not stupid. So I put the boilie on the hair and walked out of the bivvy, reeled it up and swung it out.

Suddenly Vic said: "Oi! That bait wasn't on the hook!"

I said: "Course it was!" but he wouldn't have it. He wanted me to reel it back in and show him what I was using. All due credit to him, he was sharp enough to spot that something was different.

One of my favourite memories of Vic was when I showed him how you can catch a carp with your bare hands. I had only ever done it once before and that was at Gunnersbury Park when I was a youngster. It was near the bank and my grandad had taught me how to tickle trout, so I crept up to this fish like I would a trout.

I got my hand underneath it, started tickling its belly and just scooped it out onto the bank. It was only about 3lb but I was pleased with that because I did it by hand, no rod and line nor nothing.

The next time I tried it was at Fox Pool. I had already caught this common twice so when I saw it I knew it was a twenty-pounder. It was the one with a pellet shot mark in its gill cover. Pete Springate had caught it as well.

Vic and I were over there one Close Season just looking around and I had got up in the fork of this tree and looked down and I could see the common. I thought I'm gonna try and catch this by hand. I said that to Vic and he said: "Don't be stupid!"

Tickling a 20lb carp is a bit different from doing it with a three-pounder. The principle is the same, but getting it out of the water is a different matter.

It was the one with a pellet shot mark in its gill cover.

The Good Old Days

I put my hand down, put it underneath its belly, started tickling it and it never moved. Its tail started shaking slowly and I grabbed hold of the wrist of the tail, squeezed it to lift it up in the water and it shot off like a bullet and nearly pulled me in after it. It went off with such force I couldn't keep hold of it. So I learnt that there is a limit to how big a fish you can get out on the bank by hand. That was my second attempt at carp tickling and up to now it's still been my last.

Vic may never have seen a carp tickled before, but he didn't need telling twice when he spotted the hair-rig for the first time.

Getting an edge is one thing, but keeping it is another, and when you are fishing alongside good anglers you've got to work ten times harder to get the same results you would elsewhere. So the cat was out of the bag, and when everyone knew about it, no one had an edge any more. But the real genius was in the development of it, taking the hair off different parts of the hook and developing the D-rig. It's always been my philosophy that if you come across a good idea, the first thing you should think about is how to make it even better, because that's where you get your edge from.

A few years later I was reading a book by Mitchell-Hedges, a sea fishing pioneer who caught some awesome fish, about how he used to catch tuna back in the early 1900s using a sprat that was suspended two or three inches below the hook. I just wish I had seen it earlier and known it was worth giving a try.

Once I was told about the hair-rig I stepped up to heavier leads and went from free-running rigs to line clips and rods that were put up higher. Many years ago we used to dip the tips of the rods in the water and then we had parallel rods 2 ft off the floor, unless you were fishing in Kent and then they would be 5 ft off the floor. I couldn't believe their set-ups. It was in the pre-hair-rig days and they were looking for twitchers and standing by their rods, and if the bobbin moved half an inch they would strike and be in. You had to strike so quickly that you didn't have time to bend down and pick the rod up, so there was an advantage in having the rods up high.

But back in Savay we were waiting for proper runs. One time I was thinking of taking guttering down because I thought I was too close to the water, so I was going to cast my baits out and have my rods 15 ft away from the water by my bivvy and run the line through the guttering down to the water's edge. But my mate said to me he thought that was going a bit over the top, so I left it out.

Incidentally, I read Pete Regan's chapter in the *Savay Chronicles* book, in which he describes a night in the Fisheries when he says he dived across the table at me to try to surprise me with a kiss full on the lips. He got more than he bargained for when there was a bit of tongue action, too.

I don't know if Pete's memory has started playing tricks with him, but just to give him a bit of refresher course, he got the full French kiss treatment because while I'd gone for a pee he'd filled my hat with custard. Old age can play tricks on the mind, so they tell me.

But back to the terminal tackle. All my fish were caught on 8lb main line and 6lb hook lengths. Anglers now are using braid so strong you could tow a barge with it. You don't have to play fish on that, you can just reel them in!

People say when I play fish it's like a dog on a lead. If you are playing it right then a fish isn't getting any line without having to work for it.

I remember one time at Savay when this fish was roaring off and there was a snag, but it was still quite a way away from it. I thought it's going to get there and I haven't got any way of turning it, so I just opened the bale arm.

I remember that Keith the Tooth was watching me and he said: "What you done that for?" I said: "Watch. It'll stop."

He said: "Nah." But we watched the line and it slowed down and the fish stopped and I tightened back up and was able to turn the fish.

A fish will only pull if you are pulling it. It just wants to get away from the direction of the pull. Once you open the bale arm it's got no pull so it's got to stop. When you lose a fish it doesn't keep steaming around the lake like a lunatic. It stops, and in some cases it will carry on feeding.

I've slackened off on fish loads of times, but I don't like using barbless hooks because with them you shouldn't slacken off, in case it falls out. I'm quite happy when I've hooked a fish with a barbed hook that it will stay hooked, and so I am happy slackening off.

If you are playing a fish between two beds of lilies it's no good giving it side strain from the left or the right because it's going to go straight into the other side. What you do it pull from one side and then the other and keep changing sides and the fish will come in a straight line. It did in my day, what they do today I don't know.

It takes confidence, but I'm quite comfortable in any given situation. I've always known that if you pull one way, the fish it going to go the other way. Whichever way you want the fish to go, pull it the opposite way. So if you've got a snag, pull it towards it and it will go away from it. It always has done for me, and fish don't change.

If the fish gets to the snag it's a tug of war, and on my kind of gear you're gonna get broken, though maybe these days you won't break 25lb braid. Maybe you can heave the whole snag out as well with that!

If I was fishing today I would still be using my old set-up. The fish aren't any different. When you hook a fish you aren't fighting the weight of the fish, you're fighting its stamina. A young 20lb fish will give you a much harder battle than a 50lb carp. A fish doesn't weigh anything in water, so the weight-to-line ratio doesn't mean anything to me.

Even when it's weedy, I still used 8lb Maxima main line. I did experiment with Kryston when that came out, but I liked the lighter breaking strains of braid for hook links rather than the stronger stuff.

If modern anglers could see the bite alarms that we tried to use back in those early days, they'd fall off their memory-foam-lined Indulgence bedchairs with laughter. One November I decided to do some winter nights on Longfield, which was something few carp anglers even considered, because everyone agreed that carp just didn't feed in the winter. I was the only angler on the lake and I went into the corner swim, which is the deepest swim on the lake, and I was using side-hooked spuds at the time, which was back in the late '60s or early '70s.

It was as smoggy as hell and I had three Heron buzzers that were wired up to Friedland door buzzers that were the loudest make you could get. Me and Johnny Allen had one for each rod, packed into Tupperware boxes with foam rubber to stop them vibrating so much. But they still rattled the old garden chairs that we sat in when they went off underneath, and your arse would be on top of the buzzer box so you'd know you were in.

The Good Old Days

I had a run and it was so dark I couldn't see which rod was away. I struck the first two rods before I got to the right one and by then the fish had spat the bait out, which was a shame because it would have been my first carp out of there.

Anglers these days can buy everything they need to go carp fishing over the counter, which seems easy by comparison with what we had to make and invent. But I'm sure Maurice Ingham and Dick Walker thought the same about our generation, because when they were carp fishing there was nothing, not even proper carp rods, so they had to design their own.

They probably felt that the next generation didn't have to work as hard for their fish as they did. I'm sure that there are things you can buy now that would have made my fishing a lot easier, being able to buy the best bait and having loads of information in books and magazines about how to catch carp. Back in my early days there was so much secrecy surrounding fish that you didn't even ask someone what they caught a fish on. There was no way they would tell you what bait they were using, and you'd get a funny look if you even asked.

I remember going into Cliff Glenton's tackle shop, in Northfields, in West London. He was one of the first anglers on Savay back in the very early days, and on the walls were pictures of these huge carp. I would say to him: "Where d'you catch them from?"

He'd say: "Can't tell you that, mate."

But he would tell me stories about how he caught them. He would be hiding behind the reeds and creeping up on them. Stealth was a big thing because carp were hard to catch and there weren't many of them, whereas now I think a lot of anglers are less stealthy than we were about their fishing. Places such as Longfield were hard waters.

Good luck to the people who enjoy carp fishing today, but I think from the late '50s to the mid-'90s were probably the best years that carp fishing has ever seen. There were so many massive changes to what we were using, from the hair-rig and boilies to winter fishing and the tackle we use now that you didn't dare blink in case you missed something. I don't think there will ever be a time of such excitement from so many new ideas and from wondering what was going to be discovered next. I wouldn't have missed it for the world, and those starting out today can only imagine what it was like to have someone share a secret with you that would totally transform your fishing wherever you went.

Everything you wanted in those days you had to make yourself, and we had to make our own baits. When I was a teenager and fishing Godalming and catching small fish, I was told that the way to catch bigger fish was to make a bigger bait.

So I made baits out of catfood, polony, luncheon meat and rusk, mixed up in a bowl to a firm paste, but I made the baits so big you couldn't cast them out. I had to throw them out by hand with the bale arm open.

Then I set up a billy can with a penny piece on the spool of the reel in case I dozed off. But I still caught small carp because they would all be on the bait straight away and it was the poor little sucker who got the last little bit who got hooked, or even one that picked up the bare hook.

Although I wanted to catch big carp as a kid, I didn't manage it, and I'm glad I didn't because it would have ruined me. Having to build up slowly kept me hungry for the next big fish, and that is why I've caught the fish I have, by not trying to catch too big a fish too soon.

I've fished for all sorts of species. The only fish I never fished for were eels and pike. I used to love my tench fishing as a kid, in Gunnersbury Park. I didn't think I was good enough to catch the carp there, so in the very early days I would fish for tench with a float, as close to the lily pads as I could, and watch the patches of bubbles coming up while holding the rod ready to strike.

I read an article about lowering bread off your rod tip to catch carp in the margins in among the lilies, but every fish I hooked I lost because I didn't know how to tie proper knots and I was using shoelace knots to tie the hooks on. I also remember that we had ponchos with us and if it was dry we would sit on them and if it was raining we'd put them on.

Carp fishing started getting more popular in the '80s as the baits got better and the hair-rig came in. And with people writing about their catches in magazines and books and giving talks, so the interest grew and fish started to become more easy to catch. With more food going in, the carp became more active and people began to realize that fish didn't stop feeding in winter.

I caught the first winter 'twenty' out of Redmire, and one of the reasons I managed that was because I fished it every weekend throughout the winter and caught three 'twenties' and lost a really big common. No one really fished for them then, because once October arrived the syndicate members all went barbel and chub fishing.

Now that so many people fish for carp all year round, you might think it is harder to succeed because lakes are more crowded and anglers are fishing against the anglers around them rather than the fish. They know where the fish are going to come out from, but someone else is in that swim and they can't get near to it.

But it was just as hard in my day because although there were fewer anglers, there were still enough around to make sure that the swim you wanted was taken, and often the angler in it would be fishing it wrong, even if they were someone that knew what they were doing. It only takes one angler on a lake to be where you need to be to stop you catching the fish you're after.

But one thing that has changed is that most people in my day fished at weekends. When I was at Fox Pool in the early days there would only be one other angler there on a Monday and I would do a Tuesday night but go to work the next morning and be back on Friday for the weekend. Being a window cleaner I could be there by 1pm, and other anglers would be turning up at 5pm and 6pm, so I had that little bit of an advantage.

But today from what I can gather there are so many people out of work or sponsored by tackle companies that they can stay on a lake as long as they want. I used to work for three days and fish for three days, and on a Friday evening you wouldn't be able to get a swim, but on a Monday you would have a choice of swims. On some waters now it's probably busy right throughout the week.

But I do believe that having to come up with ideas for your tackle and bait encouraged us to work hard at our fishing. When you don't have to make anything to give yourself an edge, and everyone's on the same bait so there's no creativity there, it can seem like a bit of a lottery – everyone's got the same chance of winning, so you just buy your ticket and wait for the carp to pick the winner.

No point in making any special effort because that's not going to make any difference if everyone is on the best rig and bait.

I walked on a lake recently after I was invited to have a look around and I couldn't believe it when I saw several anglers with their bivvies turned round so they had their backs to the water. Maybe it was because the wind was blowing into that bank, but I still can't see the point of fishing and not looking at the water. To me that's just not good fishing.

I wonder how many anglers climb a tree these days. I suppose it's easier today because there are more fish. I've never fished a lake where there's been more than one 'forty' in it. In my day I don't think one existed, and now you've got lakes with half a dozen 'forties' and a couple of 'fifties' and loads of 'thirties' – it should be virtually impossible to go there and not catch fish.

But I think that young anglers are missing out today if they haven't fished for other species before they get into carp fishing. I don't blame them for a minute because they want to catch big carp and there are lots about, but my first fish was a roach, on my second ever fishing trip, and I was thrilled with catching any fish.

Back in my day match fishing was probably the most popular side of the sport, with hundreds of anglers, sometimes even a thousand, in the biggest contests, and coach parties of anglers going off every weekend.

They weren't keen on us carp anglers because they would have their matches on the weekends and we would be there from the Friday, so some of the clubs said carp anglers couldn't fish on certain waters on particular weekends, which didn't go down well.

But I could see their point of view on this and I'd just go to another water. I've always had a lot of respect for match anglers because of the skills and knowledge that you need to do well at that side of the sport.

Jack Ashford said: "That looks like a nice one." I thought it was the one from Longfield because of the barbed wire behind it.

And in my day there were equal numbers of anglers fishing for other species as there were fishing for carp. At night there would always be bream anglers, which you don't see now. It seems a shame, but as long as people enjoy their fishing and look after the fish that they catch that can only be a good thing.

Certainly there is a lot more knowledge about fish care and conservation than there was a couple of decades ago, and even fish care kits, which you couldn't get in my day.

Back then you would see people standing up with fish, and unhooking mats weren't made commercially in the early days so you had to lie your fish on some long grass or the lilo that you slept on.

When I first started, if you saw someone weighing a fish, the spring balance hook was put through the gills. If you look at the old Mr Crabtree drawings you can see them doing that, so you can tell how much thing have moved on and how attitudes have changed in just a few decades.

There's no excuse for not knowing what to do any more, even when you are starting out, because there is so much more information out there than was available to past generations.

But some changes are not for the better. The two worst things that have happened to carp fishing in my opinion are the Close Season being scrapped and importing carp. Back in my day we used to get bivvied up ready for the start of the season three days before you could fish. I can remember not being able to sleep because of the excitement.

As soon as June came along you were out on the waters in the Close Season making the swims better, doing a bit of tree pruning, looking for fish and baiting up. All that has gone now.

I think the Close Season was scrapped for money, in fishing tickets and tackle sales, which is understandable. I don't think it would make an iota of difference to the wildlife. Swans are still going to nest whether you are fishing or not.

When the Close Season was first abolished, wildlife conservation was the argument against, and the welfare of the fish, but I don't think the fish suffer because of Close Season anglers. The fish may be being caught, but they're also being fed.

It's hard to say what effect angling pressure has on carp. On waters such as Redmire you could trace the history of the fish back decades, and they'd be caught by different generations of anglers, but in more recent years a lot of the famous fish have died, and maybe the increase in angling pressure has got something to do with that. All we can do is speculate, but there's always a chance that carp fishing's surge in popularity could also be one of its biggest problems.

But I'd like to think that there will be enough of the old Leney strain around to keep it going. I understand that people are bringing them on to keep the line going for future generations. It would be a shame if those classic shapes and scale patterns ever died out and were lost forever.

I never wanted to stop fishing Redmire. I loved fishing the place and I still go back there now, thanks to Les Bamford.

The problem came about because I'd had a common out of there at 28lb and also one out of Longfield, and Jack Ashford of Leisure Sports rang up and said: "I'm putting a booklet together for next year. Can we have a photo?"

He came round with a couple of bailiffs and I got a load of photos out on the table and he picked one up and said: "That looks like a nice one."

I thought it was the one from Longfield because of the barbed wire behind it, and they put it in the booklet. But then someone went to Tom Mintram and said the fish in the picture was from Redmire and at the time there was a publicity ban on fish from there.

I told them what had happened and that it was a genuine mistake, because I wouldn't put a Redmire fish in a Leisure Sports booklet.

I was told it would be best to stand down for a year and I'd be let back in the year after, as it was a misunderstanding, but after the year was up I was told I wasn't coming back in.

So I thought, right, I'll go and poach it. I rang up Dennis Davis and said: "Do you fancy going to Redmire?"

We parked up on the verge on the road above the lake and walked down the field. I said: "We'll go right round the other side, to keep ourselves hidden." Funny thing was, as soon as we were on the lake the farmer knew we were there.

He must have seen our footprints in the soft earth and he went and got a few people to find out what was going on. We could hear them looking all over the place for us, and then we heard someone walking down our bank towards us.

I've always been a believer in being on the front foot when it comes to dealing with difficult situations, whether they involve fish or humans. So I decided to do the exact opposite of what he would expect and I strolled along the bank to meet him.

"All right, Mr Davis?" I said as he appeared in front of me. He looked very surprised and you could see he wasn't sure what to make of me being there and was thrown off guard.

"How you doing?" I asked, as if I didn't have a care in the world.

He looked at me in a puzzled way: "Has the fishing season started?" He was almost apologising for disturbing me.

"Yes," I told him. "It started yesterday."

"Oh, right." He looked a bit embarrassed, and after wishing me all the best, he and the farm workers all left.

So having negotiated a successful bluff, I felt that the best policy would be to ride my luck rather than act all guilty and suspicious, and so me and Dennis moved round the other side, where we were in full view of everyone.

After I got back I rang Chris Yates up and told him I'd been back there in the Close Season and had a 31lb 8oz fish and he said: "Well done!" He was pleased for me.

I caught that fish out of the Evening Swim, and like a scrumped apple it was all the sweeter for having been poached, after I'd been edged out for something that I hadn't done.

It was the Evening Swim that had produced my first ever Redmire carp, and it was there that I caught my last one while Redmire was still being run as a syndicate. It broke my heart when they threw me out because I had the hair-rig the next year and I would have taken the place to pieces with that. I was quite successful while I was there without the hair-rig, but I was getting loads of little bleeps that I was putting down to line bites, but now I know they were takes.

Mind you, it wouldn't have been long before the fish sussed the hair-rig because as soon as you get a fish on a small lake like that, people are round to see what you're doing before you can conceal it, especially if you are fishing close to anyone.

Part Two

I went back to Redmire in September 1988, with John and Eileen Walker, and we filled our boots.

A lovely Redmire common of 26lb 8oz.

With the Richardsons, the owners of Redmire, having landing a 24lb mirror, a fish I caught ten years before while I was there with Chris Yates.

A lovely Redmire linear of 29lb 4oz.

Part Two

On the dam with Bill and Len.

Success was all the sweeter after such a long absence. This fully scaled weighed 23lb 8oz.

If I had been there I would probably not have used it when I was fishing close to people because I knew once I put it on I would catch fish straight away, because I had good bait. But that's all by the by because I didn't get the chance.

I went back to Redmire in September 1988, with John and Eileen Walker, and we filled our boots. We had 24 fish between us, and I had a 23, a 24, a 26 and a 29lb 4oz.

It's still a place that I love to visit, even if it's to spend time with good friends rather than to fish seriously now. Like a lot of lakes it changes all the time and is different from year to year, but when you stand on the bank and look across the water and think about all the things that have happened there over the past sixty years, and all the amazing fish that been landed, lost and seen, you can't help being in awe of the place.

Chapter Seven
Carping – Then and Now

I've been out of the game for twenty years, and it's like being Dr Who and travelling forward in time in a Tardis. When I walked into a show there were people in bivvies the size of small houses and others carrying radio controlled boats. I couldn't believe what was occurring.

The tackle is way and above anything I ever thought would be available. When I was fishing I had the best gear you could get, but it's way better than that now. The camo gear is fantastic, and the bedchairs are unbelievable. No wonder people want to stay in bed all day. We used to have garden furniture from the petrol station, whereas now if you buy a top-of-the-range bite alarm you need a degree in electronics to know how to work it. The tackle inventions have come on leaps and bounds. It's incredible stuff.

And the way they do the shows themselves, with the DVD screens on the stands showing people how to make rigs, is amazing. In my day you had to do it all by hand.

It's very high-tech and slick, but that's because it's a money game more now than ever before. But the great advantage of that is it's in everyone's interests to share the knowledge of the latest invention or idea because they want you to buy it.

Back in my day if you let someone in on a secret you were doing them a favour because they could then catch as well as you and you hadn't earned anything from it.

So you didn't walk up to someone and ask them if they'd caught anything because you'd just get a grunt. And you'd never ask anybody what bait they were using. You just wouldn't even ask that of people you knew. If you went to a meeting and someone had caught a big fish they wouldn't tell you where it was from.

It's better for everyone now because it's in the interest of the big companies that you catch fish, and anglers are writing about their catches and how they did it to make a name for themselves and get a sponsorship deal.

So the amount of information that's available and the way that knowledge is passed around is far better than it was in my day. Back then, most tackle dealers were either match anglers or they didn't go fishing.

I was always willing to help other anglers, especially young anglers, because I felt good if I could help someone put a fish on the bank, and I felt confident enough in my own ability to know that I would hook the fish I was after come what may.

I did the first junior carp fish-ins regularly, but I didn't do them because I wanted them to buy any products I was selling, but because I wanted them to catch fish and enjoy their carp fishing like I did.

But most of the youngsters who came along to the fish-ins had already fished for other things and were interested in carp fishing because their fathers fished for carp, or they'd seen a carp being caught. So they weren't looking for 'thirties', but a young kid today would be looking for that size of fish, which isn't how I got into carp fishing.

You can see the attraction of carp fishing when you wander around one of the shows. It's so much more glamorous now than it was when I first got involved. Just owning and handling the latest kit is like a fix now, with all the matt black, stainless, and matching luggage bags with tackle brand names that are like designer labels.

There were sleek, streamlined bait boats like miniature millionaire's yachts moored on the waterfront at Cannes, and you can get them with fish finders, global positioning and even lights for using at night! In my day at Longfield when the bream anglers turned up on the noddy bank opposite, the first thing they would do is turn their hurricane lamp on, and we'd shout: "Turn that f***ing light out!" You didn't even walk around a lake with a torch.

I was fishing Stan Talbot's one time and these two massive big blokes came along to fish. It was only a small lake that you could cast across easily and as soon as it got dark, the sun came out!

I wondered what was occurring until I saw this geezer had put a great big lamp with a massive glass lens on it in the tree. It was lighting up the whole lake.

It didn't stay that way for long, though. Back then we used to carry airguns in our kit to shoot the rats, and when they weren't looking there was a loud noise of breaking glass and darkness returned.

Even the tackle barrows are shiny these days and some even have pump-up tyres!

I had to leave my barrow at Horton the last time I packed up. I'd written my name on the side and someone had added a little cartoon character with a fag on and some smoke coming out of it.

It was too big to get in the back of my Volvo, so I had to leave it behind, but if anyone's got it tucked away at home, can I have it back please?

Plastic baits are everywhere now, and they seem like a good idea. Carp are inquisitive, and if you have got half a dozen of them in a swim and you get them feeding, you can catch them on a piece of shit.

And you can't spook feeding carp, either. I can remember being at Redmire with Chris Yates and he was up a tree and this carp came in and started feeding and he began speaking in a really high-pitched voice, so as not to spook it.

I said: "You won't spook feeding carp, only when they are patrolling." You can make as much noise as you like when carp are feeding. He wasn't convinced, so to prove the point to myself on another visit I threw a handful of corn into a depression in the bottom, out from the In-Willow swim, where the stump went out about 3 ft over the water. I was standing on this stump and the fish came from nowhere and were down on it, and as soon as it was gone so were they. I threw a load more in and when they came back and started feeding I was jumping up and down on the stump and shouting at them and not one of them spooked.

Chris is a completely different character from me. In fact he's a completely different character from anyone I've ever met. He used to call me "the Pat Cash of fishing", which I still to this day don't understand.

Part Two

When I caught the 45-12, quite a few people wanted me to claim the British record because Chris Yates' fish was still only the NASA best, but I said I can't do that. I don't need that kind of fame at someone else's expense, especially with someone like Chris, who isn't a competitive person, and I wouldn't want to steal any of his glory.

Eccentric is not the word for him. He's one of a kind. He catches fish on his own terms, using natural baits and antique tackle, but beneath the surface there's still that desire to catch fish that can tempt him into bending his own rules.

When I first started using boilies at Redmire beside him he said: "You won't catch me using those!" But as soon as I started hooking a few fish he said: "Can I have some of those baits to try?" Of course, I let him have some. No one wants to sit there watching someone else catching fish and not doing anything about it.

But as long as he isn't after the same fish as me, which is the biggest fish, and doesn't care what he catches, it doesn't bother me because I know that what I'm doing will work, and I'll get what I'm after in the end.

Glugs were just coming out when I packed up carp fishing, but I do remember trying this thing called Glow Bait, which was in a liquid form. When you put it in the water it turned really bright green, which I liked the idea of.

So I got a piece of Biro refill and catapult elastic and got some sponge and dipped it into this glow bait and cast it out 40 yards and you could see it all that way out easily. It was impressive to look at, but I didn't catch a fish on it.

When you've spent half your life looking for everything in terms of whether it would make a good bait or not, it's hard to get out of the habit. Even now I still find myself looking at things and wondering if they would work.

The other evening I was at home watching the telly and I'd bought myself a bag of Dolly Mixtures. The first taste I had took me right back to 1981 when I had the artificial sweetener for the first time and how it took every lake apart.

It worked in conjunction with the Salmon, and once it got out everybody started using it. If it hadn't been put on the market it would still be a top bait today. The success was phenomenal.

I remember getting hold of the most intense artificially sweetener that had been invented, something called Torani, which is made from sugar cane. I decided to try some to see what it was like and I got some water and poured some in. I couldn't smell it, but when I tasted it, it was so sweet it was ridiculous, and even I realized that was probably going a bit too far.

So anyway I took the Dolly Mixtures and got a needle from in my bedroom and tried pushing it through to see if they split. Then I got a bowl of water and put the needle with the bait in and a few sweets around it to see how they reacted in water.

Now bear in mind that I haven't carp fished seriously for twenty years, yet here I was with a bowl of Dolly Mixture in water watching them to see what happened.

My mate came round and took one look at me and wanted to know what on earth I was doing, staring at a bowl of water and brightly coloured sweets!

I said: "I think I've found a new bait."

In the morning I went straight to the bowl to see what had happened and a couple had come to the top but the others were just dust, so they wouldn't work as an overnight bait, but they could be a great stalking bait and once the fish got a taste for them they'd be straight on 'em, I'm sure.

It's the bright colours. I don't think fish see as well as people think. I think they feed more by smell, but if something is really bright they can find it a lot more easily. So I don't know if anglers experiment with baits in the way that we used to, but if you're the sort of person who likes to try new things, give Dolly Mixtures a go – they could be the next big thing.

Insect imitation zig rigs seem like a good idea. Back in the day on Longfield if we wanted to fish in 18 ft of water we would fish with a 9 ft tail and use a floater.

Sometimes carp are at different levels in the water because it is warmer in some areas and colder in others. I swam across Savay one summer on a red-hot day and I must have gone through three or four thermoclines. It got warmer for five or six yards and then colder again and you could tell the difference. It wasn't over bars, where you might expect the temperature to be higher, either.

Carp will feed at any depth and eat anything if it takes their fancy. There's nowhere in any lake or river where a carp won't feed, and it will take advantage of any feeding opportunity.

I remember fishing a lake where one guy was piking using a goldfish for bait and he caught a carp on it, and I was invited up to Birmingham by John Sidley, the famous eel angler, to fish for carp on a lake up there while he fished for eels. He fished at one end of the lake using a fish head and I went down the other, and he caught the only carp on it.

Natural baits based on bloodworm, krill or snails are very popular now, and it would boost my confidence if I knew I was fishing with a bait that contained things that they could be feeding on naturally.

Boilie fishing is now like particle fishing used to be. In my early days, kidney beans were the going bait at Cut Mill at one time, but if everybody is using particles you are not doing the fish any good. We would notice fin rot on the fish because they weren't getting enough protein. But mass boilie making has changed that, and natural food-based boilies are one step further.

Even baits such as hemp now come ready cooked and even flavoured now, so you don't have to do anything to prepare them and there's no risk to the fish from badly prepared bait.

I used safety lead clips that eject the lead if it gets snagged for the first time last year when I was barbel fishing and I think they're a fantastic idea. And I've heard of anglers sniffing their leads to tell what sort of material they are fishing over, which sound like a good idea to me. It's nice to know what you are fishing on.

Chemically sharpened hooks were around in my day, but I don't think I would ever use them. I still carry a hook sharpening stone and use it to get the point just right. I've heard that some anglers only use a hook for one cast, but I just sharpen mine.

But I do prefer barbed hooks to barbless. Some people say barbless hooks are easier to get out of the mouth of a fish when you are unhooking it. I've always believed that the way to take a barbed hook out of a fish is to pretend that you are taking it out of your own finger, and that's what I've always done.

No one had mobile phones on the bank in my day, or text messages. If you wanted to speak to someone opposite, you walked round the lake to where they were fishing. But we live in an era of Big Brother when everyone seems to want to be in touch with everyone and everything wherever they go.

I see people walking down the street talking out loud and I think they are talking to me, but it turns out they are on the phone with some little earpiece. It used to be that you got taken away to the nuthouse if you were talking to yourself.

I can see that phones are handy if you catch a big fish and want to get a mate to take a photo. It saves you having to find a phone box.

When I was fishing Wraysbury, Pete Springate and Ken Hodder used to have walkie talkies, because they were often fishing so far apart.

Ken Hodder and Pete Springate used to have walkie talkies when they were at Wraysbury, because they were often fishing so far apart.

I did have a mobile by the time I caught the Richmond Park fish, because I had to ring Chris Ball to come and take a photo and I couldn't leave the gear because the Copper was there.

Now I've got a smartphone, like everyone else, with loads of things on it like GPS and the internet, but I don't know how to work it. I only know how to use it for making calls.

Digital photography is a lot better than the old days of film. I used to have an Olympus OM10 camera, and before that I had a Yashica 2.25 square camera, which is a nightmare to use if you are on your own. Now I've got a digi camera and it's great to see your pictures before you put the fish back. So if the geezer taking them has messed them up and cut your head off, you can have a quick look, tell him he'd better do them again and to do the job properly this time.

I don't hunger for big carp any more, though I do hunger for big chub and barbel – a 9lb fish from the Kennet's Jam Factory stretch.

And head-torches are another great invention. I had a great big Petzl one when they first came out and it was so big it made my head ache. I would leave it 'til the last minute to put it on because it was so uncomfortable.

It was like walking round with two heads on, but it gave a great light. Johnny Walker's grandson bought one for me last year and it's even got a red light, so that you don't get bothered by mosquitoes.

Walking around the show looking at all the shiny new gear and listening to the slick sales patter, it would be easy to envy the young anglers now, starting up in carp fishing and all the huge choice of amazing inventions, brilliant tackle, incredible bait combinations and massive fish to go for. It would have been like a dream in my day.

But I don't envy them, or anybody. I don't lie awake at night wishing I could have caught a bigger carp than I did, because I had a 57lb fish at Cassien, so I know what it feels like to hold a big fish and I don't know if I'd have the strength to lift one that size up for the cameras for three or four minutes these days.

I'd like to see a 100lb French carp on the bank, and if I'm honest I'd like to catch one, but the reality is I'm like the cowboy in the westerns who hangs up his hat and belt, because if you're not fast enough on the draw any more you don't go out shooting people.

Carp fishing at the top level is hard work even when you're fit, and if I was doing it now I'd still want to be the bloke climbing trees and moving swims in the middle of the night because that's how I fish, and I know that wouldn't do me any good.

But on the rivers the fishing isn't like that, and the rivers are just like they used to be. They have stayed much the same while carp fishing on stillwaters has jumped forward by leaps and bounds, to the extent that I don't think I could catch it up.

I'm more than happy with what I've achieved in carp fishing, and I don't think I could better myself by going out and catching a couple of 'fifties' in a day, or a morning, or an hour. I don't think that would be a better achievement than what I've already done.

I don't hunger for big carp any more, though I do hunger for big chub and barbel, especially now they have increased so much in size since I've been away. My best barbel is 13lb 2oz, from the Hampshire Avon, and they take a lot of skill to hook and land when they get big.

When I'm mobile again I'll be back out there because I still want to catch the biggest fish. I've never liked catching lots of fish, just the biggest. Fish for one target fish, that's my way.

I never wanted to be famous. When I caught the Ashlea Pool record, Peter Mohan went on at me to put it in the papers. I didn't want to, and when I did, things just snowballed. I'm not saying I didn't enjoy the fame, I did. It was really nice to have people come up and to be recognized, and even today when I'm out and about it still happens.

When I was at the carping show I could see people nudging their friends and saying: "Do you know who that is?"

I didn't realize people would still recognize me after twenty years away, but when I got to the bar there were quite a few behind me ready to buy me a beer. And signing books was a nightmare. My hand was killing me by the end of the day.

It's thirty years since I started carp fishing seriously, and the changes have been so astronomical that what it's going to be like in another thirty years I can't imagine. But I believe that there are enough good people around to safeguard its future, and now that a lot of people's livelihoods depend on it, it should be in everyone's interests to keep it in safe hands.

Fishing has been my life, and I don't have many regrets. A few lost fish, a few missed chances, and a few lessons learnt the hard way, but nothing that keeps me awake at night any more.

What would I do differently if I had my time over again? I'd make a bit more money while I had the chance, I'd make the most of the company of people who aren't around now and whom I still miss, and I'd find a way of getting that barrow in the back of my Volvo.

Chapter Eight
The Last Word by Greg Meenehan

It's thirty years since I first met Ritchie. It was at a NASA Conference, back in the days when this annual gathering gave the great and the good of fishing a chance to put the world to rights over a few beers.

Most people settle for a nod and a handshake when you're introduced to them for the first time, but Ritchie, as I have since discovered, doesn't do things the way that most people do them. He looked at me for several seconds, as if he were trying to read my thoughts, and then told me and those standing with me that I had an honest face.

Maybe even back then, in 1984, when he was at the height of his fame, he was aware of the need to sort those he could trust from among those who would prove to be unreliable. He once told me that he believed you could only ever trust people who had blue eyes, so perhaps that was what he was looking for.

Whether he intended it that way, he gave me something to live up to, and hopefully I didn't let him down. Several years later and after many hours spent in his company in the UK and in France, visiting his home and sharing time on the bank, producing thousands of words in print about him, his first impressions of me had not changed. He told me during the writing of his first book, in a way that only Ritchie can, that if he came home one day and found me in his house with his wife and both of us were naked, he would automatically assume that there was a completely innocent explanation.

I took it as a compliment, though perhaps others would have been a bit less than flattered. As Ritchie is fond of saying, we are very different people. In my more fanciful moments I saw myself as a sort of Harry Carpenter to his Muhammad Ali, someone so unlike him in every way that I would seem like an unlikely ally, and yet someone able to understand what he was trying to say in print and to communicate that in a way that was entertaining and true.

I have found that if you can leave your ego at the door and just listen, often the person who you are interviewing opens up, and it's amazing what they will tell you.

It was 1985 when Allan Haines, the then Editor of *Angling Times*, approached me to ask if I would go to the South of France for a week to cover Ritchie's attempt to break the world carp record at Lake Cassien.

Until that time it was Mark Williams, a fellow reporter, who had dealt with news stories concerning Ritchie, having covered his capture of the Yateley North Lake fish at 45-12. But Mark was booked to go on a sunshine holiday with his family on that week in late September, so the baton passed to me.

Paul Regent's tour coach would provide the transport, and armed with a pair of 35 mm cameras and a notebook I was told to come back with the material for a six-part series to run through to December.

On September 24, 1985, I climbed on board the coach full of carp anglers at a Midlands service station and spent the next twenty-four hours watching the countryside outside the window change gradually from the green of southern England to the dry heat of the South of France.

We were booked into a small hotel in the backstreets of Cannes, a lengthy cast with a 3oz lead away from the glamorous La Croisette waterfront boulevard, with its grand-fronted hotels and billionaires' yachts.

Every day our coach took us to Le Lac de St Cassien, just a short drive away, dropping off its anglers and their tackle at roadside lay-byes along the South Arm to let them try to make their dreams come true before pick-up time at nightfall.

Ritchie had travelled out the previous week, and my first task was to find him. In those pre-mobile phone days that was no mean feat, standing in the blazing sun beside a 1,500-acre lake that is four and a half miles long and two miles wide and with a language barrier to overcome.

At school when I had been trying to learn French to pass an 'O' Level, and struggling to hold a conversation in French for ten minutes with a complete stranger in the form of an examiner, I had wondered whether I would ever have any use for these skills. Standing in Chez Pierre's Restaurant talking to the moustachioed Monsieur Pierre himself and negotiating the hire of one of his boats powered with an electric outboard motor (un bateau électrique), I began to appreciate the benefits of a decent education.

There was a crowd of us, all English, all anglers and all wanting to hire boats, which were in short supply, unless you fancied rowing wherever you were planning to go. But the other requests came to Pierre in a stream of broken English, and on hearing mine in something like his native tongue, he took pity on me and provided me with the transport that I needed and the chance to leave the scrum of would-be boat hirers behind.

So the search began, and one of the most surprising things about Cassien was not just its size, but how crowded it was. In most of the pictures you see it looks empty, like a warm version of a Scottish loch, with unruffled water stretching to the horizon. But it quickly became obvious that this was a playground for the French, who descended upon it in the way that British crowds pack beaches along the south coast on a hot August Bank Holiday, swimming, sailing and sunbathing.

Most distracting of all was the fact that most of the women were young, athletic and tanned… oh, and invariably topless. Groups of giggling adolescents would rush down to the water, pull most of their clothes off and plunge into the lake. Families would come down with picnic baskets and while mum and dad organised the food and comfortable seating arrangements, the sons and daughters would stroll along the shore dressed in the most microscopic of bathing briefs. And the hundreds of windsurfers would glide by just a few feet away, one moment covered from the legs up by a large white sail and the next moment revealed to be practically naked.

To a twenty-three year old raised on family holidays of the seaside donkeys, knotted handkerchiefs and candyfloss variety at Weston-super-Mare, it was almost frightening.

Thankfully, Ritchie had found himself a haven from all of these goings-on, half way down the West Arm, where the lack of road access and dense forests close to the rocky shoreline kept all but an occasional passing windsurfer away. The line of rods, polystyrene swim markers and Lafuma beds betrayed his presence from a distance, and the familiar sarf London accent raised in greeting confirmed that the first hurdle of my mission had been overcome.

He told me he recognised me by the fact that I was the only one wearing a shirt, and one of his aims on the trip, while trying to catch a world record carp, was to go home with the sort of suntan that turns heads with envy in the high street.

I've never been a sun-worshipper. I once got burnt just preparing for a sunshine holiday by lying under a sunbed, having hired a set up tubes, much to the amusement of those who witnessed my lobster-coloured midriff. And with a job to do and only six days to get everything in the can, I knew that sunstroke or sunburn would be a major handicap to the success of my visit, so the hat and long-sleeved shirt became essential attire during the hottest part of each day.

It was strange to be in such unfamiliar surroundings with someone who sounded so English as Ritchie. I had forgotten how alien everything is to your senses when you are abroad. On the way there the road signs, the cars, the voices and the smells were all constant reminders of how removed I was from a normal routine, and even beside the lake, the power of the sun was unlike anything that the UK could provide.

I've heard that photographers seek out the South of France for its wonderful light, which has a richness that cannot be matched further north. Certainly, the camera exposures needed to be adjusted for the intensity of the light, and I began to understand why experienced photographers sought out the shade or arranged to work early in the morning or late in the evening, when the sun has lost or not yet gained its intensity and the burning rays have mellowed into a golden light, like that of the glow from a candle in a darkened room, flattering faces and smoothing away wrinkles.

For this reason Cassien was also a popular location among adult film makers, and many a British carp angler packed a pair of binoculars in his fishing kit in the hope of being entertained during the long wait between runs by more than just leaping carp.

Ritchie was also aware of the potential entertainments of shapely windsurfers and film shoots, but he asked me not to mention them in the first book or the articles, which is why they don't appear, on the grounds that his wife wouldn't have liked it if she had known about the floor-show on display while he was fishing in France.

It also surprised me how cold it became at night. By day the main occupation was how to stay cool, but even before the sun had set, a chill had descended that would send a shiver through anyone still dressed for midday.

Every morning I hired a bateau électrique and joined Ritchie, Johnny Allen and Bob Tyrell in their extended swim on the rocky shoreline of the West Arm. The weather was the same every day, a cloudless blue sky with a glassy surfaced lake that I cut through with the boat as I pointed it at the same spot and it hummed in the early morning stilly quiet, the cold air refreshing and the sun beginning to assert itself with a foretaste of an intensity to come.

Night fishing at the time was not allowed, but Ritchie and his companions figured that with time so short and the night-time being potentially the best feeding opportunity given the heat of the day, getting caught was a risk they had to take. At night they retreated to the edge of the woods, to be out of sight of any patrols checking for anglers, so when I arrived each morning it was with a sense of anticipation of hearing what action, if any, they had enjoyed in the night.

On some days there were fish sacked up for me to photograph, which was done straight away to make the most of the early light and return the fish as soon as possible. After that it was a case of sitting and awaiting a run while working through the list of picture ideas that I had assembled on the way down, looking for dozens of ways of illustrating a series that had yet to be written.

While Ritchie fished and rolled boilies, he talked me through all the lessons he had learnt, about taking to the boat as soon as a fish was hooked, using strings of boilies to imitate crayfish tails and checking bags for scorpions and spiders before putting his hand inside.

When a daytime run did finally happen, getting an action photo proved a lot more difficult that expected. The sun was so strong that facing towards it sent the needle off the scale of my Olympus OM10 and was blinding to look at, so the boat had to be coaxed around so that Ritchie and the fish on the end of his line were both 'down-sun' of the camera, but not in my shadow.

No sooner was everything in position than the fish would dive deep and be out of sight for the picture, or it would kite to one side, swinging the boat around to face the sun again, which meant putting down the camera and picking up an oar. And when Ritchie tried to net his fish, pushing the net towards the carp just made the boat go further away from it, out of reach, so I had to give up on that and help with the net myself.

Back in those days *Angling Times* was printed in a combination of black and white and colour, so we carried two cameras, one loaded with Fujichrome 100 film and the other with Kodak Tri-X 400 black and white. I had packed a dozen rolls into the outer pocket of my small camera bag, which I had to load into the luggage hold of the Regent coach each morning ahead of the drop-off trip to the lay-byes along the road.

Arriving at Chez Pierre's on the second morning, which was one of the final drop-off destinations for anglers, I looked into the luggage hold while standing beside the road only to find it empty. Desperately I scanned my fellow English travellers to see if they had picked it up, but there was no sign of it. Nor was it on board in the seating area.

The coach driver shrugged, climbed aboard and left me to it, as did the other anglers. I stood alone above the lake on the dusty roadside under the strengthening sun minus my cameras, film, notebook and water.

As the bag had been there when the coach had set out, I knew that it must be somewhere between where I stood and the hotel, so I had no choice but to start walking.

It was at the earliest lay-bye drop-off point that I spotted what at first looked like a roadside rock but on getting closer turned out to be my camera bag. With an enormous sense of relief I pounced on the bag, but I noticed that one side of it didn't look right. It had been flattened by something very heavy, and when I looked into the film pocket, two of the rolls of Tri-X had been squashed, one so badly that it was beyond being loaded into the camera. It resembled a drinks can that has been stomped on, and I kept it and still have it as a memento of that trip.

Part Two

I kept the dented canister of Tri-X film as a memento along with the battle-scarred OM10s.

The truth of what happened emerged only on the return journey to England. One of my fellow travellers had taken exception to me getting an electric-powered boat ahead of him, forcing him to make do with one of the rowing kind.

So to get his revenge, when he had been dropped off at the first lay-bye the following day, while getting his tackle out of the hold he had taken my camera bag out and kicked it under the coach wheel. Fortunately for me it had travelled further than he'd intended and the wheel had only gone over the corner when the coach had pulled away. A few inches further along and both cameras would have been reduced to scrap metal, and the whole trip would have been a wasted journey.

It would be dark each night when I fired up the motor to leave the anglers and steer the boat back towards the lights of Chez Pierre's to catch the coach back to the hotel. Ritchie, John and Bob would have recast their rigs and baited up their markers prior to retreating to the bushes for the night, and having watched their careful preparations, I was determined to avoid causing them any problems and so chose a course exactly between the two white markers that John had arranged, to avoid the chance of fouling one. Unfortunately I discovered much later that he had a third marker that was smaller than the other two and it was positioned exactly between the larger ones, and my careful manoeuvring took the electric engine right over it every time with uncanny accuracy, inadvertently undoing one-third of his hard work in the process. If you're reading this, John, I apologise. It may not have seemed like it, but I had your interests at heart.

When the time came to head home on the following Monday, I gave my spare francs to Ritchie to help tide them over for as long as they could, to try to catch the fish that they had come for. My biggest regret was that I wasn't there when John hooked his 200lb catfish, which took him ninety minutes to bring to the shore in temperatures so high it made him hallucinate and his mind wander to thoughts of what would be happening back home.

The capture caused a sensation when the story broke and the pictures showed its size, for these were the days before the Ebro had turned into a nursery for giant catfish, and anything over 50lb was mind-boggling to imagine.

I'd left Ritchie my unused film and when he got back he posted it to us at *Angling Times* to process. In these days of instant digital images, it is difficult to remember what it was like waiting for films to be ready, wondering what they would reveal. When they were laid out on the light-table, we scanned them for a picture that would do justice to the story, and there at the end of the roll, after lots of frames of the catfish in the water that gave no indication of its size, was the one that we wanted, number 36 and a half on the roll of 36, so close to the tag that joined it to the canister that the perforated edge for the film sprockets was slightly crumpled.

It appeared in colour in the paper and in the first book, but Ritchie sent the original to John, where he now lives in Thailand, as a memento, so a black and white scan of the original book's negative page plate, on page 124, is the best we could do this time.

The news of that fish provided the perfect springboard for the series, which ended up being read by anglers whether they fished for carp or not, and gave the paper's circulation a healthy boost to break the one hundred thousand copies a week figure, which is three or four times what the biggest selling weeklies command now.

Ritchie got Mark Williams to sneak a thank-you into the last words of the final episode, which ended with Ritchie's return on his own to bag the fish that he felt the lake owed him and come home having landed a new personal best of 57lb.

It showed a lot of character for him to go back again, single-handed and for no extra cash, just for the satisfaction of finishing the job in style and showing what he could achieve with unshakeable determination. I think that was what won him the admiration of so many anglers who had never fished for carp, how pride drove him to achieving his aim.

Amongst all the interest created by those articles, it was perhaps inevitable that the idea of a book would be mentioned. Rod Hutchinson wrote me a nice letter saying how much he enjoyed the *Angling Times* series, and Ritchie asked me if I'd help write the story of his fishing career and his rise to fame.

We approached The Crowood Press with an outline of the content, but by then Ritchie was working for Mike Davis, who owned Penge Angling, and Mike said he would like to publish it.

All we had to do, then, was write it. Frequent trips down from where I lived in Peterborough to Michels Row in Richmond followed, along with week-long holidays bivvied up alongside Ritchie on the Copse and Car Park Lake at Yateley.

Those were heady times of long nights listening to his stories while scribbling his words down in shorthand, fuelled by take-aways from his favourite curry house just a two-minute walk around the corner washed down with cans of Fosters and cups of tea.

My biggest regret was not being there when John caught his 200lb catfish.

The Last Word by Greg Meenehan

The six-part series in Angling Times boosted the circulation to over one hundred thousand.

Anglers read it who had never fished for carp, caught up in the drama of what would happen next.

When someone as famous as Rod put pen to paper to say how much he liked the series, it was a huge buzz.

When he was working in the shop at Penge or Rayleigh Ritchie would drive me over there in the morning to sit and read a book while he served customers, before another white knuckle ride back again through the traffic for a further session on the book in the evening.

To follow him in your own car isn't much better. When Ritchie drives he rarely leaves the outside lane, and when he puts his foot to the floor on a dual carriageway, it stays there. I would catch him up only to see him rapidly disappear into a dot on the horizon, knowing that the next change of lights between him and me would leave me stranded and not knowing the way to where he planned to go.

At least when I was following him home I knew where he was heading for when he lost me. He would be there, looking as if he'd been indoors for hours, playing with the kids, showing them his breakdancing skills, wrestling with Sabie, his Staffordshire bull terrier, or chatting to someone who had called round. Sabie is the only animal I've met that could walk into your legs while hurrying to get past and knock your feet from under you without even noticing you were there. She must have had a forehead made of reinforced concrete, but the whole family loved her.

His place was always something of an open house to visitors. There was a time when a youngish couple who were friends of the family came round with their baby while we were working. Declaring suddenly that it was time for the youngster's feed, the woman whipped her top off while sitting on the sofa and left us to chat amongst ourselves while the infant tucked in.

We were working on the book alone one evening when a friend called round and asked if she could leave her young son with him. He couldn't have been more than two or three and my heart sank, having driven a hundred miles to get some writing done, but Ritchie didn't bat an eyelid. The lad was sitting on the carpet in the middle of the living room floor, playing with a toy that he had brought with him, when he heard the clunk of the front door closing and looked up to see his mum gone.

His face creased into a wail and he took a huge breath, like children do when they want to make a big impression, preparing to give vent to his feelings at full volume. I winced and prepared myself for the full blast of his vocal chords, but before he could exhale, Ritchie had interrupted.

"Now you can cut that out for a start! We ain't gonna be listening to none of that, mate," he told the toddler, who was so taken aback at this straight talking, man to man, that he froze, open mouthed, before the wail had fully formed on his lips.

"Your mum's not gonna be away long but I ain't gonna listen to your grizzling so you can just leave that out."

They say that the tone of a voice transcends the language barrier, communicating your mood to animals and infants who don't understand the words, and it was clear from this lad's face that not only did he realize that he was dealing with someone who was in a different league from anyone he had ever met before, but this was clearly someone not to be messed with. Ritchie turned back to me from the figure on the floor saying: "Now, where were we…", and apart from occasional glances at the door and up at Ritchie, the lad hardly made a sound until his mother returned, but sat playing with his toy, as good as gold.

"Has he been good?" asked his mother half an hour later, when she came back in to scoop him up.

I don't think he's had any choice, I felt like saying, but another side of Ritchie and his many talents had been revealed.

It was fascinating to watch Ritchie fishing. One of the great bonuses of being an angling journalist has been to observe at close quarters some of the finest that Britain has ever produced, and possibly the best in the world at their style of fishing.

The very best are like magicians, conjuring fish up out of nowhere and seeming to be like magnets to anything with fins, such that it all seems incredibly, laughably easy. And that confidence can seem like wonder dust, rubbing off on anyone close to them and bringing success as if talent were contagious, though only until things go wrong and then comes the realisation that unlike them, we have feet of clay.

Ritchie had about him a preciseness of action that was infectious. At the top of his game his every move would be careful and exact, right down to the folding of a towel or the arranging of a seat. He had the most immaculate swim on the lake, without a bobbin or a bivvy peg out of place, his Dictaphone on his bivvy table ready to record his thoughts, looking as calm and controlled when playing a fish as he was when waiting for a run.

But there were always distractions. On the week I spent on the Car Park Lake, Ritchie decided to go to see Rod up in Lincolnshire for a couple of days, though I was entertained by witnessing the capture of Heather by Keith Byatt, down in weight at 34 lb 12 oz, while I was there.

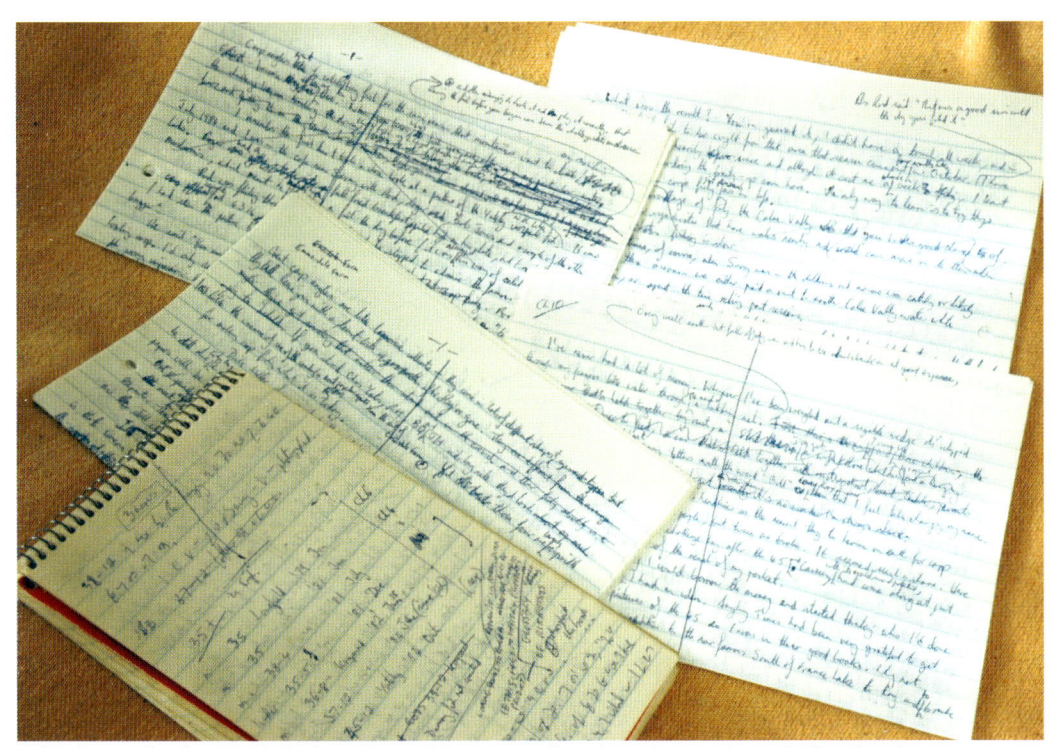

I filled a notebook with Ritchie's stories and then wrote them into chapters in an A4 lined pad.

In those pre-computer days, a portable typewriter and a bottle of Tipp-Ex were the tools of the trade.

Sometimes talent can be contagious. A 22lb 5oz mirror from Deeping St James AC's Maxey No.1 Pit, near Peterborough, in September 1985.

Part Two

And on the Copse Lake he planned an assignation with his young lady hairdresser, but a problem with his car lights meant he couldn't drive at night. He asked if he could borrow my car to go and see her. How could I refuse? He returned at dawn and a couple of days later we loaded up our cars and went our separate ways early, before the roads became busy, him back to Richmond and me back to Peterborough. Only when I went to start mine did I discover that the battery was flat. The headlights were still switched on from two days before, but by then, Ritchie had gone. A long wait for the AA to jump start my car was followed by a difficult journey through all the traffic back up to the East Midlands.

This was when things were starting to go wrong for him at home, as the first cracks started appearing. A phone call out of the blue at my home turned out to be his wife, asking me if he was seeing anyone behind her back. Caught on the spot I said no, but felt guilty about it. I told Ritchie and he looked surprised. He had come to know me as someone who was always honest, and it was the first time he had heard of me lying about something. I told him that he couldn't guarantee I would do it again.

But sometimes when I came for the weekend to work on the book and sleep on the sofa overnight, the arguments between them would begin. It would be the early hours of the morning and she would say she was going to leave and he would stand in front of the door and say she wasn't going anywhere, and I wondered whether I ought not to be there at all, and would soon be driving home without any sleep before it was light. But in the morning it was as if nothing had happened, though the fear of things flaring up again made me wonder whether each visit would be the last.

At the same time one of my colleagues on *Angling Times* was splitting up with his wife, and listening to his stories as I drove him into work made me shudder. Maybe I got too close to those two break-ups and got singed by the flames, but that was back in 1987 and ever since then I've avoided risking that kind of emotional trauma after seeing their worlds turned upside down.

I had been asked to go to Redmire for a feature in *Angling Times*, and it would have been an ambition achieved for me. But the offer was transferred to my colleague and without any carp tackle he asked if he could borrow mine.

When he got back, he and his wife had an almighty row and he left in just the clothes he stood up in. She sold everything of his, including my fishing tackle, so my Tri-Cast 2.25lb test curve carp rods, Abu Cardinal 155 reels and Optonics with Bamford conversions went west, and I haven't been carp fishing since.

Sometimes on book writing sessions at his home, Ritchie would disappear to see someone and not come back for an hour, or at other times he would just not be in the mood to work, but slowly the book took shape and with a guest chapter by Tim Paisley, the sixty thousand words were enough to make the project a goer.

There were times when I wondered whether it was ever going to happen, but when Ritchie was in the zone and in full flow, wonderful stories came tumbling out, one after another, all original and described so well that you almost felt you were there at the time that they happened.

As a journalist there are moments when you are told things that are so good, they make the hairs on the back of your neck stand up because you are aware immediately how much they will be enjoyed when you've weaved them into a chapter or a news story and presented them to readers.

One chapter in particular from the first book, Four-legged Friends, just flowed like hot oil, and I can't read the ending even now without getting goosebumps. When I had finished it, having written it from the shorthand notes taken in Ritchie's front room, I was sitting at home alone in Peterborough and it was 11pm. When you lose yourself in writing that is going really well, time seems to cease to exist, and I knew as I finished that I had to ring Ritchie just to tell him about it.

The phone rang quite a few times before I heard his voice, and even before I said anything I heard him say: "I bet that's Greg."

I asked him how he knew and he said he'd been in bed and said to Yvonne: "I bet that's Greg ringing up. No one else would be ringing at this time of night. I bet he's just finished a chapter of the book and can't wait to tell me."

No wonder the carp stood no chance against Ritchie. It wasn't watercraft, it was mind reading.

With a successful slide show tour completed and a book to his name, life was good for a while for Ritchie, and I bowed out of his life to move to London to take a job with the BBC on *Radio Times*. I'd been there for a couple of years, and angling journalism was becoming just a fond memory, when a call came through to me at the office out of the blue. It was Ritchie, and he'd just caught two 40lb carp in a week. He wanted to write the story for Big Carp magazine and Rob Maylin, but he wanted me to help "because you do my writing and you put it down better than I can."

So we met up again, just like old times, only this time the journey wasn't so far. He told the story with all the old Ritchie swagger and it appeared in the June/July 1991 edition.

When I left the BBC a year later to go freelance and was offered work by *Angler's Mail*, I got back in touch with Ritchie to find out how he was doing. He had got a ticket for Horton Church Lake, which had just formed its first syndicate, but his home life was unravelling. I remember going to Horton to see him, parking in the car park just inside the famous big gates and walking down the left-hand bank, past the Salt Circle swim that now takes its name from him.

He was half a dozen swims down, and from a distance things looked normal – the same neat set-up, rods ready for action, Ritchie sitting sideways on his bed looking out at the water. But he could have been looking at a wall for all his interest in the lake. All he wanted to talk about was what he was going to do to the one-time friend who had split his marriage apart. He wouldn't be distracted by talk of fishing or dissuaded by being told that his burning desire to get even would only add to his misery and not make anything better. I wish I could have helped, but he was hell bent on a path of destruction and nothing I could say or do, not even just sitting and listening, did anything to help.

I walked away, not having the tools to heal wounds as deep as the ones with which he was afflicted. I used to visit people on behalf of the church, having been given training in counselling and listening therapy, but what was eating Ritchie was out of my league.

Fragments of rumours found their way back to me on the fishing journalism grapevine, how Ritchie had gone inside, how he had given up fishing and sold all his tackle and how he lived alone, having cut himself off comprehensively from almost everyone he had once known.

Part Two

A call came through to me out of the blue. It was Ritchie, and he'd just caught two 40lb carp in a week.

Horton Church Lake was embarking upon a new era of syndicate carp fishing, but Ritchie's mind was elsewhere.

From one of his close friends I heard that he had made a couple of appearances from time to time at funerals over the years, notably that of Bill Quinlan and Pete Broxup. I asked for a number where I could get in touch, having lost contact completely when he left the family home. I was told that they would pass my regards on to him, saying I would like to get in touch, but that he guarded his privacy and had asked that his phone number not be passed on. Whenever I came across someone who knew him, the answer would always be the same.

Many years on, an email arrived at *Angler's Mail* from Ritchie McDonald's sister, saying he had seen the mention he had received in the Top 100 Angling Legends series in the magazine and was pleased to see that he was still remembered fondly.

I got in touch with her via her email address of Lady Luck, but still no contact was forthcoming.

It began to look as if he was part of my past, and I couldn't help wondering whether my next contact with Ritchie would be the news being broken to me that he had gone the way of those he admired most. Maybe the final chapter of his story had already been written.

But then I spoke to someone who sounded more optimistic about him, and when I once again asked for a phone number to get in touch, although he said he couldn't promise anything, he returned with a number and told me I was welcome to give the man a ring.

It was strange, sitting there in the *Angler's Mail* office, having waiting until late in the evening, when everyone else had gone home, lifting the receiver to dial a number that I had hoped to get hold of for over a decade, and hearing that same distinctive voice answer and then shift in tone to one of surprise and welcome as I announced who it was who was calling.

We arranged to meet, and he gave me the address of his flat, not so very far from where he used to live in Richmond. I wondered whether the years had taken their toll, but most of all it was the old Ritchie spirit that I hoped to find, and while the hair is thinner and more grey (join the club) and the face more lined, the old Ritchie spark is undimmed.

His life of manual labour can be read in his hands, and glasses now perch on his nose when he reads or ties a knot. But ask him about fishing or the rights and wrongs of what goes on in the world and you will discover that his opinions are held with the same determined strength that used to subdue 40lb carp.

When I typed his name into Google and started looking at the chat forum comments, it emerged that there was a great fondness for Ritchie, fuelled partly by his sudden disappearance, a once bright star, lighting up the slide show circuit, fading to complete anonymity in next to no time, which many found puzzling. How could someone at the very top of his game suddenly give it all up?

And there were complimentary comments about the book on the internet, coupled with frustration at the high price commanded by the few copies available to buy second hand. People wanted to read it, having heard about Ritchie, but not if it meant paying £90.

It was a couple of years short of twenty-five since the first book was published, which was also the time when Ritchie would be sixty. So a plan was put together to update the old book with all the things that had happened since Cassien, this time with pictures throughout.

A large suitcase full of transparencies, prints, black and white images and negatives was entrusted to me, and many hours of sorting and scanning later I closed it and handed it back having converted the five hundred most usable images into digital files.

That was the easy bit. Now all we had to do was find out which fish was which, and from what decade, and when the person in the picture isn't sure either, head-scratching becomes a habit.

I think we got there, and I think people's curiosity about "what happened to the great Ritchie Mac" will have been assuaged. I'm just glad we were both still around and still in possession of sufficient marbles between us to tell it like it is, hopefully without too many mistakes.

How is Ritchie today? Not without his demons entirely, though he knows how to keep them in check, and the welcome he has received from those in the angling world who missed him has lifted him. He knows now he's better off on the inside of that extended family, instead of out in the cold.

He has many challenges ahead, but he knows where he wants to go now, and how he can get there, and angling will play a part in that. The fact that he goes to Redmire every year and still gets a sense of peace from being back on the banks, enjoying verbal sparring matches with Les Bamford, tells you that angling is still in his blood.

He always says he never looked for fame from his fishing, and that it was thrust upon him. But when it came, he soaked it up, and he says that walking on stage at the height of his powers to the sound of hundreds of cheering voices chanting his name, and basking in the warm glow of the affection that comes from that level of adulation, is something that he will never forget.

Perhaps, just like the rest of us, he only ever wanted to earn the respect of those whose opinions mattered to him, the average person who just loves to fish for carp, and maybe now, with this book, he will get a second chance to see that happen.

The Last Word by Greg Meenehan

ALL THE BEST!